INTERCULTURAL
BUSINESS
COMMUNICATION

INTERCULTURAL BUSINESS COMMUNICATION

Lillian H. Chaney
The University of Memphis

Jeanette S. Martin
The University of Mississippi

Prentice Hall Career and Technology
Englewood Cliffs, New Jersey 07632

Library of Congress Cataloging-in-Publication Data

Chaney, Lillian H.
    Intercultural business communication / Lillian H. Chaney,
Jeanette S. Martin
        p.   cm.
    Includes bibliographical references and index.
    ISBN 0-13-038753-3
    1. Business etiquette.   2. Corporate culture   3. Business
communication.   4. Intercultural communication.   I. Martin,
Jeanette S.   II. Title.
HF5389.C47   1995
395'.52—dc20   94-17297
                                                    CIP

Acquisitions editor: Elizabeth Sugg
Editorial assistant: Maria Klimek
Editorial/production supervision
   and interior design: Linda B. Pawelchak
Cover design: Marianne Frasco
Production coordinator: Ed O'Dougherty

© 1995 by Prentice Hall Career and Technology
Prentice-Hall, Inc.
A Paramount Communications Company
Englewood Cliffs, New Jersey 07632

Printed in the United States of America
10   9   8   7   6   5   4   3   2   1

ISBN 0-13-038753-3

Prentice-Hall International (UK) Limited, *London*
Prentice-Hall of Australia Pty. Limited, *Sydney*
Prentice-Hall Canada Inc., *Toronto*
Prentice-Hall Hispanoamericana, S.A., *Mexico*
Prentice-Hall of India Private Limited, *New Delhi*
Prentice-Hall of Japan, Inc., *Tokyo*
Simon & Schuster Asia Pte. Ltd., *Singapore*
Editora Prentice-Hall do Brasil, Ltda., *Rio de Janeiro*

Contents

1

The Nature of Intercultural Communication   1

2

Universal Systems   18

3

Contrasting Cultural Values   40

4

Oral and Nonverbal Communication Patterns   55

5

Written Communication Patterns   74

8

Country-Specific Information   132

9

Cultural Shock   153

10

Intercultural Negotiation Process   171

11

Intercultural Negotiation Strategies   195

12

Laws Affecting International Business and Travel   219

Foreword

With the globalization of the world economy, it is imperative that managers, both present and future, be sensitive to differences in intercultural business communication. Professors Lillian H. Chaney and Jeanette S. Martin have done an admirable job in addressing a broad range of issues and skills that are crucial to effective intercultural encounters. In the book, the most significant issues pertaining to cross-cultural interaction are covered: culture, intercultural (both verbal and nonverbal) communication, and cultural shock. In addition, the book contains practical guidelines and information on how to conduct negotiations across countries and write business letters in different societies, as well as other general do's and don'ts in international business. College students and businesspeople new to the international business scene can certainly benefit from such practical advice.

This book can also sensitize readers to the dynamics of international diversity. With the increasing multiethnic composition of the North American labor force and the growing participation of women in the professional and managerial ranks of organizations, it is equally important that students, the managers of the future, be attuned to the issues associated with managing and valuing diversity within a domestic context. The book addresses the issues of gender differences and how these impact on communication styles and patterns.

While recognizing the significant differences that can exist across cultures and subcultures, it is important to acknowledge the existence of individual differences within any given society. Just as it is naive to assume that all cultures are similar, it is equally fallacious to fall into the trap of "cultural stereotyping." To quote Lao Tzu, the famous Chinese philosopher who is usually considered to be the spiritual leader of Taoism, "The one becomes the many." Although people in a given society may share certain common values and characteristics, there can be important differences in how these are applied and exhibited in specific situations. In addition, these intranational differences can be exacerbated by religious influences, exposure to Western philosophies and ideas through education at universities abroad, overseas travel, and social and business contacts with peoples from other cultures. Furthermore, it is significant to note that cultural values and norms do evolve over time, however slowly. Some of the cultural characteristics alluded to in this book may be changing or have changed. A cursory review of the dramatic upheavals that have taken and are still taking place in virtually all aspects of societal and organizational functionings in many socialist and former socialist countries will attest to the fact that culture is not static; rather, it evolves over time.

Judicious application of the principles and techniques introduced in this book will enable readers to develop a proficiency in managing diversity, both cross-nationally and internationally.

Rosalie L. Tung
The Ming & Stella Wong Professor
of International Business
Simon Fraser University
Canada

Preface

PURPOSE

With the increasing number of multinational corporations and the internationalization of the economy, intercultural business communication continues to become more important. Government leaders, educators, and businesspersons agree that internationalizing the curriculum is important to maintaining the competitive position of the United States in the world economy. Since all international activity involves communication, students need a knowledge of intercultural business communication to prepare them for upward mobility and promotion in tomorrow's culturally diverse domestic and international environments.

CONTENTS

Topics selected for *Intercultural Business Communication* were those considered important or essential by three Delphi panels of experts: international employees of multinational corporations, college professors who teach intercultural communication, and members of the Academy of International Business.* We know of no other book on intercultural communication that has used research involving experts' perceptions of the importance of topics to be covered as a basis of content selection.

The topics include

*Martin, J. S. (1991). Experts' Consensus Concerning the Content for an Intercultural Business Communication Course. (Doctoral dissertation, University of Memphis). Major professor, L. H. Chaney.

- The nature of intercultural communication
- Universal systems
- Contrasting cultural values
- Oral and nonverbal communication patterns
- Written communication patterns
- Language
- Business and social etiquette
- Country-specific information
- Cultural shock
- Intercultural negotiation process
- Intercultural negotiation strategies
- Laws affecting international business and travel

Each chapter contains objectives, terms, questions and cases for discussion, and activities. Also provided are exercises to be used for self-evaluation of material covered and illustrations to depict various aspects of the content.

Both authors have traveled or worked in a number of countries or multinational corporations and, therefore, have firsthand knowledge of many of the topics covered.

PROPOSED USE

Intercultural Business Communication is designed to be used as a text for a college-level course in intercultural business communication or to augment courses in which intercultural communication is a major component.

ACKNOWLEDGMENTS

Appreciation is expressed to the following persons who reviewed the manuscript and offered helpful suggestions: Marie Dalton, San Jacinto College, Pasadena, TX; Lynn Fitzgerald, New England Banking Institute, Boston, MA; Marie Flatley, San Diego State University, San Diego, CA; Richard F. Tyler, Anne Arundel Community College, Arnold, MD; and Carolyn Rainey, Southeast Missouri State University, Cape Girardeau, MO.

Appreciation is also expressed to the following persons who provided models for the illustrations used in the text: Bill Cooper, freelance artist, and Tom Foster and other members of the University of Memphis Department of Graphic Design and Production, as well as Doug French, who adapted them for the book.

About the Authors

Lillian H. Chaney is a Professor of Management and Distinguished Professor of Office Management at the University of Memphis. She received both the M.S. and the Ed.D. from the University of Tennessee. She is coauthor of a textbook on office management and has published numerous articles on communication and office management in professional journals. Dr. Chaney teaches graduate/undergraduate courses in business communication, executive communication, and international business communication and negotiation. She has teaching experience at a South American university and has conducted training programs on communication, corporate etiquette, and business ethics for international corporations, educational institutions, and government agencies.

Jeanette S. Martin is an Assistant Professor at the University of Mississippi. She received her B.A. from Michigan State University, M.B.A. from the University of Chicago, and her Ed.D. from the University of Memphis. She has considerable corporate experience in both U.S. multinational corporations and foreign multinational corporations. Dr. Martin has published several articles involving intercultural business communication, education, and management information systems. Her current research and consulting interests include NAFTA and the effects intercultural communication has on such international agreements.

INTERCULTURAL
BUSINESS
COMMUNICATION

1

The Nature
of Intercultural
Communication

OBJECTIVES

Upon completion of this chapter, you will:

- be able to define such terms as intercultural, international, intracultural, multicultural, and ethnocentric.

- understand how communication barriers affect intercultural communication.

- understand the differences between norms, rules, roles, and networks.

- be able to distinguish between subcultures and subgroups.

- understand the concept of business globalization.

- be able to differentiate between ethnocentric, polycentric, regiocentric, and geocentric management orientations.

More than 2 million North Americans work for foreign employers, and the number of foreign companies that have built plants in the United States is increasing. Evidence that the world is becoming more cosmopolitan can be seen in the number of international products, such as Coke, McDonald's hamburgers, the Sony Walkman, and Honda automobiles, that are common around the world. The new economic bonanza is apparent in the universal appreciation of food, such as sushi; fashion, such as U.S. jeans and Mexican bajas; and music, such as U.S. jazz and rock. Because of the global boom, more and more business will involve international activities, which will require the ability to communicate across cultures.

To gain a better understanding of the field of intercultural communication, a knowledge of frequently used terms is important. Such terms as *intercultural, international,* and *multicultural* are often used interchangeably. However, certain distinctions should be made.

The term *intercultural communication* was first used by Edward T. Hall in 1959. Hall was one of the first researchers to differentiate cultures based on how communications are sent and received. Hall defined **intercultural communication** as communication between persons of different cultures.

Intercultural business communication is a relatively new term in the business world and is defined as communication within and between businesses that involves people from more than one culture. Although we generally think of the United States as one culture, a great deal of cultural diversity exists. For example, more than 30 percent of the residents of New York City are foreign born, Miami is two-thirds Latin American, and San Francisco is one-third Asian. In fact, African Americans, Asians, and Latin Americans make up 21 percent of the U.S. population. An increase in the Asian and Latin American populations is expected during the next decade. Many U.S. citizens communicate interculturally almost daily because the communication is between people of different cultural backgrounds (Copeland, 1988).

With the increased globalization of the economy and interaction of different cultures, the concept of a *world culture* has emerged. A **world culture** is the idea that as traditional barriers among people of differing cultures break down, emphasizing the commonality of human needs, one culture will emerge, a new culture to which all people will adhere.

The United States continues to welcome a large number of immigrants each year and has been referred to as a melting pot society. **Melting pot** means a sociocultural assimilation of people of differing backgrounds and nationalities; the term implies losing ethnic differences and forming one large society, or **macroculture**. While the idea of everyone's being the same may sound ideal, the problem with this concept is that many U.S. citizens wish to maintain their ethnic-cultural heritage. Rather than being one melting pot society, therefore, the reality in the United States is that many U.S. cities are made up of neighborhoods of people with a common heritage who strive to retain their original culture and language. If you travel to San Francisco, a visit to Chinatown with signs in Chinese and people speaking Chinese will verify this reality. Many street signs in other U.S. cities, such as New York, Miami, or Honolulu, are in another language in addition to English. The result has not been the melding of various cultures into one cultural group as idealists believed would happen. Because we have cultures within cultures (**microcultures**), communication problems often result.

Intracultural communication is defined as communication between and among members of the same culture. Generally, people who are of the same race, political persuasion, and religion or who share the same interests communicate intraculturally. Having the same beliefs, values, and constructs facilitates communication and defines a particular culture (Gudykunst & Ting-Toomey, 1988). However, due to distance, cultural differences may exist within a culture, such as differences in the pace of life and regional speech patterns between residents of New York City and Jackson, Mississippi. Distance is also a factor in the differences in the dialects of the people of other cultures, such as in northern and southern Japan.

The terms *intercultural communication* and *international communication* should not be used interchangeably. Intercultural communication, as stated previously, involves communication between people of different cultures. **International communication** takes place between nations and governments rather than individuals; it is quite formal and ritualized. The dialogue at the United Nations, for example, would be termed *international communication.*

Since all international business activity involves communication, a knowledge of intercultural communication and international business communication is important to prepare you to compete successfully in international environments. In fact, upward mobility and promotion in tomorrow's corporate world may depend on your knowledge of intercultural business communication.

GLOBALIZATION

Although globalization has come to the world, most of the world's businesses are not globalized. Business **globalization** is the ability of a corporation to take a product and market it in the entire civilized world. International firms have subsidiaries or components in other countries; however, control of the foreign operations is maintained at the home country headquarters. Multinational firms allow their foreign operations to exist as domestic organizations. Most firms are international, either sourcing, producing, or exporting. Many times the product may also be partially or completely manufactured somewhere other than the United States (Rhinesmith, 1993). The top multinational firms listed in *The Economist* (Emmott, 1993) earned 31 to 93 percent of their total revenues from foreign sales. The United Nations estimated there were 35,000 multinationals; and the largest 100 multinationals, excluding banking and finance, accounted for $3.1 trillion of worldwide assets in 1990. U.S. dependency on exports is confirmed by the fact that one of every six manufacturing jobs is related to exports. Export crops account for 40 percent of farm production, and exports account for one-third of all U.S. corporate profits (Emmott, 1993). In the past some U.S. corporations have been largely insulated from globalization due to a strong domestic market and an absence of foreign competitors. However, this trend is changing as foreign corporations enter the U.S. market.

The personnel of an organization must have a global mindset in order for the firm to succeed in the international marketplace. Laurent (1986), in a study of multinational corporations, found that successful multinational corporations do not submerge the individuality of different cultures completely in the corporate culture, that intercultural contact can promote a determination not to adjust to other cultures, and that new management theory and practice can be presented only to individuals who are culturally able and willing to accept it. Rhinesmith (1993) states that "The corporate culture contains the values, norms of behavior, systems, policies, and procedures through which the organization adapts to the complexity of the global arena" (p. 14). Successful corporations have found that the values, beliefs, and behaviors of the parent corporation do not need to be the beliefs, values, and behaviors of the offices in other cultures. Hofstede's (1991) study of IBM determined that managers had to adjust the corporate management philosophy to fit the beliefs, values, and behaviors of the country in which they were working. Companies with franchises abroad have had to make certain adjustments to accommodate the tastes and preferences of individual countries; for example, Tex-Mex cuisine is prepared kosher in Israel. According to Rhinesmith (1993), "Diversity—both domestic and international—will be the engine that drives the creative energy of the corporation of the 21st century. Successful global managers will be those who are able to manage this diversity for the innovative and competitive edge of their corporations" (p. 5). Evans, Doz, and Laurent (1990) state that the

> five elements critical to building a successful corporate culture are: (1) a clear and simple mission statement, (2) the vision of the chief executive officer, (3) company-controlled management education, (4) project-oriented management training programs, and (5) emphasis on the processes of global corporate culture. (p. 118)

While the United States is dependent on foreign economic opportunities, the multinational firms have had problems with U.S. citizens working in foreign assignments. The failures to adapt included differences in lifestyle, language, and business philosophy as well as financial problems, government problems, cultural shock, and problems with housing, food, and family. Ruch (1989) found the ability to blend with the host culture and explain one's own culture is more important than having product, price, or quality advantages. Although many of the people sent on foreign assignments know their U.S. market, they do not have the ability to accept another culture on that culture's terms, even for short periods.

CULTURE

Whereas communication is a process, **culture** is the structure through which the communication is formulated and interpreted. Culture deals with the way people live. When cultures interact, adaptation has to take place in order for the cultures to communicate effectively. In dealing with intercultural business communication, awareness of the symbols of each culture, how they are the same and how they are different, is important.

Dimensions of Culture

In order to communicate effectively in the intercultural business environment, being knowledgeable about all cultural factors that affect the situation is essential. The following graphical representation of culture (Figure 1.1) has three primary dimensions—languages, physical, and psychological (Borden, 1991, p. 171).

FIGURE 1.1   Dimensions of Culture

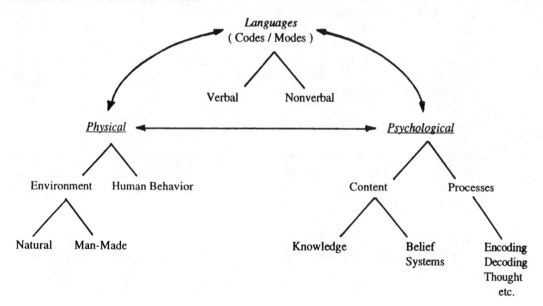

The languages, physical, and psychological dimensions of culture are interdependent. As we are born into a society, no one dimension is more important than the others. The individual dimensions develop in harmony with each other.

First, the language dimension is used to communicate with others who have values and beliefs like our own. Second, the physical dimension relates to the physical reality of our environment and what people do within the culture. The physical dimension is measured objectively. Third is the psychological dimension, which relates to what we have learned and believe as well as to mental activities. The psychological dimension is measured subjectively. While we can alter these dimensions and our way of communicating with others, we must first understand our own personal characteristics and why we are the way we are.

Glen's (1981) cognitive approach to studying culture suggests that different cultures structure knowledge differently and that these differences determine aspects of behavior and communication, such as information that is accepted as proof for an opinion or argument, the syntax of the information, and the topics that are considered appropriate to discuss.

If you find that a particular cultural attitude is constant across cultures, then you do not have to be concerned about that particular cultural trait. However, if you find that a particular cultural attitude varies for specific cultures, you will want to consider the effect it will have on communications with cultures that do not possess this attitude. A cultural symbol is a word or object that represents something in the culture. Cultural symbol variability may be included in social cognitive processes such as information processing, persuasive strategy selection, conflict management styles, personality, social relations, and self-perceptions as well as habits, norms, rules, roles, networks, language, and environment. All of the factors interact and influence each other. An example of cultural symbol variability is the use of the dove as the symbol of peace or the valentine as a symbol of love in some cultures. In order to communicate effectively in the intercultural business environment, a knowledge of all cultural factors that affect the situation is important.

Stereotypes of U.S. Culture

Stereotypes, perceptions about certain groups of people or nationalities, exist about people in the United States as well as people of other cultures. In *American Ways*, Althen (1988) describes typical U.S. businesspersons as people who tend to

- be informal in their relationships.
- be rather formal in their business attire (suits for men and dresses or suits for women); however, many firms are becoming more relaxed in their dress codes or have a casual day when employees can dress more casually.

- be workaholics because they spend more time working than they do with their family or social engagements; U.S. executives tend to put in long hours at the office.
- embarrass foreign businesspeople by doing manual labor (for example, mowing their own lawns) or tasks that would be done by the lower class or servants in their country.
- be overly concerned with time, money, and appointments; people of other cultures interpret the need of U.S. businesspeople to begin meetings on time and start business discussions immediately as an indication that they are unfriendly, impersonal, and cold.
- make decisions on hard, objective facts rather than on personal feelings, social relationships, or political advantage.
- consider contracts and the written word as very important and to be taken very seriously.
- be aware of the status differences within the organization; however, generally no display of superiority or inferiority is made that tends to make rank-conscious foreigners uneasy.
- be mobile; they rarely work for one company all their life, which is very different from many countries in the world.
- convey superiority in their actions and attitudes because they feel the United States is a superior nation.*

Axtell (1991) identified these stereotypes of persons in the United States: arrogant, loud, friendly, impatient, generous, hard working, and monolingual. These descriptions, admittedly, are stereotypes.

Stereotypes of Persons in Other Cultures

Axtell (1991, pp. 83–84) asked people in the United States who conduct business with persons outside the United States to give one-word descriptors of their impression of people of other nationalities. Some of these stereotypes follow:

Culture	Image
English	conservative, reserved, polite, proper, formal
French	arrogant, rude, chauvinistic, romantics, gourmets, cultural, artistic
Italians	demonstrative, talkative, emotional, romantics, bold, artistic

* Adapted from Althen, Gary, *American Ways: A Guide for Foreigners.* Used by permission of Intercultural Press Inc., Yarmouth, ME. © 1988.

Latin Americans	mañana attitude, macho, music lovers, touchers
Asians	inscrutable, intelligent, xenophobic (fear/hatred of strangers/foreigners), golfers, group oriented, polite, soft-spoken

By recognizing differences as well as similarities, businesspersons can adjust their mode of communication to fit the individual culture with which they are communicating.

ENCULTURATION

Enculturation is the socialization process you go through to adapt to your own society. When you grow up in one culture, you learn one way of classifying, coding, prioritizing, and justifying reality. Cultural information that you are willing to share with outsiders is considered **frontstage culture**, while cultural information that is concealed from outsiders is considered **backstage culture**. An example of frontstage culture would be a sales representative who loudly announces: "We got the Hunter Fan account." This information is readily shared. An example of backstage culture would be the sales representative who conceals the fact that his child is mentally retarded. Frontstage and backstage culture vary by culture and by individuals within the culture because some people are inherently more open than others. As a representative of your company, you need to learn what the culture with which you are working considers acceptable frontstage information that can be shared, and what is considered backstage information that is not to be shared with others.

Datan, Rodeheaver, and Hughes (1987) use the concept of *scripts* to explain the cognitive imprinting that happens during enculturation.

> Individuals experience events in their lives as "scenes"—organized wholes combining people, places, time, actions, and in particular, affects that amplify these experiences and provide a sense of urgency about understanding them. Out of early scenes, the individual develops sets of rules for interpreting, evaluating, producing, predicting, or controlling future scenes. These rules—"scripts"—are initially innate but are supplemented and replaced by learned scripts. Higher-order scripts are created when scenes are combined and instilled with fresh affect—"psychological magnification." . . . The order in personality development, then, derives from the individual's need to impose order—the script—on the critical events, or scenes, in life. And, finally, scripts that initially arise from scenes begin to give rise to scenes instead, as the individual's construction of experience affects experience itself. (p. 164)

Examples of such scripts are the inability of the Japanese to say the word "no" directly but instead to say "it would be difficult," and the difficulty for someone of a strong Christian background to lie to save face when for a Christian lying is never condoned.

ACCULTURATION

People do not want to abandon their past; therefore, they *acculturate* new ideas into their existing culture. **Acculturation** is the process of adjusting and adapting to a new and different culture. If people of two different cultures absorb a significant number of each others' cultural differences and have a number of similarities, **cultural synergy** takes place with the two cultures merging to form a stronger overriding culture. Corporate cultures are an example of a synergy of diverse cultures. People who learn more than one culture are **multicultural** and can move between two cultures very comfortably. An example of cultural synergy is the royal Grimaldi family of Monaco. Princess Grace was a U.S. citizen and married Prince Ranier of Monaco. The Grimaldi children were raised in Monaco; however, due to the time they spent in the United States, they were acculturated to this country. While acculturation increases the interconnectedness of cultures, differences are sources of potential problems. All differences will probably not be absorbed by either culture.

ETHNOCENTRISM

Ethnocentrism is the belief that your own cultural background, including ways of analyzing problems, values, beliefs, language, and verbal and nonverbal communication, is correct. Ethnocentrists believe their culture is the central culture and other cultures are incorrect, defective, or quaint. When we evaluate others, we do it through our self-reference criterion because it is what we know. In his research, Fisher (1988) refers to ethnocentrism as *mindsets*. **Mindsets** are ways of being that allow us to see and perceive things through our own filter. Mindsets are learned by growing up in a particular culture. We learn to be open or closed to others and their way of living; however, mindsets can be altered.

The U.S. mindset includes the concept that the American way is best. ("American" as used in the United States is an example of ethnocentrism because the term *American* actually refers to all the people in North, South, and Central American countries.) Although this is mainly a U.S. concept, people who are born in smaller countries feel the same way about their own country—that it is the best place to live. The belief that one's own culture is best is a natural phenomenon common to all cultures. While it is natural to be ethnocentric and have a particular mindset, when we judge other mindsets we need to look at them from the perspective of the people who hold them before we judge them as good or bad. However, we must be careful about generalizing to other cultures or making assumptions about how others view the United States. The term *Ugly American* was derived from the behavior of U.S. travelers observed by persons in other cultures who judged them to be inconsiderate of the culture they were visiting.

NORMS, RULES, ROLES, AND NETWORKS

Norms, rules, roles, and networks are situational factors that influence encoding and decoding of both verbal and nonverbal messages within a culture. They are unwritten guidelines people within the cultural group follow. **Norms** are culturally ingrained principles of correct and incorrect behaviors, which, if broken, carry a form of overt or covert penalty. **Rules** are formed to clarify cloudy areas of norms. The U.S. Supreme Court is an excellent example of an organization that looks at the intent of a rule and determines how strongly or loosely it should be followed. A **role** includes the behavioral expectations of a position within a culture and is affected by norms and rules. **Networks** are formed with personal ties and involve an exchange of assistance. Networks and the need to belong are the bases of friendships and subgroups. An example of a political network is the exchange of votes between U.S. legislators needed to support their projects. When the United States decided to help the Kuwaitis defend themselves against Iraq in 1992, the U.S. ambassador to the United Nations called in the other ambassadors within his network for their concurrence. The ability to develop networks in intercultural situations can enable you to do business more effectively in multicultural environments. In some cultures, such as the Arab, Spanish, and Japanese, networking is essential since they prefer to conduct business with people they know or with associates of people they know (Gudykunst & Ting-Toomey, 1988).

SUBCULTURES AND SUBGROUPS

Subcultures are groups of people possessing characteristic traits that set them apart and distinguish them from others within a larger society, or macroculture. The macroculture may be a country, a city, or a business. For example, U.S. citizens belong to many different religions, yet they belong to the macroculture of U.S. citizens. Examples of subcultures (or microcultures) in the United States include senior citizens, teenagers, baby boomers, African Americans, Latin Americans, Catholics, Jews, disabled individuals, trade associations, and self-help groups. All these groups will have similarities to the macroculture but will also have some differences. The subculture members will all have the same self-perception and agree that they belong to the subculture (Dodd, 1987).

Intercultural business communication necessitates working with subcultures. The subcultures form a diversity of ethnic identities with which managers will have to learn to work harmoniously.

Subgroups, while also part of the macroculture, are groups with which the macroculture does not agree and has problems communicating. Members of these groups often engage in communication behavior that is distinctively different from that of the dominant culture. Examples of subgroups include youth gangs, prostitutes, saboteurs, embezzlers, and other groups that have unique experiences and/or characteristics not sanctioned by the macroculture (Dodd, 1987).

COMMUNICATION BARRIERS

When encountering someone from another culture, communication barriers are often created when the behavior of the other person differs from our own. **Communication barriers** are obstacles to effective communication. An example of such a barrier is the cultural differences of the head nod, which indicates understanding in the United States, but in Japan it means only that the person is listening. By understanding intercultural communication, we can break down barriers and pave the way for mutual understanding and respect.

Bell (1992) identified the following barriers to communication:

1. Physical—time, environment, comfort and needs, and physical medium (e.g., telephone, letter) of communication
2. Cultural—ethnic, religious, and social differences
3. Perceptual—viewing what is said from your own mindset
4. Motivational—include the listener's mental inertia
5. Experiential—lack of similar life happenings
6. Emotional—personal feelings of the listener
7. Linguistic—different languages spoken by the speaker and listener or use of a vocabulary beyond the comprehension of the listener
8. Nonverbal—caused by how something is said and other nonword messages
9. Competition—the listener's ability to do other things rather than hear the communication

INTERCULTURAL CONSTRUCTS

Borden (1991) lists seven constructs that individuals must possess if they are going to succeed interculturally: The degree to which we can understand intercultural communication depends upon the degree to which

1. We are aware that our intent to communicate, either as communicator or communicatee, may result in only expressive behavior or information gathering respectively.
2. Our cybernetic (self-concept) in one culture can operate independently of our cybernetic in the other culture.
3. We are competent in the language of each culture.
4. We are able to work within the constraints (personal, situational, and cultural) of the human communication system established by the communication from the two cultures.
5. We are culturally literate in our own and the other's culture.
6. We know the position of our culture and the other's culture on the four universal value dimensions and their interaction with the cultural orientation model.
7. We know the cultural orientation of our culture and the other's culture on the associative-abstractive, particularistic-universalistic, and closed-minded/open-minded dimensions and can use it as the first approximation of the cognitive style of the communicants (pp. 210–213).

The components of Borden's constructs will be discussed in later chapters.

MULTINATIONAL MANAGEMENT ORIENTATIONS

To compete successfully in a global economy, a knowledge of management styles used by international corporations is also important. With the emergence of the concept of *world culture* has come a heightened awareness of the interdependence of nations and the need to break cultural barriers and find ways to work harmoniously with people of all cultures.

Multinational firms, those located in more than one nation, generally will follow either an ethnocentric, polycentric, geocentric, or regiocentric form of management. Multinational firms, such as Sony, Quaker Oats, Exxon, Robert Bosch, and Nissan, may follow a single management style at all global locations or may use various styles of management to increase productivity, while maintaining worker morale. All multinational or global corporations are **transnational**, which means they cross the borders of countries in conducting their business (Moran & Stripp, 1991).

Not all of these management styles consider the diversity of cultures working within them nor are they managed to take advantage of the surprises that surface in multinational management. As Rhinesmith (1993) has stated, global managers have a mindset that allows them to take advantage of and manage the complexity, adaptability, teams, uncertainty, and learning that the global organization requires. Since people are the most critical factor, for an

TABLE 1.1 Comparison of Domestic and Global Mindsets

Domestic Mindset	*Global Mindset*
Functional expertise	Bigger, broader picture
Prioritization	Balance of contradictions
Structure	Process
Individual responsibility	Teamwork and diversity
No surprises	Change as opportunity
Trained against surprises	Openness to surprises

Source: Rhinesmith, 1993, p. 27. Used with publisher's permission.

organization to succeed globally, people are also the restraining factor in the firm's ability to survive and grow. Human resource development personnel must be involved in the education and changing of the mindsets. The global mindset differs from the domestic mindset as illustrated in Table 1.1.

The person who can manage a domestic operation does not necessarily have the competencies to manage a global operation. People who have a global mindset tend to live life in many ways that may be physically, intellectually, emotionally, or spiritually different depending upon the culture with which they are interacting.

When a firm is located in one country and all its sales are in the same country, **ethnocentric management** practices will be employed. Ethnocentric management does not account for cultural differences in the workforce. All workers will be treated the same. Many times the management practices employed will rely on one person's views of how the organization should be run. Some domestic corporations that purchase abroad for resale at home, are financed from abroad, or buy technology abroad still need to think globally due to their international activities (Moran & Stripp, 1991). For example, U.S. car manufacturers complained that their cars were not selling in Japan. These manufacturers, however, had not changed the position of the steering wheel from the left to the right for driving on the opposite side of the road from the United States, and they had not downsized their cars in consideration of the limited space available to park cars in Japan. When a company expands internationally, it has to consider the consumers who are targeted to buy its products.

Polycentric management practices consider the culture of the country in which the firm is located. The people in charge consider the cultural needs of the workers in the area in which the firm is located. A melting pot effect may seem to exist because the majority's culture is considered in management decisions. In the United States, you will see this particularly in small firms. Leaving the polycentric management practices one is used to in one's home country is part of the problem workers have when they move to a foreign country to work because they were comfortable in the old management style (Moran & Stripp, 1991).

Regiocentric management considers the region rather than the country in which the firm is located, realizing that countries can and often do have many different cultural backgrounds. The regional theory acknowledges that in the United States all areas are not the same. For example, running a production facility in Michigan with high unionization and a facility in Mississippi with low unionization and different ethnic bases calls for different management strategies. Management strategies will consider the diversity of the workforce (Moran & Stripp, 1991). Unions tend to keep the workers from interacting directly with management. Many firms now wish to use Total Quality Management, which utilizes interaction between workers and management. The Saturn automotive company built its plant in Springfield, Tennessee, because it could implement Total Quality Management. Although Saturn now has a workforce that is unionized, the union works with management, and the quality and sales of the Saturn automobile have been better than any other General Motors' product.

Geocentric management requires a common framework with enough freedom for individual locations to operate regionally in order to meet the cultural needs of the workers. *Geocentric* refers to a synergy of ideas from different countries of operation. The most successful multinational corporations use integrated geocentric management. Corporations have common control practices that the individual locations are free to modify. To compete successfully in a global economy, being able to recognize the management style used is helpful (Moran & Stripp, 1991).

The ability of different cultures to communicate successfully in a business environment, to assimilate their cultures and conduct business, and to do this either within the United States or abroad is what intercultural business communication is about. Different cultures do present communication problems; differing business practices and negotiation strategies pose additional problems. Intercultural business communication involves a knowledge and understanding of other cultures, including their subcultures and subgroups and standards of behavior. With the emergence of the concept of a world culture has come a heightened awareness of the interdependence of nations and the need to break cultural barriers in order to find ways to work harmoniously with people of all cultures.

Exercise 1.1

Instructions: Match the following terms with their definition.

___ 1. Belief that your own culture is superior

___ 2. The socialization process we go through to learn a culture

___ 3. A sociocultural assimilation

___ 4. Cultural information concealed from outsiders

___ 5. Absorption of new ideas into existing culture

___ 6. Between members of the same culture

___ 7. Between persons of different cultures

___ 8. Between nations and governments

___ 9. Groups having traits differing from the macroculture

___ 10. Culturally ingrained principles of correct/incorrect behavior

A Acculturation
B. Backstage culture
C. Enculturation
D. Ethnocentrism
E. Frontstage culture
F. Intercultural
G. International
H. Intracultural
I. Melting pot
J. Norms
K. Subcultures

TERMS

Acculturation
Backstage culture
Communication barriers
Cultural synergy
Culture
Enculturation
Ethnocentric management
Ethnocentrism
Frontstage culture
Geocentric management
Globalization
Intercultural business
    communication

Intercultural communication
International communication
Intracultural communication
Macroculture
Melting pot
Microculture
Mindsets
Multicultural
Multinational firm
Networks
Norms
Polycentric management
Regiocentric management

Roles   Subgroup
Rules   Transnational
Stereotypes   World culture
Subculture

QUESTIONS AND CASES FOR DISCUSSION

1. The United States has long been called a *melting pot*. What does this term mean?

2. What does it mean for a firm to be global?

3. Give examples of how products have been globalized.

4. Explain the differences between norms, roles, rules, and networks.

5. Explain what a subculture is and give examples of U.S. subcultures.

6. What is cultural synergy?

7. Distinguish between intercultural communication and intracultural communication.

8. Identify the dimensions of culture.

9. Identify types of barriers to communication.

10. Are business cultures necessarily aligned to national cultures?

Case 1   At a reception for a U.S. political candidate, the guests appear to be divided into groups. People in some groups are all African American, others are Latin American, and others are Asian. Explain the cultural phenomena that are operating at this political gathering.

Case 2   The U.S. automotive manufacturers have complained about Japanese automotive imports and the fact that they are locked out of the Japanese market. The Japanese have countered that the U.S. firms have not done their homework; they offer cars that are too big or are fuel inefficient. While U.S. car sales have decreased in the United States, Japanese sales have increased. Japanese manufacturers have begun to assemble cars in the United States; many U.S. firms are moving part of their operations to Mexico. Discuss the implications to these firms as they globalize.

ACTIVITIES

1. Clip a story from the local newspaper that is related to some aspect of intercultural communication, such as problems encountered by persons of other

cultures in the acculturation process or problems between subgroups; give a short report to the class.

2. Ask a member of the class who is from another culture to discuss how cultural norms and rules in his or her culture differ from those in the United States.

3. Invite a member of the business community who conducts business globally to address problems encountered when dealing with representatives of other cultures whose form of management (ethnocentric, polycentric, geocentric, or regiocentric) may be different from that in the United States.

4. Interview a foreign student on roles of women and children in their culture. In a report to the class, make comparisons between these roles and those in the United States.

5. Write a one-page proposal for improving relationships between U.S. students and students from other cultures in your school.

6. Analyze a multinational corporation's annual report and determine where it is producing and selling goods and what the profit margins of those goods are compared to other multinational firms.

REFERENCES

Althen, G. (1988). *American ways*. Yarmouth, ME: Intercultural Press, Inc.

Axtell, R. E. (1991). *The do's and taboos of international trade*. New York: John Wiley & Sons, Inc.

Bell, A. H. (1992). *Business communication: Toward 2000*. Cincinnati, OH: South-Western Publishing Co.

Borden, G. A. (1991). *Cultural orientation: An approach to understanding intercultural communication*. Englewood Cliffs, NJ: Prentice Hall.

Copeland, L. (1988). Making the most of cultural differences at the workplace. *Personnel, 65*, 52.

Datan, N., Rodeheaver, D., & Hughes, F. (1987). Adult development and aging. In M. R. Rosenzweig & L. W. Porter (Eds.), *Annual Review of Psychology, 38*, 153–180.

Dodd, C. H. (1987). *Dynamics of intercultural communication*. Dubuque, IA: Wm. C. Brown.

Emmott, B. (1993). Multinationals: The non-global firm. *The Economist, 326* (7804), 5–20.

Evans, P., Doz, Y., & Laurent, A. (Eds.) (1990). *Human resource management in international firms: Change, globalization, innovation*. New York: St. Martin's Press.

Fisher, G. (1988). *Mindsets*. Yarmouth, ME: Intercultural Press, Inc.

Glen, E. S. (1981). *Man and mankind*. Norwood, NJ: Ablex Publishing Corporation.

Gudykunst, W. B., & Ting-Toomey, S. (1988). *Culture and interpersonal communication*. Newbury Park, CA: Sage Publications.

Hall, E. T. (1959). *The silent language*. Garden City, NY: Doubleday.

Hofstede, G. (1991). *Cultures and organizations*. London: McGraw-Hill Book Company.

Laurent, A. (1986). The cross-cultural puzzle of human resource management. *Human Resource Management, 25*(1), 91–102.

Moran, R. T., & Stripp, W. G. (1991). *Dynamics of successful international business negotiations*. Houston, TX: Gulf Publishing Company.

Rhinesmith, S. H. (1993). *A manager's guide to globalization*. Homewood, IL: Richard D. Irwin, Inc.

Ruch, W. V. (1989). *International handbook of corporate communication*. Jefferson, NC: McFarland.

2

Universal Systems

OBJECTIVES

Upon completion of this chapter, you will:

- increase your understanding of systems that are universal to all cultural groups and their relationship to communicating and negotiating in a global setting.

- understand the role that economic and political systems play in communicating interculturally in business settings.

- see the relationship between educational systems and global communication.

- gain insight into social systems and hierarchies that affect effective intercultural business communication.

Cultural systems have an impact on multicultural communication. **Cultural universals** are formed out of the common problems of all cultures. The following systems are found in all cultures: economic and political, education, marriage and family, and social hierarchies and interaction. A knowledge of how cultural systems in the United States differ from those of other cultures can enhance communication effectiveness when conducting business with persons of other cultures. Although these systems are universal to all cultures, different cultures may deal with an issue in a significantly different way. In communicating interculturally, the variabilities are equally as important as the similarities.

ECONOMIC SYSTEMS

A culture develops an **economic system** in order to meet the physiological needs of its people. The way in which the products that meet the physiological needs of the people are produced, distributed, and consumed is referred to as the economic system. All societies not only work out ways of producing or procuring goods, they must also determine the procedure for distributing them.

The different economic systems in the world today include capitalism, socialism, agrarianism, and barter. The United States and Japan are capitalistic; Sweden and China are socialistic; Belize and Cambodia are agrarian; and Laos and the Marshall Islands use the barter system. The relationship between the public and private sectors, and which sector dominates, may make some economic systems a blend of the first three systems. No single correct economic system exists. The U.S. method of distributing goods is based on the capacity to pay, while such countries as Cuba distribute goods according to need. A brief description of the economic and political systems of the United States and other selected countries follows.

United States

The U.S. economic system is capitalistic with socialistic overtones. Free market principles tempered by government regulations operate the economy. In addition, the United States is a financial center, and its economy affects the world. The U.S. capitalistic system is affected by inflation (brought about by the change from an industrially oriented economy to a service and technical economy), unemployment, and the economy of other countries since many U.S. corporations have become multinational. Inflation in late 1993 was 2.8 percent, and unemployment was 6.3 percent.

Canada

Canada's economy is very strong worldwide. A 3 percent growth rate is normal, but it was slower in 1991–1993 due to the global recession. The economy is capitalistic with socialistic controls in the areas of health care and the retirement system. Unemployment has been high in recent years; in 1992 it was about 8 to 10 percent and inflation was around 5 percent. The economy is driven by industrial plants, mining, fishing, agriculture, and food processing. Canada is the world leader in wood pulp and timber.

England

England's economy is based on capitalism; however, many sectors of the economy were nationalized or socialized between 1945 and 1980. Since the 1980s, some of the sectors have been privatized, and less regulation of industry has been encouraged. Currently England's inflation is 8 percent, and unemployment is 11 percent. England is still a major industrial power in the world.

Japan

Japan's economy is a capitalistic/free market one, based on manufacturing, fishing, and exporting. Except for fish, Japan must import over half of its food supply. Japan must also import most of its raw materials for manufacturing, and over 95 percent of exports are manufactured goods. An early 1990s recession caused businesses to have to lay off or retire employees early. Inflation in late 1993 was about 1 percent; unemployment was 2.8 percent.

Mexico

Mexico's economy is dependent on that of other countries. The oil industry, agriculture, tourism, and maquiladoras (Mexican assembly facilities often near a major U.S. market) employ most of the working people; however, there is still a great deal of unemployment. The government is attracting foreign investment by selling state-owned companies and deregulating trade in order to combat unemployment, high inflation, and high debt. Mexico's growth rate is currently 3 percent, and inflation is below 20 percent. Projecting the impact of the North American Free Trade Agreement (NAFTA) on Mexico's economy is purely speculative. According to de Forest (1994), some predict that U.S. manufacturers will take advantage of the low wages of Mexican workers and will move their operations to Mexico. Others predict that many manufacturers will not consider a plant in Mexico because of problems with working within Mexican behavioral expectations. Currently only about 10 percent of *maquiladora* programs are profitable by U.S. standards; profitability probably would be increased if U.S. manufacturers were more sensitive to Mexican mores and values.

POLITICAL SYSTEMS

The **political system** is the governing system of the country and can be based on dictatorship, inherited rights, election procedures, consensus, or conquest. A person's age, economic ability, or marital status may be considered when selecting people for political positions in some countries. In other countries, oratory skills and the ability to sway public opinion may be factors. Group members may even select a political leader because they believe the person to have supernatural powers. A description of a few political systems follows.

United States

The U.S. political system is made up of a federal government with the states having numerous rights. The president is elected by the electoral college, and other positions are voted on by the people. U.S. citizens tend to be very proud of their political system yet may not be well informed about politics. However, U.S. citizens do not like their system to be criticized.

Canada

Canada has a parliamentary system. The people elect the prime minister and members of Parliament. Elections can be held any time a no-confidence vote occurs in Parliament, requiring the prime minister to call a general election. The central government has power in the areas of national health insurance, trade, the military, and development. The country is divided into provinces; each province controls its region.

England

England is ruled by a constitutional monarchy with a parliament. The House of Lords, which is composed of life appointees, members of the nobility, and Church of England bishops, is both a legislative body and the highest judicial court, but it has little legislative power. The House of Commons is elected by citizens over the age of 18. The prime minister is the leader of the majority party in the House of Commons and appoints a cabinet that runs the government.

Iran

Six religious leaders and six lay leaders make up the Council of Guardians in Iran. The council approves presidential candidates, and the voting age is 15. The council members vote on the feasibility of all legislation passed by the legislature.

Japan

A constitutional monarchy is part of the political system of Japan; however, the emperor has no power. The prime minister, lower house, and upper house are elected by the people. The prefectures (equivalent to states in the United States) have governors who are elected by the people.

Mexico

Mexico has a federal government with the president elected by those over 18 years of age. Voting is obligatory. While the president may serve only one term, the senators and deputies may serve more than one term, but the terms cannot be consecutive. The federal government controls education and some industries in the Mexican states.

Morocco

Morocco is ruled by a king who appoints a prime minister and the other members of the government. A legislature is elected by those over 20 years of age.

Saudi Arabia

The Saudi Arabian political system consists of a series of regions called gover-norates that are headed by an emir who reports to the king. The current king inherited his position; however, after the current crown prince serves, all future kings will be elected by all the princes (over 500), which will eliminate the inherited monarchy; however, there will continue to be an elected monarch. In 1992 the king issued a written body of laws that guarantees the common citizens basic rights.

Companies worldwide have become increasingly affected by economic, political, and competitive pressures from companies in other countries. The recent recession in the United States was not only a U.S. problem but a world-wide problem due to the economic interrelationships. While it is well known that the automobile, steel, textile, and electronic industries face worldwide competition, it may not be as well known that many small- and medium-sized firms are also having to compete in world markets (Nath, 1988).

The United States maintained a substantial technological lead after World War II and during the 1950s, 1960s, and the beginning of the 1970s. Today this competitive edge is gone, and the macroeconomy of the world affects the perfor-mance of U.S. industry. Many U.S. industries were not prepared for this change in the macroeconomy, and the U.S. government had to provide temporary pro-tection for industries and negotiate with foreign firms to limit their exports to the

United States. In addition, the Justice Department relaxed antitrust rules allowing more joint ventures (Garland & Farmer, 1986). When a particular industry is caught in the growing complexity of global economics, many smaller firms, regions, and communities may face adverse economic times. Although U.S. companies are facing intensive foreign competition, the groundwork has been laid to increase productivity, reduce capacity requirements, and increase flexibility, making the United States able to compete in the long run.

Although the United States had a trade deficit of –$86.6 billion in 1991, direct foreign investment in the United States that year was $66.98 billion (*Economic Indicators*, 1992). During the 1980s the inflow of foreign funds was due to high interest rates in the United States, the value of the dollar, stock prices of U.S. firms, and the formation of joint ventures. The influx of foreign investment has made it difficult to distinguish a U.S. firm from a foreign firm. Many companies now have no allegiance to a given nation but are truly multinational firms in their thinking and actions. The actions multinational firms take are in the best interest of their corporation rather than the best interest of their originating country. If a corporation can manufacture a product cheaper in another country, it will do so by closing the current plant and opening a new plant in another country. Many product lines are produced almost entirely outside of the United States today, including televisions, camcorders, electronic components, tires, and clothing.

The multinational firm also has to deal with a very complex political environment. A successful domestic firm learns and operates within the existing political situation. A firm that moves into the international environment has to learn how to manage and predict politics in other nations. The multinational firm deals successfully with many diverse and conflicting political environments. Some people are concerned that due to the size, wealth, resources, and knowledge some multinational companies have, they will become political bodies themselves. In many countries, the multinational firm exercises power that parallels the powers of the country's government. For example, in the Middle East, corporations within the oil cartels exert power that equals the government's power. Some multinational managers view the world as a single marketplace ignoring national boundaries. The multinational company may well be an agent of change in the future.

Multinational companies also must be concerned with supernationalism, international politics, and international relations of the nations in which they operate. Decrees by such organizations as the United Nations, the European Economic Community, and the North American Free Trade Agreement are only a few examples of **supernationalism** today. Regionalism and economic interdependency are common in international politics, and it is projected that more regional trade agreements will be formed in the near future (Reich, 1991).

Companies also have to be concerned with subnationalism and the strife and political havoc that can result. **Subnationalism** exists when a political body attempts to unite diverse people under one government. With the Eastern European countries' discarding of communism, one of the results has been that sub-nationals want their own countries and their own government once again (Reich, 1991).

Nationalism, supernationalism, and subnationalism are all active forces multinational companies have to consider because such factors affect the politics and the economics of the areas of the world in which they operate their businesses. Although the form and content of the "isms" may vary from region to region, the possibility of upheaval is something multinational companies must consider. A company must analyze the political environment's positive and negative aspects before expanding into the environment. Other economic differences that may need to be considered before doing business in another nation include chronic high inflation versus low inflation, developed banking systems versus primitive systems, an agricultural economy versus an industrial economy versus a technological economy, low employee productivity versus high employee productivity, favorable versus unfavorable balance of payments, and currency exchange rates. To secure additional information related to conducting business in other countries, the following sources are recommended:

The Economist Business Traveller's Guides, Prentice Hall, Englewood Cliffs, NJ, 1987, are available for Britain, Japan, and the Arabian Peninsula. The guides provide maps of key cities; names of hotels and restaurants; and economic and political background, such as business structure, major industries, and social factors that affect business.

Culturgram '94, Brigham Young University, provides information for a number of countries. The *Culturgram* covers a variety of topics, such as greetings, visiting, eating, gestures, the people, the lifestyle, land and climate, history, commerce, government, economy, education, transportation, communication, health, and information for the traveler.

EDUCATIONAL SYSTEMS

The **educational system** may be formal, informal, or a combination of the two. Some societies, such as the Maoris of New Zealand and the Aleuts of Alaska, still pass on a great deal of information concerning their cultural heritage by word of mouth; other societies, such as the United States and Canada, include most of their cultural heritage in textbooks. Other societies have some of both. However it is accomplished, every society has a way of passing on its cultural heritage. **Cultural heritage** is the body of customary beliefs, social forms, material traits, thoughts, speech, and the artistic and intellectual traditions of a society.

Formal Education

Because societies are different, formal education varies between countries. The types of educational training in business also vary between and within countries and may include liberal arts, technical training, and apprenticeships. Liberal arts training teaches the humanities and considers learning important in its own right. Technical business training is generally narrowly focused along specialized lines, such as marketing, management, finance, economics, accounting, or management information systems. A problem with technical training is that there is very little human training and thought given to the people part of the business process. The apprenticeship program offers students practical experience and theory.

As the population of third world nations receive training beyond the secondary level, these nations become more developed and similar in their use of technologies (Victor, 1992). One of the arguments for the North American Free Trade Agreement (NAFTA) is that it will help Mexico to train and educate its population and not allow foreign companies to take advantage of an illiterate workforce. NAFTA requires that a company going into Mexico from the United States or Canada provide the same safety standards within its plants as in its home country and contribute to water treatment facilities and sewage treatment plants. The costs of such standards make the advantages of a workforce willing to work for low wages deteriorate quickly.

Accessibility to education varies from country to country. Much of Europe operates on a two-track system in which at approximately age 12 children are assigned to a vocational track or a university track. While the United States, Japan, and the Russian states have open access to the educational system for all children, the importance the family places on education, the child's ability, and the quality of the child's teachers all play an important role in how far a child will go in the educational system (Victor, 1992).

The value of an education, once it is received, varies again from country to country. A description of educational systems in the United States and other selected countries is given in the following sections.

United States

In the United States, education for those who are 5 to 16 years old is compulsory and free. Although not highly competitive up to the secondary level, the U.S. education system is somewhat competitive at the postsecondary level at such schools as Harvard, MIT, and Yale, where intellectual demands may be quite rigorous. Since education is a state's right, competition between and within state educational systems may vary. The literacy rate varies by region in the United States from 80 to 97 percent. Even though graduating from certain prestigious institutions of higher learning may help in securing initial corporate positions, what a person does on the job determines the person's career and the companies for which the person will work. University ties then become less important (Victor, 1992).

Canada

In Canada the provinces are responsible for education; however, in all the provinces education is free and compulsory for eight years to age 15. The literacy rate is 99 percent. In Newfoundland the primary and secondary education is free but operated by different religious groups. In Quebec, Catholic and Protestant boards are supported by the government to direct school curricula. About 40 percent of the population attend a university; approximately 10 percent have college degrees. A number of students who wish to enter the workforce early complete a two-year technical training program (*Culturgram*, 1994).

England

The educational systems of England and Canada are similar. England has free and compulsory education from ages 5 to 16. England's literacy rate is 99 percent. "At age 16 students take an exam to earn the General Certificate of Secondary Education, which is used basically as an entrance exam by England's universities and colleges" (*Culturgram*, 1994). Members of England's upper class tend to go to the elite educational institutions. Although it is possible for someone in the lower classes to attend such schools, primarily those with alumni connections attend them. Therefore, in Britain one's position in society determines one's education.

France

France's educational system has several unique aspects. Education is free and compulsory for ages 6 to 16. The literacy rate is nearly 99 percent. The Catholic schools enroll 20 percent of the children and are subsidized by the government. Secondary school begins at age 11 and lasts seven years to age 18. The secondary education is offered by lycées and colleges. The lycée equals a U.S. junior college education. Upon completing secondary school, students take a comprehensive exam for the university. Most university training is also free in France except for the marketing schools (*Culturgram*, 1994).

The French also consider the university graduated from to be very important. While positions in business and government are not limited to a few institutions, alumni of the Grandes Écoles are considered more favorably. In France where a student goes to school determines her or his position in society. The Grandes Écoles and the alumni of the Grandes Écoles control business in France; and to be successful in business dealings in France, one must network through alumni of those schools (Victor, 1992).

Germany

In Germany's educational system, people must determine their careers early in life. Education is free from kindergarten through the university. School begins with preschool at age 4; however, it is mandatory from ages 7 to 14. Literacy is 99 percent in Germany. People of Germany are required to choose between technical training and college training at the age of 13. The entrance exam for the university is very difficult and can only be completed successfully after finishing the college preparatory school.

Iran

In Iran the literacy rate for the population is 54 percent. Religious instruction receives more support than secular education. The rural areas particularly are lacking in primary education. Studies in science and mathematics are popular when they are available.

Japan

The education system in Japan is very competitive; entrance exams to private schools and universities are rigorous. Competition is keen for acceptance to the prestigious schools since graduating from these schools usually assures the person a position in a top corporation. Japan's literacy rate is 99 percent. Education for ages 6 to 15 is generally free and compulsory, and after age 15 tuition must be paid. Math and science are stressed. In addition, the heavy intellectual demand on the students occurs during the primary and secondary education years rather than in the college years. After high school, a very competitive university entrance exam is taken. The university a student graduates from determines the company for which he or she will work; therefore, the better the university the better that person's life will be. A close allegiance (i.e., sense of loyalty) is maintained between graduating classes, employee careers, alma mater, and year of graduation.

A comparison of Japanese and U.S. educational systems as reported by Moran (1985) follows:

Japan	*United States*
240 school days per year	180 school days per year
Less than 1% illiteracy	8% illiteracy
99% complete high school	80% complete high school
Pragmatic thinking	Creative thinking
Memorization	Logical thinking
No verbalization in class	Verbalization in class

Mexico

Education in Mexico has only recently reached the masses. Mexico has compulsory and free education for persons between the ages of 6 and 14. Although the literacy rate is reported to be 90 percent overall, figures on various subcultures, such as the Amerindian, vary. After six years of primary education, students choose to enter the secondary school for 3 years, 5 years for college preparatory education, or 6 years for teacher training. After secondary school the student must take the entrance exam to attend the university; only one-third of the students pass the exam. A university education lasts from 3 to 7 years.

Saudi Arabia

Saudi Arabia's educational system is funded by the government. In Saudi Arabia the literacy rate is 62 percent. Children 4 to 6 attend kindergarten with boys and girls in the same classroom. After age 6, boys and girls attend separate schools. Six years of primary school are followed by 3 years of intermediate school, and 3 years of secondary school. During the second year of secondary school, the student follows either a science or a literary track (*Culturgram*, 1994). Although the males and females attend the same university, they have separate classes and are given hours they can use such common facilities as the library.

How people are expected to learn may be seen on a continuum from very involved in the learning process (much interaction between teachers and students) to little involvement (no interaction between teachers and students). In the Israeli kibbutz, for example, children are expected to react spontaneously, and the classrooms are noisy. This behavior, however, is not interpreted as a lack of reverence for knowledge. Chinese classrooms, on the other hand, are silent due to the reverence paid to knowledge, truth, and wisdom (Samovar & Porter, 1991).

Informal Education

Countries that do not have an entrenched formal educational infrastructure for all people will tend to have two classes of people: the small wealthy upper class and the majority who live in poverty. The wealthy who attend school, and in many cases go to college abroad, will have a very different view of the world and their cultural heritage. The masses will hold a strong allegiance to the cultural past. Depending on the country involved, the literacy level of the masses can vary widely. A person cannot take for granted that everyone can read, has a knowledge of mathematics, or is familiar with technology. Many times what is important in one nation may be very unimportant in another nation (Victor, 1992).

Examples of cultures that place more emphasis on informal rather than formal education include the Gambia, with 25 percent literacy, no universities; Mali, with a literacy rate below 35 percent (only 25 percent go to school), no universities; and Bangladesh, with a literacy rate of 35 percent (less than half of all children attend school), few attend universities (*Culturgram*, 1994).

MARRIAGE AND FAMILY SYSTEMS

Marriage and family systems are made up of the attitudes, beliefs, and practices related to marriage and the family held by people in a culture. In order to survive, all societies must procreate. Since human infants must depend on adults for their basic needs for a significant period of time, cultures have defined how the children in their culture will be reared and who is responsible for their care. Consequently, all cultures have devised rules as to who can marry and have set conditions or procedures to be followed whereby people can marry and raise families. Anthropologists have researched and categorized much of this information for us (Ferraro, 1990).

While many different ways of being a family exist on our globe, people will tend to consider their own background first when they consider the concept of family. In many parts of the world, the concept of family is so strong that it is of paramount importance in each person's life. This is true in the Japanese, Chinese, Spanish, African, Arab, Indian, Italian, and Turkish cultures. In some cultures the association of the family is so strong that sharing the family wealth with outsiders or protecting outsiders is an unknown concept. In the United States and parts of Europe, work and family life are often combined; business guests are invited to the home. The Japanese, Taiwanese, and people of many Arab nations, on the other hand, would not invite business guests to their home.

However, the word *family* has very different connotations around the world. Definitions of a family in the United States include the nuclear family and the extended family. The **nuclear family** consists of the father, mother, and children; the **extended family** consists of grandparents, uncles, aunts, and cousins (Samovar & Porter, 1991).

In many countries the family may include second-, third-, and fourth-generation relationships. The Arabs may have over a hundred close relatives, and in Mexico godparents are considered family. Family can mean your immediate biological family, or it can mean the entire culture. In some parts of the world, the children are reared and taught communally, as in parts of Israel. Each community member takes part in raising and educating each child. The family unit, as the culture views "family," will help to foster individual and/or group dependency (Victor, 1992).

In Italy the most important affiliation is to the family, which also is responsible for a large number of self-employed people and small businesses. A necessity of Italian life is to be affiliated with at least one prime interest group (such as a political party or trade union) in order to live and work.

The ability to be hired and work in many countries depends on your relatives, and nepotism and favoritism are considered a way of life. However, in large U.S. corporations nepotism and favoritism are viewed with disfavor because the person being hired under such circumstances is often considered unqualified or corrupt. Corporations may need to adjust their views of family relationships in multicultural business relationships in order to be successful (Victor, 1992).

Family systems originally evolved to meet the needs of the society, and the following forms developed: **polygyny**, one man with many wives; **polyandry**, one woman with many husbands; **monogamy**, one husband and wife; and **serial monogamy**, a number of different monogamous marriages (Dodd, 1987; see Figure 2.1).

Many Arab countries and followers of Islam practice polygyny. The Arab countries currently have the highest birth rate in the world; however, they also have a very small population base. In the United Arab Emirates (UAE), 75 percent of the people who live there are not Arab. The UAE has had to import people to fill the jobs that are available; therefore, the government encourages men to have large families and many wives. Polyandry would help reduce the birth rate and has been practiced by many of the Polynesian nations. Monogamy is practiced in North America, South America, in some parts of the Orient, Europe, and parts of Africa. Serial monogamy is practiced where people are able to remarry after divorce or death of a spouse.

Another aspect of family is who is in control, or who plays the role of an authority figure. Families can be **patriarchal** (father-oriented) or **matriarchal** (mother-oriented) (Figure 2.2). Inheritance rights and the naming of children help in determining whether a society is matriarchal or patriarchal (Dodd, 1987).

Jewish families are matriarchal due to the Judaic Code of inheritance through the mother, although the father's name is used. Christians and followers of Islam tend to be patriarchal, and the father's name is also given to the children. Spanish women, however, maintain their maiden name hyphenated to their married name although the Spanish culture is patriarchal. Many professional women in the United States are now retaining their maiden name when they marry.

A brief description of marriage and family customs in the United States and in other selected countries follows to give you an idea of how family structures and customs vary from culture to culture.

FIGURE 2.1   Family Systems

Patriarchal   Matriarchal

FIGURE 2.2   Family Authority Figures

United States

Dating in the United States begins as early as 13 to 15 years of age. Premarital sex is common, and many couples choose to live together prior to or in place of marriage. The age for marriage averages 26 for men and 24 for women. In the United States you will find a nuclear family, consisting of either monogamous or serial monogamous parents or single parent families. The nuclear family generally maintains a close relationship with members of the extended family. The traditional family includes a mother, father, and one or two children. However, one out of four children is born out of wedlock (*Culturgram*, 1994). Some women are choosing not to marry the father of the baby or are using sperm banks if they prefer to be solely responsible for the child. Almost half of all U.S. women work, which affects decisions on family size. Many older members of the extended family live in private or government institutions rather than with their immediate families, partly due to the mobility of the family and changes in living conditions.

Canada

The Canadian family system is similar to that in the United States in that dating begins before 16 years of age. Canada is generally a patriarchal society; frequently both parents work outside the home. The divorce rate is low in Canada, which makes for a largely monogamous society (*Culturgram*, 1994).

France

France tends to have an elitist attitude toward the family. Dating begins around 15 years of age. In France social class, wealth, and level of education are important in the choice of a spouse. The nuclear family is common in France. The average family has fewer than two children, with many couples choosing to have no children. Many of the French have moved away from their extended family to work or study.

Germany

The German family system includes dating, which is dutch treat (each gender pays his or her own expenses). Marriage occurs generally after 20 years of age, but Germans usually believe they must have some financial security prior to marriage. Living together before marriage is not unusual. The family is generally patriarchal; one or two children are the norm. In what was East Germany, it is common for both parents to work; while in what was West Germany both parents working is less common (*Culturgram*, 1994).

Japan

In Japan, the family system is quite different. In the past, most marriages were arranged; now, however, most of the people from Western cultures choose their own spouse. Dating begins around 15 years of age, but the average age for marriage is 27 for men and a little younger for women. Men feel they must be financially secure before taking a wife and assume financial responsibility for the wedding. The family is an extended family with a strong sense of obligation and responsibility. One's actions reflect strongly on the family as well as on one's self. While the father is the breadwinner, the mother runs the house. In the past, it has been considered improper for women to work outside the home; however, many of the younger women have chosen a career over a family and marriage. Families tend to be small with fewer than three children. Having a male heir is important in Japan as well as in most Asian countries. The divorce rate is very low, and the marriages are monogamous.

Mexico

In the Mexican family system, dating is allowed; however, a boy often meets the girl at a prearranged place rather than picking her up at her home. Marriage follows the customary Catholic traditions. The Mexican family tends to be large by U.S. standards (more than three children), and family unity is very important. The divorce rate is low, so monogamous families are the norm. In the rural areas, particularly, households include members of the extended family. While the family is patriarchal, the mother runs the household. Family responsibilities come before all other responsibilities (*Culturgram*, 1994).

Saudi Arabia

The family system in Saudi Arabia is very different from that of the United States. Saudi Arabian marriages are arranged, although a minority of men and women are being allowed to choose their mates. Because of the separation of the genders, there is no dating. Islamic law allows a man to have four wives with the wives' permission; however, most Saudi men have only one wife. Most Saudi families live as extended families with strong patriarchal authority but are matriarchal in the home. The family is the most important part of a Saudi's life. Women and men are separated in most aspects of life. Women do not socialize in public with men and are always accompanied by a male relative when in public. Women do not interact with men outside their family and do not drive a car or ride a bicycle (*Culturgram*, 1994).

SOCIAL HIERARCHIES AND INTERACTION

Although human behavior is never totally controlled, society through social order limits its randomness. People learn through enculturation what is and is not proper social behavior. Generally the learning is introduced by the older family members to the younger family members; however, most of the social ideals arise in society in general and not in the family directly. Many times there are family and nonfamily orientations. A good starting point to learn about another culture is from children's literature, television shows, and games that are enjoyed by the culture. The social structure of a society tends to be enduring and is shared by the members of the culture. Social values are changed very slowly when dealing with an entire society. What are considered proper **social hierarchies** and **social interactions** are being tested as business becomes multinational and people meet and have to deal with other ways of living. We either adapt or remain restricted in the cocoon of our own culture. If you are to communicate successfully in a multicultural environment, you learn that different is simply different, not better or worse, and that the actions of the foreign people are correct for them.

In examining social hierarchies and social interactions, consideration must be given to the five sets of structures into which society can be divided: social reciprocity, group membership, intermediaries, formality, and property (Condon & Yousef, 1975).

Social reciprocity refers to the way formal and informal communications are handled. Someone who believes in independent social reciprocity tries to avoid commitment; under symmetrical-obligatory social reciprocity, people have an equal obligation; and under complementary-obligatory social reciprocity, people are forever indebted to others.

Group membership has two extremes: People can belong to many groups or very few groups, and there is a middle ground between the two. People belonging to many groups generally are not strongly associated with any of them and do not want to give up their personal freedom; likewise, people who belong to a few groups for a long time may tend to subordinate themselves to the group. The people in between try to balance group affiliation and personal freedom.

The use of **intermediaries** in societies can tell you a great deal about the makeup of the society. Intermediaries are people who act as go-betweens with other people. If no use is made of intermediaries, you will have a great deal of directness and independence. If intermediaries are always used, you will have a society that dislikes confrontation and is very group oriented. In the middle are the people who can sometimes be direct and sometimes want someone else to intervene.

Formality is the degree of preciseness, regularity, or conformity expected within the society. Formality is particularly troublesome between cultures because even the most formal culture also has some informality, and the most informal culture has some formality. Selective formality, which is the middle ground between the two extremes, can be very different in various cultures.

The last structure is **property**, which is something that is or may be possessed. Property can be viewed as private, utilitarian, or community. U.S. citizens think of property as an extension of the self; Mexicans think of property ownership in relation to feelings and need. In the past communist countries had community property. Native Americans also believed that land was community property. Even in private property cultures, there will be common property such as parks, land grant colleges, and hospitals. The three values of the five structures discussed are capitalism, socialism, and communism.

True equality does not exist in any country in the world due to the power, wealth, and privilege that exist in all countries. Although the United States considers equal opportunity important, the differences in children make it clear that not all grow up with equal opportunity for wealth or position. Human beings do not choose their cultural interaction and social hierarchical foundations; they are born or adopted into them. Hierarchical divisions can be social classes, ethnic groups, castes, or tribes. Although aristocracies or monarchies may not be active in many nations in the world, they still form a very large network. Through this network, many members are still in positions to influence the public. Religion and legal systems are used in many cultures to enforce class distinctions.

Laws, rules, or religion may preserve or dictate social interaction and the social hierarchies that may evolve within a given culture. All cultures have punishments that are administered when cultural norms are violated. Although punishment is universal, the scope of punishment for the same crime may vary significantly among cultures and include fines, incarceration, or death.

When working interculturally, you may need to adjust your approach to work to that of people in the host country in such areas as speed and efficiency, time, rules of work, kinesics, friendships, work-role expectations, social acceptance, the showing of respect, correct body posture, knowledge, the showing of empathy, role behavior, management interaction, and ambiguity tolerance. By taking the time to learn about the characteristics of a culture, you show your sincerity and friendship. Management skills that consider differences among cultures will more successfully solve business problems. Friendships in many cultures are necessary before any business will ever be conducted. In fact, friendship and work may be interrelated. Examples of social hierarchies and interactions for the United States and other selected cultures follow.

United States

In the United States people like to believe that they can rise above cultural bias and change themselves; yet at the same time many find security in the social hierarchy and social interaction patterns into which they were born. In the United States wealth is related to social class. However, the U.S. society still admires achievement above all else. Persons who invent, discover, or make it on their own are widely admired. U.S. people enjoy socializing and are frank and outspoken; they will discuss most subjects except for personal issues. U.S. people tend to be informal, belong to very few groups, do not use intermediaries, and are possessive of property (Althen, 1988).

Canada

Canadians view themselves as very separate from the United States and do not like being considered as U.S. people living in Canada. French-Canadians are very proud of the cultural heritage that they maintain. Canadians in general are very proud to be Canadian and take special pride in their own province. Canadians are generally more formal than U.S. Americans but are very friendly and kind to guests. They tend to be social but conservative, and etiquette is important.

Japan

The Japanese are very concerned with social reciprocity, which can be seen in the importance of gift giving. Gift giving says how one respects the recipient. The peak of gift giving is the end of each year. Formality and conformity in life, work, and family are all very important aspects of the social hierarchy of the society. The Japanese are very social and devoted to their families, employers, and superiors. Friendships are not made easily but are made for life and not taken lightly. The Japanese like to use intermediaries particularly in negative situations in order to help everyone save face. Property is very important but very expensive since so many people live in such small geographic areas (Condon & Yousef, 1975; Moran, 1985).

Mexico

Mexicans view social reciprocity as very important. Mexicans are good hosts and place great importance on being a good employer, a good employee, and a good friend. People of Mexico involve religion in their social interactions. The majority of Mexicans are Catholic and take their religion and religious celebrations very seriously. Much of their life is informal, other than their religion. Their attitude toward property is an aspect of their social attitude of sharing. Property is viewed in a utilitarian way as belonging to those who need it. A possessive attitude toward property is infrequent (Condon & Yousef, 1975).

Saudi Arabia

For the people of Saudi Arabia, life moves at a slower pace than in Western nations. Social reciprocity is very important. Although the people are friendly and hospitable, their personal privacy is important. The social hierarchy has been maintained by formal and conservative traditions. Saudi Arabians are devoted to their extended family and their religion. The Islamic religion is their way of life (*Culturgram*, 1994).

TERMS

Cultural heritage
Cultural universals
Economic system
Educational system
Extended family
Formality
Group membership
Intermediaries
Marriage and family system
Matriarchal
Monogamy
Nuclear family

Patriarchal
Political system
Polyandry
Polygyny
Property
Serial monogamy
Social hierarchies
Social interaction
Social reciprocity
Subnationalism
Supernationalism

Exercise 2.1

Instructions: Circle the T for true or the F for false.

1. T   F   Most countries have similar economic systems.
2. T   F   No true universal governmental body exists.
3. T   F   Political systems in England and Japan are dissimilar.
4. T   F   Multinational companies are responsible only to the country in which they are based.
5. T   F   Enculturation means learning about other cultures.
6. T   F   Educational systems throughout the world vary widely.
7. T   F   The university from which you graduate is very important in France.
8. T   F   A major family system in the United States is serial monogamy.
9. T   F   Followers of Islam tend to be matriarchal.
10. T   F   Social reciprocity is relatively unimportant in Japan and Saudi Arabia.

QUESTIONS AND CASES FOR DISCUSSION

1. Define universal cultural systems and identify them.
2. Why do societies develop economic/political systems and what do these systems do for the members of the society?
3. Compare the economic systems of Japan and Canada.
4. Compare the political systems of England and Mexico.
5. Discuss differences in educational systems in various cultures.
6. Explain how marriage and family systems in the United States are different from those of other cultures.
7. How important is social reciprocity in Mexico, Japan, and Saudi Arabia?
8. What are intermediaries? In which countries are intermediaries used?
9. Explain cultural variations in the way property is viewed.

10. Explain what is meant by equality in the United States. Does the term mean the same thing in other countries?

Case 1   Education is offered to everyone in the United States; however, 25 percent of the people who enter school as five-year-olds never graduate from high school. In Japan the high school graduation rate is 95 percent, and in Germany and England it is equally as high. However, in countries such as Mexico and third world nations many people never complete the equivalent of a high school education. The percentage of people who attend college after high school varies from country to country as described in the text. Currently many nations are sending a large number of students to U.S. universities, and many foreign companies are giving grants to U.S. "think tank" universities (such as MIT, Stanford, Chicago, and Harvard).

1. In light of this information, what do you see as the future role of U.S. universities in the world?
2. Is the fact that 25 percent of the U.S. population does not graduate from high school important in comparison to percentages in other countries of the world?
3. Is the fact that so many foreign students are attending college in the U.S. positive or negative? What do you see as the long-term effects?

Case 2   Many Korean children and children of other nationalities have been adopted by U.S. Americans. Generally these children were reared in homes where the parents were not of the nationality of the adopted child. Sometimes after the children become adults, they return to their native country to learn about people of their own ethnic heritage. Would language differences pose a problem? What cultural problems would they have?

Case 3   Many of the former communist countries are trying to change their economic and political systems. Examples are the Russian states, Czechoslovakia, and the former East Germany. What cultural changes will be necessitated in their educational system in order to have a smooth transition?

Case 4   Since more and more firms are becoming multinational and must deal with a number of monetary systems, what is the feasibility of developing one monetary system to do away with exchange rates? Do multinational firms have the ability to help bring about a world currency?

_____ **ACTIVITIES** _____

1. Interview an Asian or a Latin American student to determine the educational system in his or her country and the relationship between educational training and positions in business and society. Be prepared to share your findings with the class.
2. Research the economic system of a country you would like to visit. Prepare a one-page summary for class discussion and submission to the instructor.
3. Research the marriage and family system of a country of your choice. In a one-page written summary, make comparisons with the family lifestyle in the United States.
4. Prepare a list of countries with patriarchal family systems and those with matriarchal family systems to gain a better understanding of the role of women in various cultures.
5. List at least two countries that practice the following family systems: polygyny, polyandry, monogamy, and serial monogamy.

_____ **REFERENCES** _____

Althen, G. (1988). _American ways_. Yarmouth, ME: Intercultural Press, Inc.

Condon, J. C., & Yousef, F. (1975). _An introduction to intercultural communication_. New York: Macmillan Publishing Company.

Culturgram '94. (1994). Provo, UT: Brigham Young University, David M. Kennedy Center for International Studies.

de Forest, M. E. (1994). Thinking about a plant in Mexico? _Academy of Management Review, 8_(1), 33–40.

Dodd, C. H. (1987). _Dynamics of intercultural communication_. Dubuque, IA: Wm. C. Brown Publishers.

Economic Indicators. (1992, September). Prepared for the Joint Economic Committee by the Council of Economic Advisers. Washington, DC: U.S. Government Printing Office.

Ferraro, G. P. (1990). _The cultural dimension of international business_. Englewood Cliffs, NJ: Prentice Hall.

Moran, R. T. (1985). _Getting your yen's worth_. Houston, TX: Gulf Publishing Co.

Nath, R. (Ed.). (1988). _Comparative management_. New York: Ballinger Publishing Company.

Reich, R. B. (1991). _The work of nations: Preparing ourselves for 21st century capitalism_. New York: Alfred A. Knopf.

Samovar, L. A., & Porter, R. E. (1991). _Intercultural communication: A reader_. Belmont, CA: Wadsworth Publishing Company.

Victor, D. A. (1992). _International business communication_. New York: HarperCollins Publishers.

3

Contrasting Cultural Values

OBJECTIVES

Upon completion of this chapter, you will:

- appreciate the role that values play in communicating effectively with persons from other cultures.

- understand differences in word meanings among cultures.

- learn how attribution and perception play a role in cultural values.

- appreciate attitude differences toward men and women in various cultures.

- understand how attitudes toward work and ethics vary with the culture.

- learn how religious influences have an impact on cultural values.

- understand how individualism and collectivism play a role in cultural values.

Values, according to Thiederman (1991), form the core of a culture. **Values** are social principles, goals, or standards accepted by persons in a culture; they establish what is proper and improper behavior as well as what is normal and abnormal. Values are learned by contacts with family members, teachers, and religious leaders. What you hear, read, and watch on television influences your value system.

People in various cultures hold different attitudes toward women, ethical standards, and work. Semantic differences and attribution affect cultural values, as do religious influences. **Attribution** is something seen as belonging to or representing something or someone. Understanding these differences in cultural values is essential not only when communicating with persons from other countries but when communicating with persons in the workplace who come from different cultural backgrounds. According to an article in *The Wall Street Journal* (Solomon, 1990, pp. B1, B9), "the workplace is becoming less a melting pot than a mosaic." Since the U.S. workplace is becoming increasingly diverse culturally, managers need to be aware of the values of all workers so that they will understand what motivates people of different cultures and how to deal effectively with problem situations.

Some values held by people in the United States are not shared by people in other cultures. In his book *American Ways*, Althen (1988) identifies a number of U.S. values and assumptions, including equality, informality, individualism, directness, and attitude toward the future, time, and work.

People in the United States may claim that all persons are equal and that no person is superior to another simply because one has more money or a better education or was born to a family of high social standing. In reality, subtle distinctions are made within a group to acknowledge status differences, many of which are nonverbal. Because of this belief in equality, U.S. persons are uncomfortable with displays of respect that are common in some cultures, such as bowing. In the United States men and women are considered equal (though inequalities exist), and many women hold positions of power and influence in education, government, and industry.

People in the United States also are rather informal when compared to people of other cultures. They may dress more casually—it is not unusual to see the president of the United States in jeans or jogging attire. The posture of U.S. people is often informal; a slouched stance or putting one's feet on a desk or chair is not uncommon. Their speech is also rather informal; they often address people they hardly know by their first names.

Another quality that people in the United States value is directness. They prefer that people be open and get to the point. Such sayings as "What is the bottom line?" and "Put your cards on the table" illustrate the importance placed on directness in the United States. In some cultures, such as Asia, people do not value directness. They will not reveal their emotions using the same nonverbal cues as westerners; therefore, people in the United States have difficulty reading Asian body language. People in the United States generally believe that honesty and truthfulness are important unless they believe the truth would hurt a person's feelings or that they did not know the person well enough to be candid. They are less concerned than people in Asia with saving face.

People in the United States value time and study time management principles to learn how to get more work done in a day. They are concerned with being on time for work and appointments and study ways of working more efficiently. The success of the fast-food industry in the United States is directly related to eating on the run rather than wasting time lingering over meals. In other parts of the world, mealtime is very leisurely. In many South American countries, businesses close for two hours in the middle of the day for a long meal and a rest (siesta), but people often work into the evening. The importance of time is directly related to religious dogma. The Puritans who came to the United States were very concerned with wasting time and with the future more than the past or present. Native Americans, African Americans, Latin Americans, and Asians, however, come from a different combination of religious biases and cultural differences and are occupied with the past and present. One of the reasons Deming's theory of management was adopted in Japan before it was in the United States was the amount of time it takes to formulate group decisions as opposed to individual decisions.

People in the United States do not place as great an emphasis on history as do people of many other cultures; they look to the future and consider change to be desirable, particularly if they are Christians. In the Asian, Arab, and Latin cultures, the past is revered. Their future is determined by fate or, in some religions, by the Almighty. People of the Islamic faith believe that if they work very hard and pray, everything will be as Allah desires. They simply try to live in harmony with whatever changes occur, rather than seeking change, as is true in the U.S. culture. The following list contrasts the priorities of cultural values of U.S. Americans, Japanese, and Arabs ("1" represents the most important value; Elashmawi & Harris, 1993, p. 63).

U.S. Americans	Japanese	Arabs
1. Freedom	1. Belonging	1. Family security
2. Independence	2. Group harmony	2. Family harmony
3. Self-reliance	3. Collectiveness	3. Parental guidance
4. Equality	4. Age/Seniority	4. Age
5. Individualism	5. Group consensus	5. Authority
6. Competition	6. Cooperation	6. Compromise
7. Efficiency	7. Quality	7. Devotion
8. Time	8. Patience	8. Patience
9. Directness	9. Indirectness	9. Indirectness
10. Openness	10. Go-between	10. Hospitality

In the United States, as the number of Asians, Arabs, and Latin Americans increases, U.S. companies are having to recognize the differences in values that exist in their workforces.

SEMANTIC DIFFERENCES

Semantics is the study of the meaning of words; it involves the way behavior is influenced by words and nonverbal means used to communicate.

Words in the English language often have multiple meanings, some of which are contradictory. The word *sanction*, for example, may mean either to restrict a particular activity or to authorize it. Semantic differences are compounded when interacting with people of other cultures. Even when both people speak the same language, a word may have a different meaning and implication in each culture.

Although England and Australia are English-speaking countries, words are often used in a different way in these cultures from the way they are used in the United States. The word *homely*, for example, means plain in the United States, while in England it means friendly, warm, and comfortable. To the English a *sharp* person is one who is devious and lacking in principles rather than one who is quick, smart, and clever, which is the meaning in the United States. A situation recorded by Winston Churchill and reported by Axtell (1991) illustrates how a misunderstanding over the meaning of one word during an important meeting in World War II caused quite an argument between U.S. Americans and the British. The problem was caused by the British interpretation of the phrase "to table an item," which to them meant to bring up the item for immediate consideration. The U.S. interpretation, on the other hand, was to shelve or postpone the subject. Australian English also holds some surprises for people in the United States. In Australia you would hear such terms as *bloke* for *man, lollies* for *candy,* and *sandshoes* for *sneakers.*

Language problems are compounded when conducting business with persons in non–English-speaking countries. Differences in the meanings of words are often lost in translation. Sometimes a word has no real counterpart in the other language, and the translator must select a word that he or she believes is similar to the meaning intended.

Brand names for U.S. products have caused problems when translated into another language. The Spanish translation of Ford Motor Company's *Fiera* truck means *ugly old woman,* not a very flattering name for a vehicle. Another well-known Spanish translation problem was the introduction of General Motors' *Nova* automobile, which in that language means *doesn't go,* not a quality car buyers in any country would appreciate. A slogan adopted for Pepsi, *Come alive!,* would have translated in several countries as *come out of the grave.* U.S. firms have had to exercise greater care when introducing products in non–English-speaking countries because of marketing errors made in the past when product names and slogans were translated into another language (Axtell, 1991).

When conversing with people of other cultures, make sure your meaning is clear by avoiding slang, contractions, and idioms; by paraphrasing what the other person has said; and by speaking slowly and distinctly.

ATTRIBUTION AND PERCEPTION

Attribution, or the ability to look at social behavior from another culture's view, can cause communication problems since known experiences from your own culture are used in explaining unknown behaviors of those in another culture. **Perception**, the learned meaning of sensory images, may involve learning a new reaction to an old learned stimulus.

To lessen anxiety when communicating with someone in an unfamiliar culture, reducing uncertainty and increasing predictability about your own and the other person's behavior are important. The **uncertainty-reduction theory**, according to Gudykunst and Ting-Toomey (1988, p. 22) "involves the creation of proactive predictions and retroactive explanations about our own and others' behavior, beliefs, and attitudes." People who have high uncertainty avoidance prefer to specialize, avoid conflict, want clear instructions, and do not want competition. Some ways to reduce uncertainty about other people are to observe them, try to get information about them, and interact with them.

Uncertainty avoidance can be used to determine whether people who have different convictions can be personal friends. People from countries with weak uncertainty avoidance are more likely to remain close friends in spite of differing opinions while those in countries with strong uncertainty avoidance would be less likely to remain friendly following open disagreements. Some key differences between weak and strong uncertainty avoidance societies follow:

Weak Uncertainty Avoidance	*Strong Uncertainty Avoidance*
Citizen protest acceptable	Citizen protest should be repressed
Civil servants positive toward political process	Civil servants negative toward political process
Positive attitudes toward young people	Negative attitudes toward young people
One group's truth should not be imposed on others	There is only one truth—ours
Human rights: people should not be persecuted for their beliefs	Religious, political, and ideological fundamentalism and intolerance
Scientific opponents can be personal friends	Scientific opponents cannot be personal friends*

*Hofstede, G. (1992). *Cultures and organizations*. London: McGraw-Hill Book Company. Copyright © 1992. Reproduced with permission of McGraw-Hill.

Attribution training involves making people aware of their own cultural context and how it differs from the cultural context of the country to which they will go. Measuring employees' attributional confidence, then training them to be cognizant of their personal differences with the assignment culture, is often used to prepare employees for overseas assignments. The training is accomplished by forcing participants to evaluate behavior from the viewpoint of the host nation by providing short scenarios that summarize problems that they may encounter while living in another culture. Participants are then asked to select the one response considered correct from the viewpoint of the native of the country being studied. With feedback from the trainer and exposure to numerous situations, participants are better able to understand and work within the cultural variations in behavior and to look at the situation from the other culture's view.

ATTITUDES TOWARD WOMEN

A society's attitudes toward women are influenced by its cultural roots. In some cultures, such as the United States, women are supposed to have the same rights as men. In others, such as Libya and Kenya, women are considered subordinate to men.

This attitude toward a woman's role in society carries over into the workplace. In the United States gender differences in the workplace have been deemphasized. The women's rights movement has worked for such legislation as fair employment laws requiring that men and women must be given equal pay for equal work. Even though differences in pay still exist, treating men and women equally is expected in U.S. firms. The acceptance of women at higher levels is evidenced by the appointments of Sandra Day O'Connor and Ruth Bader Ginsburg to the U.S. Supreme Court and Janet Reno as U.S. Attorney General. The number of women appointees to top national and state level positions continues to increase. In large corporations women executives are also on the increase.

Naisbitt and Aburdene (1990) in their book *Megatrends 2000* have identified the 1990s as the decade of women in leadership positions in business. They point out that during the past two decades, women in the United States have taken two-thirds of the new jobs created and that women are starting new businesses at twice the rate of men. Compared to this U.S. trend, in France one-fifth of small businesses are owned by women while in Canada the rate is one-third. In Britain the number of self-employed women has increased three times as fast as the number of self-employed men in the past decade.

While the number of women in government, business, and the professions is increasing rapidly in the United States, most other countries are just starting to accept women at managerial levels. According to Rossman (1990), women fill only 10 percent of the managerial posts in Great Britain, 13 percent in Portugal, and 6 percent in Spain. Countries in the Far East are beginning to advance women in business, while in the Middle East, progress is rather slow.

In such countries as Saudi Arabia, the Islamic belief in the subordination of women has impeded the progress of working women. In many Latin American countries, women hold positions in politics and business. Women in Mexican businesses are respected, but they are expected to compete on an equal footing with men and prove their competence. Although Mexican businesses have historically been male dominated, this seems to be changing as many Mexican businesswomen are now enjoying success at managerial levels.

Women in Japan, according to a Labor Ministry survey published in May 1993, hold only 1.2 percent of senior company positions. Only 6.4 percent of women employed had reached low-management positions, and 2.3 percent had advanced to section chief (Sekimitsu, 1993). Even though the 1986 equal employment law clearly bars firms from discriminating against women, no penalties are involved for companies that do not comply with the law. Japanese professional women, therefore, still face many hurdles in their climb up the corporate ladder (Rossman, 1990).

Although some women in various countries may have received their first job opportunities from family or political connections, others advanced through professional qualifications and job competence. Major problems women in the workforce have faced, such as child care and trying to combine a career and family, are common to all cultures. As more women are successful in managing multiple priorities and demands on their time and can demonstrate that they are equally effective in high positions in business and politics, it will be easier for women in all cultures to advance to positions of prestige, importance, and responsibility. However, women continue to face credibility problems in some cultures that do not consider women as equal to men. For example, in fundamentalist Islamic cultures, the women are allowed to work only with other women.

WORK ATTITUDES

Attitudes toward work are culturally diverse. The term **work attitudes** refers to how people of a culture view work. **Work**, defined as mental or physical activities directed to socially productive accomplishments, in some societies is associated with economic values, status and class, and cultural values.

People in the United States value work and tend to subscribe to the **work ethic**, which means that hard work is applauded and rewarded, while failure to work is viewed negatively. U.S. Americans admire people who work hard and are motivated to achieve. Reward systems in many firms are based on an employee's achievement and willingness to work beyond a 40-hour week. U.S. senior-level executives often work 56 hours a week, far more than in many European countries. They average only 14 days of vacation a year, far fewer than in some countries in Europe, where people often close businesses for a month to go on vacation.

This attitude toward work and responsibility to one's job is ingrained from an early age in the United States. Parents teach their children about the American free enterprise system, which is based on the premise that you are the master of your destiny, that you can be anything you want to be if you are willing to try hard enough, and that hard work will be rewarded. In contrast, people in the Islamic countries place great importance on the will of Allah and believe that planning for the future would conflict with religious beliefs.

To people in the United States, the job is almost an identification badge. Evidence of this identification with the job is shown when making introductions. People tend to include the person's occupation or job title along with the name—for example, "I'd like to present Betty Freeman, owner of the Health Hut" or "This is Jay Hunt, president of Southern Express." Success is not only measured by the job title but by the perception of what one earns; the implication is that the high income has probably resulted from the person's willingness to work 12- and 14-hour days, seven days a week.

People in the United States are action oriented; they are often unable to relax because they feel guilty doing nothing. People from other cultures have observed that U.S. Americans even work at relaxing. Television commercials in the United States often depict an activity as leisure, such as gardening or washing the car, that persons in other cultures would consider manual labor. When they do take vacations, U.S. Americans are inclined to plan what they will do and where they will go so that the entire time is scheduled. Even those who participate in sports for recreation seem to try to make work out of it (Althen, 1988).

Unlike people in many countries, many people in the United States consider spending hours visiting with others as a waste of time and may excuse themselves from a group because they say they need to get back to work. This apparent obsession with work is viewed with both amazement and amusement by persons in other cultures.

In much of Europe, attitudes toward work seem to be more relaxed. Many businesses close during the month of August when people go on vacation. Most Europeans do not work on weekends or holidays, as they believe this is time that should be spent with family or engaging in personal activities. Although many people in the United States receive a two- or three-week vacation, the individual vacation time periods are staggered so that businesses will not be closed for an extended period. It is not unusual for people in the United States who are in upper management to not take all their vacation time each year.

The attitude toward work of Japanese men is very group oriented and it plays a major role in their lives. They work Monday through Friday; 18-hour days are not unusual. Because of the long hours, relaxation does not include working around the house. Instead, they relax by watching TV, drinking, or joining their friends at the local bar. However, this attitude appears to be changing as they become more westernized.

ATTITUDES TOWARD ETHICS

Ethical standards are guidelines established to convey what is perceived to be correct or incorrect behavior by most people in a society. According to Ferrell and Gardiner (1991), ethical conduct "is something judged as proper or acceptable based on some standard of right and wrong" (p. 2). According to Borden (1991), being ethical means keeping your values in balance; and if you compromise your values, you are unethical.

Personal ethics or moral standards may differ from societal ethics. Your own standards of what is right and wrong may be more stringent than those of your society as a whole, but problems occur when the reverse is true—that is, when your ethical standards are lower than those considered acceptable by society. And, of course, your ethical standards must meet the minimum level of behavior identified by law as acceptable.

An increased concern for ethics has been seen in the United States because of blatant misconduct of persons in government and industry. Religious leaders have been convicted of fraud and Wall Street moguls found guilty of insider trading. Naisbitt and Aburdene (1990) foresee that all countries will have to give increased attention to values and ethics in their schools so that the next generation will be better prepared to make appropriate decisions involving ethical behavior.

Ethical standards should be addressed when conducting business with persons of other cultures, especially those whose standards of ethical behavior differ markedly from our own. While we carry our frame of reference and value system with us when conducting business interculturally, we should also be aware that our values may differ from those of other countries. For example, in the United States bribery and graft are illegal. In some of the Latin American countries, however, using gifts to assure success in sealing an agreement is an accepted way of conducting business.

RELIGIOUS INFLUENCES

Religious influences have an impact on when and how business is conducted in international settings.

In some cultures, such as those of North and South Americans, Australians, and Europeans, lifestyle and religion are separate. In much of northern Africa and southern Asia, no distinction is made between lifestyle and religion, since religion is a lifestyle. Business-persons in these countries may seek the advice of religious leaders on business matters.

The United States has never had an official state church; religious observances rarely interfere with business with a few exceptions, such as Christmas. Although business is not conducted on such religious holidays as

Christmas, no one feels obligated to participate in religious ceremonies or observe religious customs. Religion is a personal matter in the United States. Members of one family often hold different beliefs and belong to different denominations.

The United States subscribes to the doctrine of "separation of church and state." According to this doctrine, the government does not lend official support to any particular religion and may not interfere with a person's practicing any religion. About 26 percent of the population is Roman Catholic; the largest Protestant groups are the Baptists, Methodists, and Lutherans (*Culturgram*, 1994). Non-Christian groups include Jews and Muslims.

Some countries have officially recognized religions and participate in religious rituals that would affect business encounters. In Saudi Arabia, for example, Islam is the official religion. Muslims observe the ritual of stopping work five times a day to pray. Meetings with persons in Saudi Arabia should be sufficiently flexible to allow for this daily ritual, which is a way of life for Muslims. Conducting business during the month of Ramadan (currently during February) would not be recommended as Muslims are required to fast from dawn to sunset. Because of the impact of religion on all aspects of life in Islamic countries, learning about religious rituals and beliefs prior to conducting business there is advisable. When working with people in countries that practice nonliterate religions (those that lack written precepts), an understanding of the logic of their beliefs is important. The Hawaiian people, for example, believe in curses and spirits; this belief should be respected. Witchcraft is practiced in such countries as Zaire; conducting business with people of these cultures may involve changing the sales and marketing techniques that you would ordinarily use.

Religious beliefs and practices affect business in many countries. Although both the United States and Italy are primarily Christian countries, religious holidays are more numerous in Italy than in the United States. Sri Lanka has a total of 27 holidays. Religious beliefs also affect consumption patterns. Beef is not eaten by Hindus and pork is not eaten by Muslims and Orthodox Jews. When conducting business internationally, religion must be considered (Terpstra & David, 1991; Victor, 1992).

INDIVIDUALISM AND COLLECTIVISM

Individualism refers to the attitude of valuing ourselves as separate individuals with responsibility for our own destinies and our own actions. Proponents of individualism believe that self-interest is an appropriate goal. **Collectivism** emphasizes common interests, conformity, cooperation, and interdependence (see Figure 3.1).

FIGURE 3.1   Individualism Versus Collectivism

Hofstede (1992) studied the IBM Corporation in 53 countries and determined the dimensions on which countries' business cultures differed. Using statistical analysis and theoretical reasoning, Hofstede developed four scales that he labeled Power Distance, Uncertainty Avoidance, Individualism, and Masculinity. The countries were then ranked according to their scores.

As shown in the following list, the United States ranks first in individualism, followed by Australia, Great Britain, Canada, and the Netherlands. Countries that ranked lowest on individualism included Colombia, Venezuela, Panama, Equador, and Guatemala (Hofstede, 1992, p. 53).

Score Rank	Country or Region	Score Rank	Country or Region
1	USA	28	Turkey
2	Australia	29	Uruguay
3	Great Britain	30	Greece
4/5	Canada	31	Philippines
4/5	Netherlands	32	Mexico
6	New Zealand	33/35	East Africa
7	Italy	33/35	Yugoslavia
8	Belgium	33/35	Portugal
9	Denmark	36	Malaysia
10/11	Sweden	37	Hong Kong
10/11	France	38	Chile

12	Ireland	39/41	West Africa
13	Norway	39/41	Singapore
14	Switzerland	39/41	Thailand
15	Germany F.R.	42	Salvador
16	South Africa	43	South Korea
17	Finland	44	Taiwan
18	Austria	45	Peru
19	Israel	46	Costa Rica
20	Spain	47/48	Pakistan
21	India	47/48	Indonesia
22/23	Japan	49	Colombia
22/23	Argentina	50	Venezuela
24	Iran	51	Panama
25	Jamaica	52	Equador
26/27	Brazil	53	Guatemala*
26/27	Arab countries		

U.S. people place great importance on individuality and self-reliance and teach their children at a very young age to think for themselves, make their own choices, and express their ideas and opinions. Well-known phrases typically used by U.S. parents to convey this emphasis on self-reliance include "Do your own thing," "You made your bed, now lie in it," and "You'd better look out for yourself; no one else will." This emphasis on individuality carries over into college/university choices as well as job choices that may take children away from friends and family members. Parents feel successful when their children are on their own and completely self-supporting. Although individualism and the value placed on the family as an important unit are often associated, evidence shows that this relationship may not always exist. Costa Ricans, for example, have individualistic tendencies but also value the extended family structure. Examining each culture separately is important. Since people of the United States value individualism, self-reliance, and independence, understanding cultures that do not value these qualities is often difficult (Hofstede, 1991).

In other cultures, such as the Japanese, emphasis is placed on the group approach, rather than the individual approach, to all aspects of life. The Chinese also value the group approach and the family.

*Hofstede, G. (1992). *Cultures and organizations*. London: McGraw-Hill Book Company. Copyright © 1992. Reproduced with permission of McGraw-Hill.

TERMS

Attribution   Semantics
Attribution training   Uncertainty-reduction theory
Collectivism   Values
Ethical standards   Work
Individualism   Work attitudes
Perception   Work ethic

Exercise 3.1

Instructions: Circle the T for true or the F for false.

1. T   F   Values are learned; they are not innate.

2. T   F   In the United States, family is a top priority.

3. T   F   A characteristic valued by U.S. persons is directness.

4. T   F   People in the Asian culture value history.

5. T   F   Semantic differences between cultures that speak the same language are rare.

6. T   F   The word "yes" means the same in all languages.

7. T   F   Women in management are treated similarly in all cultures.

8. T   F   Japan has a well-enforced equal employment law preventing discrimination against women.

9. T   F   The U.S. society is considered to have a strong work ethic.

10. T   F   Ethical standards are culture specific.

QUESTIONS AND CASES FOR DISCUSSION
---

1. Explain how values are formed.
2. In what ways are values of persons in the United States different from those of persons in other cultures?
3. Explain how semantic differences can affect intercultural communication. Give some examples.

4. Explain what is meant by the term *attribution*.

5. How are attitudes toward women culturally different? In what countries are women and men treated equally in the workplace?

6. Explain the difference between work attitudes in the United States and other cultures. Are your personal work attitudes typical of the U.S. culture or another culture?

7. How are attitudes toward ethics different in the United States and Latin America?

8. What role does religion play in conducting business in the United States and Saudi Arabia?

9. Explain what is meant by *individualism*. Give examples of cultures that are primarily individualistic.

10. Explain what is meant by *collectivism*. Give examples of cultures that are primarily collectivistic.

Case 1   Ching Lee was transferred by his Asian firm to assume a managerial position in a large automobile production plant in the United States. In his first report to his supervisor, he expressed concern that U.S. workers were not giving him the proper respect. What behaviors by U.S. workers could have led Ching Lee to draw this conclusion?

Case 2   A U.S. firm sent its senior-level manager, Laura Green, to negotiate a contract for a chain of fast-food restaurants in Saudi Arabia. What cultural attitudes and behaviors related to gender could she expect to encounter?

———— ACTIVITIES ————————————————————————————

1. Ask a person from each of the following groups this question: "What is your attitude toward work?" Report their responses to the class.

   a. blue-collar worker
   b. business professional
   c. educator
   d. high school student
   e. college student

2. Clip an article from the local newspaper related to ethics in business; summarize the article for class members.

3. Ask a professor or student from another culture to speak to the class on attitudes toward women in his or her culture.

4. Prepare a list of women in your state who have achieved high-ranking positions in either government or business. List the special qualifications these women possess that make them qualified for their position. Prepare a similar list of women in high-ranking positions in another country of your choice.

5. Prepare a list of words (other than those mentioned in the chapter) that have different meanings in other areas of the United States or in other English-speaking countries.

REFERENCES

Althen, G. (1988). *American ways.* Yarmouth, ME: Intercultural Press, Inc.

Axtell, R. (1991). *The do's and taboos of international trade.* New York: John Wiley & Sons, Inc.

Borden, G. A. (1991). *Cultural orientation.* Englewood Cliffs, NJ: Prentice Hall.

Culturgram '94. (1994). Provo, UT: Brigham Young University, David M. Kennedy Center for International Studies.

Elashmawi, F., & Harris, P. R. (1993). *Multicultural management.* Houston, TX: Gulf Publishing Company.

Ferrell, O. C., & Gardiner, G. (1991). *In pursuit of ethics.* Springfield, IL: Smith Collins Company.

Gudykunst, W. B., & Ting-Toomey, S. (1988). *Culture and interpersonal communication.* Newbury Park, CA: Sage Publications.

Hofstede, G. (1991). *Cultures in organizations.* London: McGraw-Hill Book Company.

Naisbitt, J., & Aburdene, P. (1990). *Megatrends 2000.* New York: William Morrow and Company, Inc.

Rossman, M. L. (1990). *The international businesswoman of the 1990s.* New York: Praeger.

Sekimitsu, A. (1993, June 6). Future princess gives up on career. *The Commercial Appeal,* p. A9.

Solomon, J. (1990, September 12). Learning to accept cultural diversity. *The Wall Street Journal,* pp. B1, B9.

Terpstra, V., & David, K. (1991). *The cultural environment of international business.* Cincinnati: South-Western Publishing Co.

Thiederman, S. (1991). *Bridging cultural barriers for corporate success.* New York: Lexington Books.

Victor, D. A. (1992). *International business communication.* New York: HarperCollins Publishers.

4

Oral and Nonverbal Communication Patterns

OBJECTIVES

Upon completion of this chapter, you will:

- be able to evaluate thought patterns and their relationship to intercultural business communication.

- understand how paralanguage and metacommunication affect successful intercultural communication.

- appreciate how attitudes toward time and use of space convey nonverbal messages in intercultural encounters.

- understand the role that eye contact, smell, color, touch, and body language play in communicating nonverbally in cultural situations.

- learn how silence is used to send nonverbal messages in various cultures.

Successful multicultural business encounters depend to a large extent on effective oral and nonverbal communication. Although much communication in the global arena is oral, the nonverbal aspects can contribute significantly to understanding and interpreting oral communication. **Nonverbal communication** refers to nonword messages, such as gestures, facial expressions, interpersonal distance, touch, eye contact, smell, and silence.

Costly business blunders are often the result of a lack of knowledge of another culture's oral and nonverbal communication patterns. A knowledge of these aspects of intercultural communication is essential for conducting business in the international marketplace.

THOUGHT PATTERNS

Patterns of thought or processes of reasoning and problem solving are not the same in all cultures and have an impact on oral communication.

Most people in the United States use the deductive method of reasoning to solve problems. The **deductive method** goes from broad categories or observations to specific examples to determine the facts and then the solution to the problem. The line of reasoning used by people in many other cultures, such as Asians, is typically the **inductive method**. People who use this approach start with facts or observations and proceed to generalizations (Samovar & Porter, 1991a).

Thought patterns also include the pace or speed with which problems are solved or decisions made. Making quick decisions is a characteristic of an effective manager in the United States, while this behavior would be viewed as impulsive by the Japanese. The slower method of problem solving of the Japanese is often a source of frustration for U.S. managers. Thought as an aspect of language is discussed in Chapter 6.

Recognizing that people from other cultures may have different thought patterns is important to communicating and negotiating successfully in the global business environment.

PARALANGUAGE/METACOMMUNICATION

Paralanguage is related to oral communication; it refers to rate, volume, and quality, which interrupt or temporarily take the place of speech and affect the meaning of a message. Paralanguage conveys emotions. Negative emotions of impatience, fear, and anger are easier to convey than more positive emotions of satisfaction and admiration. An increased rate of speech could indicate anger or impatience; a decrease in rate could suggest lack of interest or a reflective attitude. An increased volume could also indicate anger; a lower volume is nonthreatening and sympathetic.

In the United States people usually have no difficulty in distinguishing the speech of persons from specific regions of the country, such as the North and the South. Although rate of speech and dialect may vary from region to region, they rarely cause major problems in the communication process.

Learning the nuances in speech that affect verbal messages will help when communicating with persons of other cultures. Differences in loudness of speech, for example, are culture specific as well as gender specific. Arabs, for example, speak loudly, as this shows strength and sincerity. People from the Philippines, however, speak softly as this is an indication of breeding and education. Males usually speak louder than females; they also speak in a lower pitch than females. Differences also exist in the rate at which people speak. U.S. Northerners usually speak faster than U.S. Southerners; Italians and Arabs speak faster than do people of the United States. People who speak slowly sometimes have difficulty understanding the speech of those who speak rapidly.

Metacommunication is the intentional or unintentional implied meaning of a message. Metacommunication, though not expressed in words, accompanies a message that is expressed in words. In both speaking and writing, people who receive messages are sensitive to not only the expressed message but the implied message as well. "You look nice today" could be interpreted as a compliment or the meaning conveyed could be that you usually do not look nice. Depending on context difference between cultures, the metacommunication can easily be misinterpreted. In Japan if a company is interested in doing business with you it will bring a large contingent of people in order to show its interest; however, in the United States only one or two people would be sent. The Japanese would interpret this to mean that the U.S. company is not very interested in doing business with the Japanese firm.

CHRONEMICS

Chronemics, attitudes toward time, vary from culture to culture. Two of the most important time systems that relate to international business are **monochronic** and **polychronic** time. Countries that follow monochronic time perform only one major activity at a time; countries that follow polychronic time work on several activities simultaneously.

The United States is a monochronic culture; other monochronic countries are England, Switzerland, and Germany. In monochronic cultures time is spoken of as something tangible; people use such terms as *wasting time* or *losing time*. In these cultures it is considered rude to do two things at once, such as reading a journal during a meeting.

Polychronic cultures include people of Latin America and the Mediterranean, as well as the Arabs. These people are well adapted to doing several things at once and do not mind interruptions.

The following listing summarizes generalizations related to monochronic and polychronic time systems (Hall, 1966).

Monochronic People	*Polychronic People*
Do one thing at a time	Do many things at once
Concentrate on the job	Are highly distractible and subject to interruptions
Take time commitments seriously	Consider time commitments more casually
Are committed to the job	Are committed to people
Show respect for private property; rarely borrow or lend	Borrow and lend things often
Are accustomed to short-term relationships	Tend to build lifetime relationships

Being on time for work, business appointments and meetings, and social engagements is very important in the United States. Punctuality is considered a positive attribute that conveys the nonverbal message of being respectful of other persons. Tardiness is interpreted as rudeness, a lack of consideration for others, or a lack of interest in the job or meeting. Being late also sends the nonverbal message that you are not well organized.

People of Germany and Switzerland are even more time conscious than are people from the United States. Being on time is important to the people of Singapore and Hong Kong (except at banquets in Hong Kong—nobody arrives at the time stated on the invitation). Being punctual is also important in Malaysia and Indonesia, particularly when meeting with a person of superior status, even though that person may be late.

In Algeria, however, punctuality is not widely regarded. In Latin American countries the "mañana" attitude (putting off until tomorrow what does not get done today) has been a source of frustration for time-sensitive U.S. executives when conducting business with people of that culture. People in the Arab culture also have a more casual attitude toward time; this attitude is related to their religious beliefs that God decides when things get accomplished (Engholm, 1991).

To work harmoniously with persons from other cultures, consider these different attitudes toward time. When conducting business with persons from cultures whose attitude toward time differs from your own, such as Bolivians, it is advisable to verify whether the meeting time is Latin American time or U.S. time.

PROXEMICS

Communicating through the use of space is known as **proxemics.** The physical distance between people when they are interacting, as well as territorial space, is strongly influenced by culture.

Consideration should be given to interpersonal space when conversing with others. Hall (1966) reports that psychologists have identified four zones within which U.S. people interact: the intimate zone, the personal zone, the social zone, and the public zone. The **intimate zone**, less than 18 inches, is reserved for very close friends; it is entered by business colleagues briefly, such as when shaking hands. The **personal zone**, from 18 inches to approximately 4 feet, is used for giving instructions to others or working closely with another person. The **social zone**, from 4 to 12 feet, is used for most business situations in which people interact more formally and impersonally, such as during a business meeting. The **public distance**, over 12 feet, is the most formal zone; therefore, fewer interactions occur because of distance.

People of the United States tend to need more space than do people of other cultures, such as Greeks, Latin Americans, or Arabs. When interacting with persons of these cultures, U.S. people will back away because the person is standing too close. On the other hand, the Japanese stand farther away than do U.S. people when conversing. Negative nonverbal messages often conveyed by standing too close to a person who requires more space include being pushy or overbearing; standing too close may also be interpreted as unwelcome sexual advances.

People also communicate through space by the arrangement of desks and chairs. When U.S. people are conversing, they generally prefer the face-to-face arrangement or chairs placed at right angles to one another. People of other cultures, such as the Chinese, prefer the side-by-side arrangement; this preference may be related to the custom of avoiding direct eye contact in that culture.

In the United States, nonverbal messages are sent by office and desk size, as well as the location of the office. Offices with windows have more status than inside offices; large offices have more status than small ones. Offices on the fourth floor have more status than offices on the first floor. The top floors of office buildings are generally occupied by the top-level executives not only in the United States but in Germany as well. However, French top-level executives would occupy a position in the middle of an office area, with subordinates located around them. The purpose of this arrangement is to help the superior stay informed on activities and to maintain control over the work area. The Japanese also do not consider private offices appropriate. In traditional Japanese firms only executives of the highest rank have private offices and may also have desks in large work areas (Gudykunst & Ting-Toomey, 1988; Victor, 1992).

OCULESICS

Some cultures place more emphasis on **oculesics** (gaze and eye contact) than others. People in the United States, as well as those in Canada, Britain, and Eastern Europe, favor direct eye contact. The eye contact, however, is not steady; it is maintained for a second or two, then broken. Eye contact is considered a sign of respect and attentiveness in these countries. People who avoid eye contact may be considered insecure, untrustworthy, unfriendly, disrespectful, or inattentive.

In other cultures, there is little direct eye contact. The Japanese direct their gaze below the chin; they are uncomfortable with maintaining direct eye contact throughout the conversation. People in China and Indonesia also lower the eyes as a sign of respect, as they feel that prolonged eye contact shows bad manners. In the Middle East, on the other hand, the eye contact is so intense that it exceeds the comfort zone for people in the United States. Prolonged eye contact with women, however, is considered inappropriate.

Thiederman (1991) summarized the cultural variations in eye contact as follows:

Very direct eye contact:	Middle Easterners
	some Latin American groups
	the French
Moderate eye contact:	Mainstream Americans
	northern Europeans
	the British
Minimal eye contact:	East Asians
	Southeast Asians
	East Indians
	native Americans*

Very direct eye contact can be misinterpreted as hostility, aggressiveness, or intrusiveness when the intended meaning was that of appearing interested. Minimal eye contact may be misinterpreted as lack of interest or understanding, dishonesty, fear, or shyness, when the intended meaning was a desire to show respect or to avoid appearing intrusive.

The eyes can be very revealing during negotiations. The pupils of the eyes constrict or dilate in response to emotions. Well-trained negotiators will watch the pupils for signs that you are willing to make concessions (Borden, 1991).

A prolonged gaze or stare in the United States is considered rude. In other cultures, such as Japan, Korea, and Thailand, staring is also considered

* Adapted with the permission of Lexington Books, an imprint of Macmillan, Inc., from *Bridging Cultural Barriers for Corporate Success* by Sondra Thiederman. Copyright © 1991 by Sondra Thiederman.

rude. In most cultures, men do not stare at women. In France and Italy, however, men do stare at women in public. In the United States, staring at a person of the same or opposite gender is considered a sign of interest and may even be interpreted as sexually suggestive.

OLFACTICS

Olfactics or smell as a means of nonverbal communication is important. A person's smell can have a positive or negative effect on the oral message. The way someone smells remains in our memory after the person has gone.

Most people of the United States respond negatively to what they consider bad odors, such as body odor, breath odor, or clothes that emit unpleasant aromas, such as perspiration. They place great importance on personal hygiene and consider it normal for people to remove body odors by bathing or showering daily and by brushing teeth to remove mouth odors (Althen, 1988). Advertisements on U.S. American television and in newspapers and magazines for underarm deodorants, perfumes, colognes, and mouthwash emphasize the importance U.S. Americans place on personal hygiene. In a television commercial that epitomizes the feelings that U.S. Americans have about body odor, a young woman states: "If a guy smells, it's such a turnoff." People in the United States are not comfortable in discussing the topic, however, and generally will not tell other people that their body odor is offensive; they will simply avoid being close to the person and will end the discourse as quickly as possible.

Other cultures have quite different concepts of natural odors; they consider them as normal and think attitudes of people in the United States are unnatural. Arabs are quite comfortable with natural odors and typically breathe on people when they talk. Other cultures in which smell plays an important role include the Japanese, Burmese, and Samoans. Cultures that include little meat in the diet, such as the Chinese, say that people who consume a lot of meat, such as U.S. Americans, emit an offensive odor (Samovar & Porter, 1991a).

To maintain harmonious intercultural business relationships, remember these diverse attitudes toward smell and, if possible, adopt the hygiene practices of the country in which you are conducting business.

HAPTICS

Haptics or touch refers to communicating through the use of bodily contact. Some cultures are very comfortable with bodily contact; others avoid it. People in the United States are taught that appropriate touch includes shaking hands but that in business situations giving hugs or other expressions of affection to supervisors and co-workers encourages familiarity that is generally considered inappropriate. Since touching may be interpreted as a form of sexual harassment, in order to avoid the appearance of impropriety refraining from touching in business situations is necessary.

In *Gestures* (1991b), Axtell has classified the following cultures as "touch" and "don't touch":

Don't touch	*Middle Ground*	*Touch*
Japan	France	Middle East countries
United States	China	Latin countries
Canada	Ireland	Italy
England	India	Greece
Scandinavia		Spain and Portugal
Other northern		Some Asian countries
European countries		Russia*
Australia		
Estonia		

In touch-oriented cultures, such as Italy, Greece, Spain, and Portugal, both males and females may be seen walking along the street holding hands or arm-in-arm. In some cultures, such as in the Latin American countries and the Middle East, touching between men is considered quite acceptable (Figure 4.1). Mexican males will stand close to a male colleague and even hold him by the lapel or shoulder. Behavior between men in the Middle East is similar, but

FIGURE 4.1 Touch-Oriented Culture

you would avoid touching the person with the left hand because the left hand is considered unclean and is reserved for personal hygiene. In other countries, such as the United States, touching between men may be construed as an indication of homosexuality.

An additional aspect of tactile communication has to do with the location of the touch. In Thailand it is offensive to touch the head, as this part of the body is considered sacred. In fact, avoid touching all Asians on the head, including small children. Even placing a hand on the back of an Asian worker's chair is considered inappropriate. While Muslims hug another person around the shoulders, in Korea young people do not touch the shoulders of their elders (Axtell, 1991b). Tactile behavior is highly cultural; learning cultural differences is important to conducting business globally.

KINESICS

Kinesics is the term used for communicating through various types of body movements, including facial expressions, gestures, posture and stance, and other mannerisms that may accompany or replace oral messages.

Facial Expressions

The face and eyes convey the most expressive types of body language. Research conducted by Leathers (1976) determined these ten types of meaning that can be communicated by facial expressions: happiness, surprise, fear, anger, sadness, disgust, contempt, interest, bewilderment, and determination. People of all cultures learn how to control facial expressions to mask emotions that are inappropriate in a specific setting, such as crying when being reprimanded or yawning when listening to a boring presentation. In some cultures, such as China, people rarely show emotion. The Japanese may smile to cover a range of emotions, including anger, happiness, or sadness, while the smile to people in the United States means happiness. Asians will smile or laugh softly when they are embarrassed or to conceal any discomfort (Samovar & Porter, 1991a). The following proverb in the Korean culture illustrates the Asian attitude concerning the meaning of a smile: "The man who smiles a lot is not a real man" (Thiederman, 1991). To interpret facial expressions correctly, you should take the communication context and the culture into account.

Gestures

Gestures are another important aspect of body language. Gestures can be emblems or symbols ("V" for victory), illustrators (police officer's hand held up to stop traffic), regulators (glancing at your watch to signal that you are in a hurry), or affect displays (someone's face turns red with embarrassment).

Gestures are used to add emphasis or clarity to an oral message. Although the meaning of gestures depends upon the context, here are some general guides to interpreting the meaning of gestures in the United States (Axtell, 1991):

- Interest is expressed by maintaining eye contact with the speaker, smiling, and nodding the head.
- Open-mindedness is expressed by open hands and palms turned upward.
- Nervousness is sometimes shown by fidgeting, failing to give the speaker eye contact, or jingling keys or money in your pocket.
- Suspiciousness is indicated by glancing away or touching your nose, eyes, or ears.
- Defensiveness is indicated by crossing your arms over your chest, making fisted gestures, or crossing your legs.
- Lack of interest or boredom is indicated by glancing repeatedly at your watch or staring at the ceiling or floor or out the window when the person is speaking.*

Although regional differences exist, people in the United States typically use moderate gesturing. They rarely use gestures in which elbows go above shoulder level as this is interpreted as being too emotional or even angry; one exception is waving hello or goodbye. Italians, Greeks, and some Latin Americans use vigorous gestures when speaking, while Chinese and Japanese people tend to keep their hands and arms close to their bodies when speaking. Most cultures have standard gestures for such daily situations as greeting someone and saying goodbye; learn and respect such gestures when conversing with persons of another culture.

Here are some additional guidelines for gesturing in various cultures (Axtell, 1991):

- The "V" for victory gesture (Figure 4.2), holding two fingers upright, with palm and fingers faced outward, is widely used in the United States and many other countries. In England, however, it has a crude connotation when used with the palm in.
- The vertical horns gesture (raised fist, index finger and little finger extended, Figure 4.3) has a positive connotation associated with the University of Texas *Longhorn* football team. This gesture has an insulting connotation in Italy, but in Brazil and Venezuela it is a sign for good luck. In other cultures, such as Italy and Malta, the horns are a symbol to ward off evil spirits. This symbol has various meanings in U.S. subcultures, such as Satanic cults (cult recogni-

---

* Axtell, R. E. (1991). *Gestures.* Copyright © 1991 by John Wiley & Sons, Inc. Reprinted by permission of John Wiley & Sons, Inc.

FIGURE 4.2 "V" for Victory Gesture

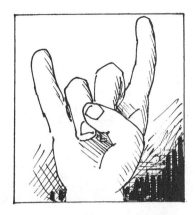

FIGURE 4.3 Vertical Horns Gesture

tion sign signifying the Devil's horns), and should be used only when you are sure the other person understands its intended meaning.

- The thumbs-up gesture (Figure 4.4) has been widely recognized as a positive signal meaning "everything is O.K." or "good going." Although well known in North America and most of Europe, in Australia and West Africa it is seen as a rude gesture.
- The "O.K." sign (Figure 4.5), with the thumb and forefinger joined to form a circle, is a positive gesture in the United States, while in Brazil it is considered obscene. The gesture has still another meaning in Japan; it is a symbol for money.
- The beckoning gesture (Figure 4.6; fingers upturned, palm facing the body) used by people in the United States for summoning a waiter, for example, is

FIGURE 4.4 Thumbs-Up Gesture

FIGURE 4.5 "OK" Gesture

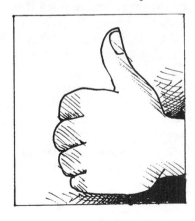

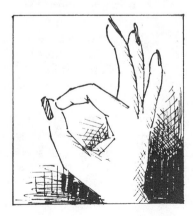

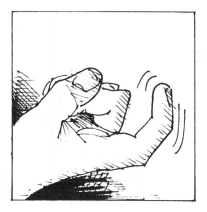

FIGURE 4.6   Beckoning Gesture

offensive to Filipinos, as it is used to beckon animals and prostitutes. Vietnamese and Mexicans also find it offensive.

• The head nod in most countries means "yes," but in Bulgaria it means "no."

Since one culture's gestures may be misinterpreted by people in another culture, avoid using gestures when communicating in international business settings until you become knowledgeable about the meaning of such gestures.

Posture and Stance

Posture, the way someone stands, sits, or walks, can send positive or negative nonverbal messages. Posture can convey self-confidence, status, and interest. Confident people generally have a relaxed posture, yet stand erect and walk with assurance. Walking with stooped shoulders and a slow, hesitating gait projects such negative messages as lack of assurance and confidence. The posture of persons of higher status is usually more relaxed than that of their subordinates. Interest is demonstrated by leaning forward toward the person you are conversing with, while sitting back communicates a lack of interest. The posture of people in the United States tends to be casual; they sit in a relaxed manner and may slouch when they stand. This behavior in Germany would be considered rude.

Posture when seated also varies with the culture. People in the United States often cross their legs while seated; women cross at the ankle and men cross with the ankle on the knee (Figure 4.7). Crossing the leg with the ankle on the knee would be considered inappropriate by most people in the Middle East. In the Arab world, correct posture while seated is important; avoid showing the sole of your shoe or pointing your foot at someone, as the lowest part of the body is considered unclean.

FIGURE 4.7   Sitting Postures

When communicating with persons of another culture, follow their lead; assume the posture they assume. Remember that in most cultures, standing when an older person or one of higher rank enters or leaves the room is considered a sign of respect.

An awareness of cultural differences in facial expressions, gestures, and posture is important to successful intercultural encounters. Body language can enhance the spoken message or detract from it. Even though we usually believe that actions speak louder than words, in intercultural interactions what the person says may give a clearer picture of the intended message than accompanying body language. However, if a gesture is used in the wrong context, it may be difficult for a foreigner to understand the intended message. The best advice is probably to keep gestures to a minimum when communicating with persons in other cultures; learn the words for "good" or "yes" in the local language rather than relying on gestures.

CHROMATICS

Chromatics or color can affect your mood, your emotions, and your impression of others. Certain colors have both negative and positive connotations. In the United States, for example, black is considered a sophisticated color, but it may also represent sadness. White is pure and peaceful, but in some cultures it is associated with mourning. Blue may represent peace and tranquility or sadness and depression, for example, "I feel blue" (Huseman, Lahiff, & Penrose, 1991).

Color may be used to symbolize such things as patriotism. People in the United States associate red, white, and blue (the colors in the flag) with patriotism. Cultural differences associated with colors include:

- Black is the color of mourning in the United States, but white is worn to funerals by the Japanese.
- In the United States white is typically worn by brides, while in India red or yellow is worn.
- Purple is sometimes associated with royalty, but it is the color of death in Mexico and Brazil.
- Red (especially red roses) is associated with romance in some cultures, including the United States. Red is not an appropriate color for wrapping gifts in Japan.
- Green is not used for wrapping packages in Egypt, since green is the nationalist color (as red, white, and blue are the nationalist colors in the United States). Men should avoid wearing a green hat in China as this signifies that their wife or sister is a prostitute.*

Determining cultural meanings associated with various colors is advised to assure that nonverbal messages associated with color are positive ones.

SILENCE

Silence is a form of nonverbal communication that may be interpreted in various ways, depending upon the situation, the duration of the silence, and the culture. Interpretations of silence include agreement, lack of interest, or contempt. Silence can also mean that the person is giving the topic some thought. Silence can be used to indicate displeasure in both the United States and in other cultures.

Other aspects of silence should also be considered: the duration, appropriateness, and relationship between people who are conversing. A prolonged silence following a question could be interpreted to mean that the person does not know the answer. Silence following an inappropriate statement, such as telling a tasteless joke, would usually be interpreted as disapproval or lack of understanding. Silence following a conversation with someone you know well could be interpreted as dissent or disapproval (Samovar & Porter, 1991a).

People of the United States are rather uncomfortable with periods of silence, except with people they know well. They will use fillers, such as comments on the weather, to avoid silence.

In some cultures, periods of silence are appropriate when communicating. The Japanese are comfortable with silence and use it as a bargaining tool when negotiating with persons from the United States. They know that U.S. persons are not comfortable with long periods of silence and that the U.S. businessperson will offer a price concession just to get the discussion going again. Learn to remain silent when negotiating with the Japanese; they like periods of silence and do not like to be hurried. People who converse with no pauses are

* Axtell, R. E. (1991). *The Do's and Taboos of International Trade*. Copyright © 1991 by John Wiley & Sons, Inc. Reprinted by permission of John Wiley & Sons, Inc.

viewed as having given little thought to what they are saying and that their thinking lacks focus (Axtell, 1991a). Japanese proverbs such as "Those who know do not speak—those who speak do not know" emphasize the value of silence over words in that culture.

In Italy, Greece, and the Arabian countries, very little silence exists. An appropriate caution would be to watch the behavior of the persons you are talking with and match their style. Allow pauses when speaking with Asians, and avoid pauses when dealing with Middle Easterners.

Knowing cultural variations in the use of silence and other forms of nonverbal communication is helpful when conversing with persons in another culture.

Exercise 4.1

Facial Expressions

Match the facial expressions to the meanings portrayed.

1. Disgust

2. Contempt

3. Sadness

4. Interest

5. Surprise

6. Anger

7. Happiness

8. Determination

TERMS

Chromatics   Nonverbal communication
Chronemics   Oculesics
Deductive method   Olfactics
Haptics   Paralanguage
Inductive method   Personal zone
Intimate zone   Polychronic
Kinesics   Proxemics
Metacommunication   Public distance
Monochronic   Social zone

Exercise 4.2

Intercultural Nonverbal Communication

Instructions: Circle the T for true or the F for false.

1. T   F   Asians typically use the deductive method of reasoning to solve problems.

2. T   F   People in the United States speak faster than Italians and Arabs.

3. T   F   Latin Americans need more space than people of the United States.

4. T   F   Punctuality is not widely regarded in Algeria.

5. T   F   Private offices are generally reserved for top-level executives in all cultures.

6. T   F   When conversing with the Japanese, it is best to keep steady eye contact throughout the dialogue.

7. T   F   People of all cultures respond negatively to body and breath odor.

8. T   F   More bodily contact occurs between Western men than between Arab men.

9. T   F   Touching the head of a Thai is forbidden.

10. T   F   Smiling is interpreted as happiness in all cultures.

Exercise 4.3

Instructions: Match the following terms with their definition.

___ 1. Space

___ 2. Body language

___ 3. Smell

___ 4. Gaze/eye contact

___ 5. Implied meaning of message

___ 6. Goes from facts to
     generalizations

___ 7. Time

___ 8. Color

___ 9. Volume, pitch, and rate that
     affect message meaning

___10. Touch

A. Chromatics
B. Chronemics
C. Deductive approach
D. Haptics
E. Inductive approach
F. Kinesics
G. Metacommunication
H. Oculesics
I. Olfactics
J. Paralanguage
K. Proxemics

——— QUESTIONS AND CASES FOR DISCUSSION ———

1. Explain how thought patterns and problem solving differ in the United States and other cultures.

2. Discuss differences in paralanguage and metacommunication of people in various cultures.

3. Explain how attitudes toward time vary from culture to culture.

4. Discuss differences in space needs of persons in the United States, Japan, Greece, and Latin America.

5. Identify cultures that favor direct eye contact and those that avoid eye contact.

6. Give examples to show how olfactics (smell) is an important aspect of multicultural nonverbal communication.

7. Identify cultures that are comfortable with bodily contact and those that avoid bodily contact. Give examples of appropriate and inappropriate bodily contact in the United States.

8. Discuss cultural differences in body language of people in the United States, Japan, China, Italy, Greece, and Latin America.

9. Explain how the use of color communicates nonverbal messages.

10. Identify cultures that are comfortable with silence and those that are not. Discuss possible meanings of silence in various situations.

Case 1   Barbara works for a subsidiary of a German corporation in the United States. Her job involves ordering products from Germany and following up as to why deliveries have not been made. Barbara does not speak, read, or write German; however, this is not a problem as Barbara's contact Anna speaks, reads, and writes English. Normally all of Barbara's telexes, letters, and faxes are written in English from Anna. Lately the German factory has been having difficulty, and Barbara has been sending telexes to Anna with inquiries as to where products are that should have been received. In her last telex, Barbara asks why the Germans cannot get their materials shipped on time. Barbara's answer comes back in German. Discuss what nonverbal communication was being conveyed in the situation and how you would change the behavior to be more positive.

Case 2   A U.S. company has sent one representative to negotiate a contract with a Japanese firm. The U.S. representative arrives at the appointed time for his meeting and is shown to the meeting room where six representatives from the Japanese firm meet with him. During his presentation the Japanese move their heads in an up and down motion; however, they say very little. The presentation was given in English as the representative had been told the Japanese understood English. When the representative asked if there were any questions, everyone nodded politely; however, no one said anything. After a few minutes, the representative asked if they were ready to sign the contracts. One of the Japanese said, "It is very difficult for us to sign." At this point the representative said, "Should I leave the contract with you?" The Japanese said, "Yes." The U.S. representative returned to the United States expecting the Japanese to return the contract, which did not happen. Explain what the Japanese were really saying by nodding their heads and using the word "difficult."

——— ACTIVITIES ———

1. Write a paragraph describing an incident from your own experience involving oral and/or nonverbal miscommunication with someone from another culture. Suggest a plausible explanation for the miscommunication.

2. Prepare a short skit to illustrate nonverbal communication blunders that a person from the United States might make in a country of your choice.

3. Demonstrate a gesture (such as thumbs-up or the U.S. "okay" sign) and ask class members to explain its meaning in a specific country.

4. Demonstrate the amount of space considered acceptable when interacting with persons in Latin America, the United States, and Egypt.

5. Demonstrate the amount of eye contact considered appropriate in the United States, Japan, and the Middle East.

REFERENCES

Althen, G. (1988). *American ways.* Yarmouth, ME: Intercultural Press, Inc.

Axtell, R. E. (1991a). *The do's and taboos of international trade.* New York: John Wiley & Sons, Inc.

Axtell, R. E. (1991b). *Gestures.* New York: John Wiley & Sons, Inc.

Borden, G. A. (1991). *Cultural orientation: An approach to understanding intercultural communication.* Englewood Cliffs, NJ: Prentice Hall.

Engholm, C. (1991). *When business East meets business West.* New York: John Wiley & Sons, Inc.

Gudykunst, W. B., & Ting-Toomey, S. (1988). *Culture and interpersonal communication.* Newbury Park, CA: Sage Publications.

Hall, E. T. (1966). *The hidden dimension* (pp. 107–122). Garden City, NY: Doubleday.

Hall, E. T., & Hall, M. R. (1990). *Understanding culture differences.* Yarmouth, ME: Intercultural Press, Inc.

Huseman, R. C., Lahiff, J. M., & Penrose, J. M., Jr. (1991). *Business communication: Strategies and skills.* Chicago: The Dryden Press.

Leathers, D. (1976). *Nonverbal communication systems.* Boston: Allyn and Bacon.

Samovar, L. A., & Porter, R. E. (1991a). *Communication between cultures.* Belmont, CA: Wadsworth Publishing Company.

Samovar, L. A., & Porter, R. E. (1991b). *Intercultural communication: A reader.* Belmont, CA: Wadsworth Publishing Company.

Thiederman, S. (1991). *Bridging cultural barriers for corporate success.* New York: Lexington Books.

Victor, D. A. (1992). *International business communication.* New York: HarperCollins Publishers.

5

Written Communication Patterns

OBJECTIVES

Upon completion of this chapter, you will:

- know the guidelines for writing international messages in English.

- be familiar with letter formats commonly used by U.S. business firms and how they differ from formats used in other countries.

- understand how facsimiles are commonly used for communicating between U.S. firms and those in other countries.

- understand how writing tone and style vary from culture to culture.

- understand cultural differences in other types of written communication, such as the résumé and related job-search documents.

Many U.S. companies correspond with foreign corporations; it is important, therefore, to be aware of differences in the format, tone, and style of written communication. Research results show that 97 percent of outgoing international correspondence is sent in English with about 1 percent each in Spanish, French, and German. Percentages for incoming international messages are similar: 96 percent are in English, with the remaining 4 percent in French, German, and Spanish (Green & Scott, 1992). Since English is used for most international written messages, making these messages as clear as possible is important. Understanding the business communication practices of the culture you are writing to will help you to communicate effectively.

INTERNATIONAL ENGLISH

International English is English for businesspeople who either deal with other cultures whose primary language is not English or for whom English may be a second language; it is limited to the 3,000 to 4,000 most common English words. One reference that contains these words is P. H. Collin, M. Lowi, and C. Weiland's, *Beginner's Dictionary of American English Usage*, 1991. In order to utilize international English, three cultural factors are important: an understanding of business communication in the other culture and/or residence in the other culture, an idea of how business communication is taught in the other culture, and a knowledge that content errors are more difficult than language errors for another culture to discern.

Content errors are **lexical errors** and refer to errors in meaning. **Syntactic errors** are errors in the order of the words in a sentence. A native speaker of a language will discover the syntactic errors in a sentence much more easily than the lexical errors. Business communication is not necessarily taught in other countries as it is in the United States. The course may not contain any information on the theory of communication and what happens between the sender and receiver. Many of the business communication courses taught in a country that desires to do more business with the United States will simply be translation courses.

Guidelines for "internationalizing" the English language have been developed to enable both native and nonnative speakers of the language to write messages clearly to decrease the possibility of misunderstanding between people of different cultures. The following guidelines adapted from those developed by Riddle and Lanham (1984–1985) are important for situations in which both cultures speak English, as well as for situations in which English may be a second language for one or both of the communicators.

- Use the 3,000 to 4,000 most common English words. Uncommon words, such as *onus* for *burden* and *flux* for *continual change,* should be avoided.
- Use only the most common meaning of words. The word *high* has 20 meanings; the word *expensive* has one.

- Select action-specific verbs and words with few or similar alternate meanings. Use *cook breakfast* rather than *make breakfast*; use *take a taxi* rather than *get a taxi.*
- Avoid redundancies (*interoffice memorandum*), sports terms (*ballpark figure*), and words that draw mental pictures (*red tape*).
- Choose words with singular rather than multiple meanings.
- Avoid using words in other than their most common way, such as making verbs out of nouns (*impacting* the economy and *faxing* a message).
- Be aware of words that have a unique meaning in some cultures; the word *check* outside the United States generally means a financial instrument and is often spelled *chèque.*
- Be aware of alternate spellings in countries that use the same language; for example, *theatre/theater, organisation/organization, colour/color,* and *judgement/judgment.*
- Avoid creating or using new words; avoid slang.
- Avoid two-word verbs, such as *pick up;* use *lift.*
- Use the formal tone and maximum punctuation to assure clarity; avoid the use of first names in letter salutations.
- Conform carefully to rules of grammar; be particularly careful of misplaced modifiers, dangling participles, and incomplete sentences.
- Use more short, simple sentences than you would ordinarily use; avoid compound and compound–complex sentences.
- Clarify the meaning of words that have more than one meaning.
- Adapt the tone of the letter to the reader if the cultural background of the reader is known; for example, use unconditional apologies if that is expected in the reader's culture.
- Try to capture the flavor of the language when writing to someone whose cultural background you know. Letters to people whose native language is Spanish, for example, would contain more flowery language (full of highly ornate language) and would be longer than U.S. letters.

WRITING TONE AND STYLE

The tone and writing style of correspondents from foreign countries are usually more formal and traditional than American companies typically use. When the tone and style differ greatly from that used by the recipient, the intended positive message may be negatively received.

Authors of business communication textbooks in the United States recommend the use of the direct approach for beginning good-news and direct request/inquiries, and neutral messages and the indirect approach for bad-news messages. The direct approach means simply that you begin with the good news or other positive ideas in the good-news message, the request or inquiry in request/inquiry messages, and the most important idea in neutral messages. When using the indirect approach, beginning with a **buffer** is recommended. A buffer is a paragraph that tells what the letter is about, is pleasant, but says neither *yes* nor *no*.

Although Germans use the buffer occasionally, they are usually more direct with negative news. Latin Americans do not use buffers; they avoid the negative news completely as they believe it is discourteous to bring bad news. For that reason, U.S. Americans must be able to read between the lines of letters from Latin American businesspeople. The Japanese begin letters on a warm, personal note, which is an inappropriate way of beginning a U.S. letter. The Japanese try to present negative news in a positive manner, a quality that has sometimes caused a U.S. counterpart to believe that the person was deceitful.

In the United States ending negative messages on a positive note is important, while the French do not consider this important. Beginnings and endings of French letters are very formal, but endings tend to be somewhat flowery: "Sir, please accept the expression of my best feelings"; the French organize some types of business letters differently. They recommend apologizing for mistakes and expressing regret for any inconvenience caused. U.S. business letter writers, on the other hand, avoid apologies and simply state objectively the reason for the action taken. Endings of German letters tend to be formal (Kilpatrick, 1984; Varner, 1987, 1988).

An awareness of the differences between the format, tone, and style of written communication can go far in building goodwill between cultures. If you receive a letter in which you are addressed "Dear Prof. Dr. Judith C. Simon," you need to be able to read past the unimportant style or tone differences and look for the meaning in the letter. The use of politeness, beyond that with which people in the United States are familiar, is very common for many cultures and should not distract U.S. readers. However, as a writer, keep these cultural differences in mind to avoid sounding harsh and insensitive to the reader. Also the length of U.S. letters tends to be shorter than letters written in other cultures. As a sign of friendship, it would be wise for U.S. businesspeople to change the tone of their letters when writing to businesspeople in another culture. The **parochialism** or ethnocentrism that so many U.S. people display in their writing to other cultures can easily be tempered with a knowledge of the person to whom they are writing.

LETTER FORMATS

Letter formats used by other countries often differ from styles used by U.S. businesses. Some countries still use the indented letter style with closed punctuation, while the preferred styles in the United States are the blocked (all lines beginning at the left margin) and modified blocked (date and closing begin at the center; paragraphs are blocked) styles with either standard punctuation (colon after the salutation, comma after the closing) or open punctuation (no punctuation after either the salutation or closing).

The French tend to use the indented style for business letters. The French place the name of the originating city before the date (Norvège, le 15 décembre 19—). (Learn to use the overstrike function of your word processing software to type accent marks used in both French and Spanish, the dieresis, and the eñe used frequently in the Spanish language.)

The format of the inside address may vary. In the United States, the title and full name are placed on the first line; street number and name on the second line; and city, state, and zip code on the last line. The format used in Germany puts the title (Herr) on the first line; full name on the second line; street name followed by the street number on the third line; and zip code, city, and state on the last line. The street number also follows the name of the street in Mexico and South America.

While U.S. letters always place the date before the inside address, the French sometimes place the date after the inside address. In French letters the inside address is typed on the right side, with the zip code preceding the name of the city (74010 PARIS); in U.S. letters, the inside address is on the left. The punctuation style used in French letters differs from that used in U.S. correspondence; the salutation is followed by a comma rather than a colon or no punctuation, which is used in standard and open punctuation styles of U.S. letters. The complimentary close is rather formal in French letters; the writer's title precedes the writer's name. Care should be taken to format the inside address and the envelope address exactly as it is shown on the incoming correspondence. Dates are written differently also. While people in the United States would use January 5, 19—, in many other countries the date would be written 5th of January 19— or 5 January 19—.

U.S. business letters are single-spaced, but in many other countries they may be single- or double-spaced. In U.S. letters the typed name of the writer is placed four lines below the complimentary close with the title placed on the next line. In German letters, the company name is placed below the complimentary close; the writer signs the letter, but the writer's name and position are not typed in the signature block. Within Japan and China the surname is always placed before the given name, such as Smith Jack rather than Jack Smith.

Salutations and closings are more formal in many other countries. Salutations for German letters would be the English equivalent of Very Honored Mrs. Jones; in Latin American countries, My Esteemed Dr. Green. Complimentary closings would often be the English equivalent of Very respectfully yours (Kilpatrick, 1984; Varner, 1987, 1988).

Samples of Japanese, French, Spanish, and Chinese letters that have been translated into English from the native language in which they were written are shown in Figures 5.1 through 5.4. A sample of a U.S. letter is shown in Figure 5.5.

The Japanese have a traditional format beginning with the salutation followed by a comment about the season or weather. Next will follow a kind remark about a gift, kindness, or patronage. Then they include the main message and close with best wishes for the receiver's health or prosperity (Haneda & Shima, 1982).

```
                                          AZ409
                                          April 7, 19—
Showa Machine Works Ltd.
Attention of Sales Department

                                   5-1 Moriyama Maguro
                                   Moriyamaku, Nagoya 463
                                   Asumi Trading Co., Ltd.


                                   President: Nobuaki Iwai
Allow us to open
with all reverence to you:


    The season for cherry blossoms is here with us and every body
is beginning to feel refreshed. We sincerely congratulate you on
becoming more prosperous in your business.
    We have an inquiry from a foreign customer and shall be very
happy to have your best price and technical literature for the
item mentioned below:
                        Wire Drawing Machine
                        6 units for Taiwan


Specifications:
1. Finished sizes:            0.04 mm to 0.10 mm
2. Spooler:                   Single
3. Speed:                     Min. 1500 meters/min.
4. Type of spooler:           Expanding arbor
5. Capstan:                   Must be covered with ceramic
6. Dimension of spool:
      Flange diam.            215 mm
      Barrel diam.            163 mm
      Bore diam.               97 mm
      Traverse                200 mm
    The above are all the information available for this inquiry.
We ask you to recommend a machine that can meet these specifica-
tions.
    We shall be very pleased if you will study the inquiry and
let us have your reply as soon as possible. We solicit your
favor.


                                   Let us close with
                                   great respect to you.
```

FIGURE 5.1   Japanese Letter

In the French letter notice the "we" attitude and manner of indirect apology; note also the way of explaining the situation and the format: typing the surname in all capital letters. The date, salutation, and closing also differ from the U.S. letter.

```
Marie Portafaix                        Mr. Pierre DESBORDE
7, Avenue Felix               Professeur d'économie politique
75541 Paris                      IUT BB Commercial Techniques
                                         Doyen Gosse Place
                                          38000 GRENOBLE



MTP/GM/05.52
                                  Paris, 25 September 19—
    Sir,
    We are in receipt of your letter and have given our best
attention to your request.
    We are unhappy to inform you, we are not able to give
your proposition a favorable report.
    As a matter of fact we are grateful for the interest and
your support, but we must consider essential publications here-
after for the media.
    We want to renew our regrets and thank you for your
belief. Sir, be assured our sentiments are the best.

                            Public Relations Director
                            Marie Thérèse PORTAFAIX
```

FIGURE 5.2   French Letter

Similarities and differences between the Spanish letter and the U.S. letter include the date, salutation, and closing.

---

8 June 19—

Zapatería Elegánte, S. A.
May 5 Avenue
Caracas, Venezuela

Esteemed clients and friends:

Permit us to communicate to you that the fabric of the shoes of Miss Modalo that were ordered has been discontinued. Therefore much to our regret we will not be able to serve you in this situation.

We always want to fill your catalog requests, and if you find another model from the enclosed catalog that you like we would be very glad to send them.

We regret your loss and hope to be able to serve you on another occasion as you deserve.

Very cordially yours,

CIA. LATINOAMERICANA, S.A.

José Mendoza Lopez
General Manager

FAL/age

Enclosure: 1 catalog

FIGURE 5.3   Spanish Letter

This letter from China is shown as it was received; notice how the syntactic errors develop when people are not writing in their native language. Also notice that the writer has used the U.S. format in deference to another culture.

April 5, 19—

Prof. L. S. St. Clair
71 South Perkins Extd.
Memphis, TN 38117-3211

Dear Prof. St. Clair:

I've received your letter of Jan. 30 and your report passed on to me by Dr. Jones of CSU, Long Beach. Thank you deeply for your kindness to let me have it. I have perused it and found it very creative and enlightening, I especially admire your observant and ingenious analysis. I fully support your suggestion to establish course in intercultural business communication. Never has it been so important to globalize business communication education as it is today. It is time now to join our effort in this important area.

I made a report on the development of BC in the U.S. at a convention in Chicago last month.

You are welcome to visit China and help us with the development of business communication in China.

Sincerely,

Feng Xiang Chun
Vice President

FIGURE 5.4   Letter Written in English by Chinese Writer

In the following example of a U.S. letter that conveys bad news, notice the use of a buffer in the first paragraph, which does not suggest a negative message. In the second paragraph, the bad news is placed in a dependent clause to deemphasize it. The letter ends with an action close, avoiding any reference to the bad news. The letter style is blocked with standard punctuation.

```
September 15, 19—


Mr. Larry Green
2871 Goodlett Street
Memphis, TN 38117

Dear Mr. Green:

A beautiful driveway not only enhances the beauty of a home,
but it also increases a home's value.

Although the driveway we installed at your home six years ago
is no longer under warranty, we will be glad to send one of our
service representatives to inspect your driveway and give you a
free estimate on repairing or replacing it.

Please call 767-6334 to arrange a time for one of our represen-
tatives to evaluate the condition of your driveway.

Sincerely,



Thomas L. Johnson

pl
```

FIGURE 5.5 U.S. Letter

FACSIMILES (FAX)_____

Multinational businesses in the United States have found that the facsimile (fax) machine is more dependable than the mail service in many countries. However, in some countries the telephone system is also poorly managed, which means the fax machine may not be better than the mail. Poor service of both mail and phone systems occurs during the stormy seasons that a number of countries have. In addition, many countries lack regular mail or telephone service in the remote areas of their countries. However, through telecommunication satellites, telephone service is becoming more dependable than the mail in many locations around the globe.

The fax should be written as you would write a letter. If you are sending production schedules, budgets, or other types of written information, then a cover letter or transmittal sheet should be used so that the operator knows to whom the fax is directed, from whom the material originates, and how many total pages are included. Figure 5.6 is an example of a fax.

```
To: Jim Cain, President
    Cainable Vegetables

From: Wu H. Chu


I received your fax message delightly. How is your business
doing? I really think that our election was better for all
business in Korea. If you can make a videotape of Ray
Manner'farm, that would be great. Videotape, Blueprints
together you can send me by airmail not by ship, regardlessly
special or regular with the bill I would appreciate it very
much. In designing of my vegetable farm I am take your experi-
enced advice in good consideration. Thank you. I will look for
your advices more.
```

FIGURE 5.6 Korean Fax

RÉSUMÉ AND JOB SEARCH INFORMATION_____

Globalization has definitely expanded the information people need if they intend to get a position in a country other than their own. Europeans have always lived with differences and adjusted as they crossed national boundaries. In the United States and other parts of the world, a person looking for a position could use the job-search method they were taught in school. The following is a description of job-search information needed to find a position in the United States, England, France, Germany, and Spain.

United States

According to research by Harcourt, Krizan, and Merrier (1991), U.S. hiring officials prefer the résumé to be one or two pages long. Important résumé items include personal information (name, address, and telephone number); job objective (to give the reader an idea of what type of work you would like and plans for advancement); educational background (universities attended); and work experience (current position, company name and location, job title, dates employed, responsibilities, and accomplishments). Most hiring officials prefer that you include three or four references—names of people who could verify your work experience, educational achievements, and character. Information about your family, age, religion, ethnicity, or gender should not be included, nor should you include a photograph. The résumé is accompanied by an application (cover) letter.

In the United States, good sources of positions are the Sunday edition of major newspapers in cities where you are interested in working. On Tuesdays *The Wall Street Journal* has a special employment section and also produces a weekly newsprint, *The Employment Weekly,* which is a collection of all employment advertising for the previous week in all U.S. regions. In larger cities public and private employment agencies are also good at assisting people in finding positions.

England

The résumé for managers in England is one to two pages in length, is typed, and generally does not have a photograph attached. The résumé will contain a professional objective, name, address, phone number, professional experience, education, hobbies and other activities, and references. Military service is not listed; family and other personal information is omitted. The résumé is sent with an application letter that is typed and formal. The letter would include your reasons for wanting the position and a request for an interview.

The universities in England offer career advisory services for their graduates. Check the ads in the following journals: *The Guardian* and *The Daily Telegraph* on Thursday, *The Guardian* and *The Daily Telegraph* on Tuesday for management positions, the *Daily Telegraph* on Wednesday and the *Sunday Times* for commercial and technical positions, and the *Financial Times* on Wednesday and Thursday for finance-related positions (Tixier, 1992).

France

In France the vita is much like the U.S. résumé. An application (cover) letter is included. The résumé should list your full name, address, and age. You would include a job objective, education, and experience as in the U.S. résumé. In addition, include information about your hobbies and the foreign languages in which you are proficient.

In France it is very difficult for someone directly from the university to get a position without experience. Connections are very important in obtaining the first position. Graduates of the Grandes Écoles, business, and engineering schools would have an advantage over others, as graduates of these institutions are considered the intellectual elite. Age is a factor in hiring; 40 is considered old. French laws do not prevent age discrimination.

Two daily newspapers that are a good source of available positions are *Le Cosigaro* and *Le Monde*. The magazine *L'Exprès* is also a source of potential jobs (Desborde, 1993).

Germany

The Germans expect applicants to be well educated and to have experience. The résumé is a complete dossier of the candidate. A résumé length of 20 to 30 pages is not unusual. Items included would be positions the candidate has held, photocopies of diplomas and degrees the candidate has earned, letters of recommendation from teachers, verification of previous employment, a recent photograph, and a statement of computer skills. Other information would include the names and professions of the candidate's parents; names of brothers, sisters, spouse, and children; and religious affiliation. With the diplomas and degrees, transcripts would be provided to certify all course work completed. The candidate's financial obligations would be included. Professional activities, including publications and personal references, would also be given. The résumé begins with the letter of application, which is typed and one to two pages in length. The style is very conservative and formal.

In Germany college students often enter into a contract with a company while in college. The two large journals where employment ads are placed are *le Frankfurter Allgemeine Zeitung* and *Suddeutsche Zeitung* (Tixier, 1992).

Spain

The résumé is a maximum of two pages; it is in letter form and is typed. A chronology of experience, military service, and education is given. Including information on the family, profession of parents, clubs and associations of which you are a member, and a picture is not unusual. A professional objective is mentioned. Many positions are gained through personal referral rather than through school placement or advertisements. Journals that do have some position advertisements include *El Pais* and *La Vanguardia* (Tixier, 1992).

TERMS

Buffer
International English
Lexical errors

Parochialism
Syntactic errors

Exercise 5.1

Instructions: Circle the T for true and the F for false.

1. T   F   Native speakers of a language will discover lexical errors more easily than syntactic errors.

2. T   F   The writing style of U.S. letters is more formal than that of most foreign correspondents.

3. T   F   The use of a buffer in bad-news messages is typical of the writing style of Latin Americans.

4. T   F   The Japanese try to present negative news in a positive manner.

5. T   F   Ending messages on a positive note is important in both U.S. and French letters.

6. T   F   The indented letter style for business letters is used by the French.

7. T   F   Salutations of German letters are more formal than in the United States.

8. T   F   The Japanese traditionally begin letters with comments about the season or weather.

9. T   F   Résumés submitted to a German firm would typically be longer than those submitted to a U.S. firm.

10. T   F   Spanish résumés are typically in letter form.

——— QUESTIONS AND CASES FOR DISCUSSION ———

1. Explain how the format of business letters differs in U.S. correspondence and in Latin American countries.
2. How does the tone and writing style of Japanese letters differ from those in the United States?
3. In order to utilize international English, what cultural factors do you have to understand?
4. Explain the difference between lexical and syntactic errors.
5. Explain why people from two cultures that speak the same language may have difficulty communicating.
6. Explain what a buffer is and how it is used.
7. Which countries expect the reader "to read between the lines" for meaning?
8. What in the German culture might explain the very long and detailed résumé that is required when job hunting in Germany?
9. What items are currently included in résumés in the United States?
10. Explain the major differences between résumés in the United States and other cultures.

Case 1   You work in the personnel division of a multinational organization. You have been asked to provide a list of potential candidates for a management position in the corporation's German office. Because of the laws, you want a German national for the position. How would you go about obtaining résumés to review?

Case 2   If you are dealing with a foreign corporation in which no one speaks English as a native or second language, what may be necessary in order for your corporation and the foreign corporation to work together? How does a U.S. corporation react when the other corporation does not speak its language? If the corporation has the flexibility to deal with another company in which someone speaks its language versus one in which no one does, which company would receive the order?

——— ACTIVITIES ———

1. Examine the Latin or Germanic roots of simple and difficult words in the English language.

2. Take a passage from a journal or textbook in another language and compare it, in terms of sentence and paragraph length, to a passage from a journal or textbook written in English.

3. Modify a bad-news letter so it will be effective for a reader who is Japanese, French, Spanish, or German.

4. Search the want ads of the local newspaper; bring to class a job announcement of a position with a multinational corporation, a position involving overseas travel, or a position located in a foreign country.

5. Prepare a résumé to be sent to a multinational company applying for an overseas assignment in a country of your choice.

6. Write a letter of application to accompany the résumé prepared in the preceding activity.

7. Write a letter in English to someone who speaks English as a second language following the International English Guidelines.

8. Find the errors in Figure 5.4, and explain why these particular errors may have happened.

9. Read the two facsimiles on pages 91 and 92 and determine the reader's probable reaction. What choice of words could have been improved upon? The first fax is from the U.S. corporate office to Taiwan; the second is from Taiwan to the U.S. corporate office.

10. Have an international student write a letter for you in English but with his or her native language style, tone, and format. Compare the letter to the style, tone, and format of U.S. letters.

TO: XYZ

ATTN: WU

FROM: BOB SMITH

DATE: SEPT. 4, 19—

RECEIVED THE HUGGER PACKAGE TODAY AND WAS VERY DISAPPOINTED.
FIRST I WANT TO SAY I SUSPECT YOU MAY NOT HAVE SEEN THE PARTS
BEFORE THEY WERE SENT. IT LOOKED LIKE EVERYTHING WAS JUST
THROWN INTO A BOX AND A COUPLE OF THIN PIECES OF POLYFOAM LAID
ON TOP. NOTHING WAS PROTECTIVE WRAPPED. THE HUGGER HOUSING IS
SO BEAT UP IT LOOKS LIKE SOMETHING OUT OF THE JUNK PILE.

THE HANGER BRACKETS WERE JUST THROWN INTO THE BOTTOM OF THE BOX
WITH NO PROTECTION AT ALL. MOST OF THE SCREWS FOR THE TOP OF
THE BALL WERE SCATTERED THROUGHOUT THE BOX AND NOT ASSEMBLED TO
THE BRACKETS.

I'M AFRAID WE WILL NOT BE ABLE TO USE THE HANGER BRACKET ASSEM-
BLIES TO FIELD TEST THE HUGGER BECAUSE THE BALL HOLD DOWN
SCREWS INTERFERE WITH THE TOP OF THE BALL. THE FIT IS SO TIGHT
THAT THE BALL WILL NOT ROTATE AND CENTER IN THE SOCKET. WHAT WE
REALLY NEED IS FOR THE THREE SCREWS TO CLEAR THE BALL BY
APPROX. 1/32 INCH (ABOVE THE BALL) AFTER THE SCREWS HAVE BEEN
ASSEMBLED TO THE BRACKET.

YOU MAY HAVE TO ADJUST THE VERTICAL LOCATION OF THE SCREW FROM
THE DRAWING DIMENSION TO MAKE SURE THE SCREWS JUST CLEAR THE
BALL.

PLEASE ADVISE WHEN YOU CAN SEND NEW BRACKET ASSEMBLIES SO WE
CAN GET ON WITH THE TESTING. ALSO PLS HAVE YOUR PEOPLE PROTEC-
TIVE WRAP EVERYTHING.

THANKS

BOB SMITH

```
TO: XYZ                                    DATE: 9/7/—
ATTN: MR. BOB SMITH
FROM: XYT
RE: 52" HUGGER PARTS
```

At first, we have to apologize to you for not having good package of samples. With thin polyfoam for package is easily to break out when air freight. Besides say sorry to you, we will improve the protection of samples.

1. New hanger housing was made by hand. Without mold, it needs some time. Can we just make one set?

2. Hanger bracket ball—When we revised it per drawing, we found when hanger bracket is setted on ceiling plate. The fit is too tight that the ball will not rotate and center in the socket. We will ask vendor to make proper correction to improve these problem.

3. The distance above the ball and three screws needs 1/32 inch. Will also revise it.

4. Blade iron after our shaking test. It results over 60,000 times. How about your testing result?

5. After we complete correction hanger bracket and ball, will send samples to you again. We will improve our protective wrap of samples.

Best Regards,

WU

REFERENCES

Collin, P. H., Lowi, M., & Weiland, C. (1991). *Beginner's dictionary of American English usage*. Lincolnwood, IL: National Textbook Co.

Desborde, R. (1993, July 23). Personal interview.

Green, D. J., & Scott, J. C. (1992). International business correspondence: Practices and perspectives of major U.S. companies with related implications for business education. *NABTE Review, 19*, 39–43.

Haneda, S., & Shima, H. (1982). Japanese communication behavior as reflected in letter writing. *Journal of Business Communication, 19*(1), 21–32.

Harcourt, J., Krizan, A. C., & Merrier, P. (1991, April). Teaching résumé content: Hiring officials' preferences versus college recruiters' preferences. *Business Education Forum*, pp. 13–17.

Kilpatrick, R. H. (1984). International business communication practices. *Journal of Business Communications, 21*(4), 40–42.

Riddle, D. I., & Lanham, Z. D. (1984–1985, Winter). Internationalizing written business English: 20 propositions for native English speakers. *The Journal of Language for International Business, 1*, 1–11.

Tixier, M. (1992). *Travailler en Europe*. Paris: Editions Liaisons.

Varner, I. I. (1987). Internationalizing business communication courses. *The Bulletin of the Association for Business Communication, 1*(4), 7–11.

Varner, I. I. (1988). A comparison of American and French business correspondence. *The Journal of Business Communication, 25*(4), 55–65.

6

Language

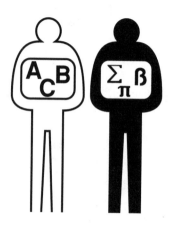

OBJECTIVES

Upon completion of this chapter, you will:

- know how language affects intercultural communication.

- understand how language construction, thought, perceptions, and culture are linked.

- understand the limits of using a second language.

- be aware that language differences exist even when people speak the same language.

- understand the importance of accurate translation and interpretation to intercultural communication.

- understand how to use parables and proverbs as insights into the culture.

- understand the concepts of the Sapir-Whorf and Bernstein hypotheses.

Language holds us together as groups, differentiates us into groups, and also controls the way we shape concepts, how we think, how we perceive, and how we judge others. When we understand how important and complex a culture's native language is, it is easier to see why in a country such as India, English is the official language. The people do, however, use over 100 native languages or dialects for communication within their microcultures.

The closest things to common languages the world has are numbers and music. Unlike mathematicians, businesspeople must be sensitive to the nuances of a language to assure understanding when communicating with people whose first language differs from their own and even with those whose language is the same as their own. Language is only part of communication. How the language is used in relationship to nonverbal communication and the beliefs and values of the culture is very important.

HIGH- AND LOW-CONTEXT LANGUAGE

The concept of high- and low-context language has been researched by Hall and Hall (1990). A **high-context** language transmits very little in the explicit message; instead, the nonverbal and cultural aspects of what is not said are very important. In high-context cultures reading between the lines in order to understand the intended meaning of the message is needed. The Japanese language and culture are an example of high-context communication.

The United States, on the other hand, provides an example of a language and culture of low-context communication. In a **low-context** language and culture, the message is explicit; it may be given in more than one way to ensure understanding by the receiver. In low-context languages, a person would state what is expected or wanted. High-context languages tend to be indirect and nonverbal, while low-context languages tend to be direct and verbal. Since people of low-context cultures favor directness, they are likely to consider high-context communications as a waste of time.

Should there be perceived disagreement between the verbal and nonverbal message within either low- or high-context societies, the nonverbal signals are believed over what is actually said. However, in high-context cultures the nonverbal signals are much more subtle and elusive to the untrained senses. An example of high-context communication is the way the Japanese indicate *no*. The Japanese would say *yes* for *no* but would indicate whether *yes* is *yes* or really *no* by the context, tone, time taken to answer, and facial and body expressions. This use of high-context communication can be very confusing to the uninitiated, nonsensitive intercultural businessperson. In the United States, a low-context society, *no* means *no*. Group-oriented, collectivistic cultures tend to use high-context languages; individualistic cultures tend to use low-context languages.

LANGUAGE DIVERSITY

Achieving successful communication is difficult due to the diversity of dialects and accents within a language. In the United States more than 140 languages and dialects are spoken currently; about 11 percent of the population speak a native language other than English in the home (Tsunda, 1986).

The diversity between languages and within the same language is arbitrary. Words in themselves have no meaning; meanings were assigned at some point by people in a culture. For example, the word *business* in the United States connotes how we choose to make and exchange commodities. In other languages, people assign other sounds to mean *business,* such as *shobai, bijinesu, shigoto, entreprise, comercio,* and *negocios.* In the English language synonyms for *business* also exist, such as *commerce, trade,* and *enterprise.*

The diversity of languages causes problems for both managers and applicants for jobs. What is the correct way to assess English-language skills of job applicants? Managers must ask themselves the question: How important are correct English-language skills in this position? Perhaps the ability to speak and write English well is not essential to job performance; on the other hand, it may be very important. Language qualifications for each position should be assessed separately. Other problems caused by language diversity include foreigners who speak their native language on the job, a practice that is not viewed favorably by the nationals. Although the main reason foreigners may use their native language is that it is easier to express their ideas that way, this behavior is interpreted as an attempt to exclude nationals from the conversation and is considered extremely rude.

SLANG AND OTHER INFORMAL LANGUAGE

English in the United States is replete with slang, colloquialisms, acronyms, euphemisms, and jargon from numerous areas, including the military, sports, computers, law, and engineering.

Slang includes idioms and other informal language. *Bottom line* and *back to square one* are examples of business slang. **Colloquialisms** are informal words or phrases often associated with certain regions of the country. Examples of colloquialisms include *y'all* (you all), *pop* (soda), and *ain't* (is/are not). **Acronyms** are words formed from the initial letters or groups of letters of words in a phrase and pronounced as one word. Examples of acronyms are *RAM* (random access memory), *BASIC* (beginner's all-purpose symbolic instruction code), *Fortran* (formula translation), and *OSHA* (Occupational Safety and Health Act). Initial abbreviations are pronounced as separate initials, such as *CEO* (corporate executive officer), *CAR* (computer-assisted retrieval), and *OJT* (on-job-training). **Euphemisms** are inoffensive expressions that are used in place of offensive words or words with negative connotations.

Taboo words are dealt with through euphemisms. Examples of euphemisms are *to pass* or *pass away* (to die), *senior citizens* (old people), and *customer service department* (complaint department). **Jargon** is technical terminology used within specialized groups, such as engineers, teenagers, and doctors. Examples of jargon include *on the ball* (on top of things), *iced* (bribe money), *oiled* (become suddenly wealthy), and *byte* (a string of binary digits) (Ferraro, 1990).

Informal language generally originates with people in a subgroup of a community who want to differentiate themselves from the masses and determine who is a member of the "in group." Informal language should be used with caution in intercultural encounters because of potential miscommunication.

FORMS OF VERBAL INTERACTION

Forms of verbal interaction include verbal dueling, repartee, rituals, and self-disclosure.

Verbal dueling is like gamesmanship; the object is to see who can gain dominance in a friendly debate rather than imparting any needed information. The competitive conversations are generally meant in jest but are also used in nonaggressive societies to release hostility. Often people who are not familiar with verbal dueling may misunderstand the subtleties of the communication taking place. In the United States, urban black adolescent males have a form of verbal dueling insult contest called *playing the dozens*. The verbal dueling begins when one male insults a member of the opponent's family. The opponent can choose not to play; however, he will normally counter with an insult of his own. The verbal dueling continues until the males become bored or one is victorious (Ferraro, 1990). In Germany, France, and England, politics is an appropriate topic for verbal dueling. Verbal dueling may also take place when discussing sporting events, such as which team is better or which team is going to win. In the business environment, verbal dueling may happen when a group is trying to decide on a new ad campaign, and members of the group are polarized as to which campaign is best. Many times when companies are interviewing candidates for positions, verbal dueling will take place over who is the best candidate for the job.

Repartee is a conversation in which the parties frequently take turns speaking, usually after the first few sentences. The speakers talk only for short time periods, then listen while the other person speaks briefly. Repartee is a favorite form of interaction for people of the United States; they become very irritated when someone speaks for too long a period. In contrast, Africans and Arabs tend to speak for extended periods of time (Althen, 1988).

Speaking well is important to the French, and repartee is admired. The speaking skill is so important that for a foreigner to function effectively in France he or she must speak French fluently (Hall & Hall, 1990).

Ritual conversation is culturally based and involves standard replies and comments for a given situation. In the United States the interchanges are superficial; little meaning is attached to what is said. U.S. people are not actually interested in learning about others or in revealing their own emotions or personal information during such rituals as greeting others upon arriving at work. Latin Americans, on the other hand, will discuss health and other personal information for extended periods during ritual conversation. Arabs in ritual conversation will invoke Allah's goodwill; however, they avoid discussions of personal situations (Althen, 1988).

Self-disclosure is another form of interaction that involves telling other people about yourself so they may get to know you better. The amount of self-disclosure a person is willing to give another is culturally determined (Althen, 1988). Foreigners who need to know a person in order to do business with that person become very frustrated with the lack of personal information provided by people in the United States. If people in a culture have the need to develop friendships prior to conducting business, doing business with U.S. persons can be very disconcerting since U.S. people are not viewed as being committed to forming friendships.

LINEAR AND NONLINEAR LANGUAGE

Linear and nonlinear aspects of language involve cultural thought patterns; they indicate how people in a specific culture think and communicate (Tsunda, 1986).

Linear language has a beginning and an end and is logical and object oriented. Linear languages, such as English, look at time on a continuum of present, past, and future. This view has affected communication patterns and business practices in the United States; an example of such business practices is short-range planning.

Nonlinear language is circular, tradition oriented, and subjective. Nonlinear languages, such as Chinese, look at time as cyclical and the seasons as an ever-repeating pattern. The nonlinear concepts are apparent in the long-range planning of the Chinese and Japanese and in the seasonal messages at the beginning of Japanese letters. The short term is unimportant in Asia. In the United States, for example, stockholders tend to sell their ownership in firms that are having short-term problems; Asians, on the other hand, look at the long-term position of the firm and hold onto the stock.

In multicultural business situations, people will respond in a dialogue based on their linear or nonlinear orientation. In the United States linear explanations are given as answers to *why* questions. The Japanese, however, would give more details that do not need lineal links. The Japanese would tell *what* happened and assume the *why*; whereas U.S. people answer *why* and assume the *what*. For example, a U.S. manager might ask a Japanese worker why the production was stopped. The manager would expect a direct answer, such as, "The parts are defective." The Japanese worker would answer nonlinearly with a very long detailed explanation including what the defects were and other related details. Miscommunication occurred because the Japanese answered with *what* was wrong instead of the *why* response expected by the U.S. manager (Tsunda, 1986).

VOCABULARY EQUIVALENCE

Because language is influenced by various aspects of a culture, exact translations for all words in one language to all words in a second language are not possible. For example, in one language the word *love* is used to mean love of another person, love of a pet, or love of an object, while in a second language different words are provided to distinguish between different types of love.

The English language is built on extremes, such as far and near, heavy and light, high and low, good and bad, wide and narrow, old and young, and long and short. The middle area between the extremes may or may not have words to describe it, forcing a person speaking English to use one of the polar ends. The Portuguese language has many words in the middle area between the extremes; however, when the Portuguese is translated to English only the

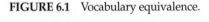

FIGURE 6.1   Vocabulary equivalence.

In the United States the word *love* is used to mean a strong preference for an object as well as physical or emotional *love.*

extremes are available. Therefore, when the translation is read in English, it may not have a vocabulary equivalence and will not be asking or saying what was said in Portuguese. The Portuguese question, "How far is it to New York?" becomes "Qual é a distancia a New York?" However, what the Portuguese are actually asking for is the location in space of New York as opposed to the translation that stresses the far or near dichotomy of the English language (Stewart & Bennett, 1991).

Language misunderstandings related to vocabulary usage are numerous, even between people who speak the same language. For example, during his 1976 presidential campaign, President Carter used the phrase *ethnic purity* to convey the message that our ethnic heritage and customs are important and should not be lost in the dominant culture. U.S. African Americans, however, interpreted it as a racist statement, and white South Africans interpreted it as support of their separatist policies. The individual cultural experiences of U.S. African Americans and white South Africans allowed for interpretations of the word *purity* that President Carter had not intended (Dodd, 1987).

Homonyms, words that sound alike but have different meanings, can be troublesome when learning a new language. The Chinese language is particularly difficult in this regard because even though the word is pronounced the same, the voice tone and pitch can change the entire meaning of a word. Within a family of languages, such as the romance languages, words with similar spellings and sometimes very similar pronunciations may have very different or very similar meanings. Assuming a similarity could be both costly and embarrassing during intercultural communication encounters (Ferraro, 1990).

PARABLES AND PROVERBS

A **parable** is a story told to convey a truth or moral lesson, while a **proverb** is a saying that expresses a common truth. Parables and proverbs deal with truths simply and concretely and teach the listener a lesson.

Parables and proverbs can help you understand a culture and can help to determine if it is a group- or individual-oriented culture. Parables and proverbs may also help in understanding what is desired and undesired, as well as what is considered correct or incorrect in the culture (Ferraro, 1990).

The U.S. proverb "The squeaking wheel gets the grease" implies that the person who stands out and is the most vocal will be rewarded. The Japanese proverb "The nail that sticks up gets knocked down" is an expression of their belief that the group is more important than the individual—the idea is that no one should stand out or be more important than anyone else.

Here are some other proverbs of selected cultures:

U.S. Proverbs

The early bird gets the worm.

Waste not, want not.

He who holds the gold makes the rules.

An ounce of prevention is worth a pound of cure.

Chinese Proverbs

Man who waits for roast duck to fly into mouth must wait very, very long time.

He who sows hemp will reap hemp; he who sows beans will reap beans.

Man who says it cannot be done should not interrupt man doing it.

Give a man a fish, and he will live for a day; give him a net, and he will live for a lifetime.

German Proverbs

No one is either rich or poor who has not helped himself to be so.

He who is afraid of doing too much always does too little.

What's the use of running if you're not on the right road.

Other Proverbs

Words do not make flour. (Italian)

He that wishes to eat the nut does not mind cracking the shell. (Polish)

Why kill time when one can employ it? (French)

Wealth which comes in at the door unjustly, goes out at the windows. (Egyptian)

Parables and proverbs can provide important information concerning the nature of the culture and what is valued.

CONVERSATION TABOOS

Conversation taboos are topics considered inappropriate for conversation with people in certain cultures or groups. Braganti and Devine (1992), Devine and Braganti (1986, 1988), and Baldrige (1993) discuss the culturally preferred topics of conversation as well as those that are considered taboo. Meeting another person usually involves a certain amount of "small talk" before getting down to business; therefore, knowing what topics are considered appropriate and inappropriate is important.

In the United States the most popular topic of small talk seems to be the weather or comments on some aspect of the physical surroundings, such as the arrangement of the meeting room, the landscaping or some other aspect of the building, or the location. Topics that are included later in the encounter include favorite restaurants, television programs, cities or countries visited, one's job, recreational interests or hobbies, and news items. Topics people in the United States have been taught to avoid discussing include religion and politics, even in family situations, because they are too controversial. In the United States family members often belong to different religions and political parties. The avoidance of such topics has caused people in other cultures to erroneously conclude that people in the United States are not intellectually capable of carrying on a conversation about anything more complex than weather and sports.

Some topics are considered too personal to discuss, such as the state of one's health or the health of family members, how much things cost, a person's salary, and personal misfortunes. People in the United States have been taught never to ask another person questions related to sensitive areas, such as age, weight, height, hair color, or sexual orientation or behavior.

Topics considered inappropriate in the United States are, however, considered appropriate in other cultures. People in Germany and Iran, for example, consider discussing and arguing about politics to be completely acceptable. The state of one's health and well-being and that of family members is an appropriate topic when people from Spanish-speaking countries meet for the first time. People from Saudi Arabia, on the other hand, would consider questions about the family inappropriate on an initial meeting.

Here are some appropriate and inappropriate topics of conversation in selected countries (Braganti & Devine, 1992; Devine & Braganti, 1986, 1988):

Country	Appropriate Topics	Topics to Avoid
Austria	professions, cars, skiing, music	money, religion, divorce/separation
Germany	travel abroad, international politics, hobbies, soccer	World War II, questions about personal life
Great Britain	history, architecture, gardening	politics, money/ prices, Falklands War
France	music, books, sports, the theater	prices of items, person's work, income, or age
Mexico	family, social concerns	politics, debt/inflation problems, border violations
Japan	history, culture, art	World War II

General guidelines for conversing with someone from another culture include the following (Baldrige, 1993):

- Avoid discussing politics or religion unless the other person initiates the discussion.
- Avoid highly personal questions, including "What do you do?," which is considered impolite by the British.
- Keep the conversation positive. Avoid asking questions that would imply criticism; phrase questions so they can be answered in a positive manner.
- Avoid telling ethnic jokes because of the possibility of offending someone.*

A good rule to follow is to take your cue from the other person. Let the other person initiate the discussion, particularly with culture-sensitive topics. Be a good listener, and stay informed on a wide variety of topics to expand your conversational repertoire.

TRANSLATION PROBLEMS

When languages are translated, the intended meaning may be lost. The word or concept may not have an exact duplicate in the other language. All languages do not have the same verb tenses, and many verbs have multiple meanings. In English, for example, the verb "get" can mean to buy, borrow, steal, rent, or retrieve. When a language is the person's second language, slang, euphemisms, and cultural thinking patterns can cause problems.

One type of translation assistance is **Group Decision Support Systems**, which allow people to communicate in a meeting using computers; to use multilingual communication; and to comment on a topic at the same time, order the comments, and vote on the comments. People can write in their own language, which will be translated into other languages just as those languages will be translated into their own. Words that do not translate directly are put in quotation marks to alert the reader to a possible translation problem. Pocket translators are also available to aid in learning and understanding another language.

Those who need oral or written translations in the United States can contact a local university for names of competent translators or consult the *Translation Services Directory*, published by the American Translators Association, 109 Croton Avenue, Ossining, New York 10562. Rates for on-the-spot verbal translations are charged by the hour, while written translations are charged by the word and the nature of the material being translated. AT&T has a Language Line Service (800-752-6096) at which you can reach language professionals who interpret more than 140 languages; they are available 24 hours a day, 7 days a week. Another source of translation assistance is the GDSS multilingual software, which can be obtained from the University of Mississippi, School of Business, University, MS 38677 (601-232-5777).

INTERPRETER USE

To be useful in a negotiation situation, an interpreter must be bilingual, bicultural, thoroughly familiar with the business culture of both sides, and able to use the correct meaning in all situations. However, what often happens is that interpreters are supplied by the host culture, are bilingual but not bicultural, and understand at least some business in their own culture and perhaps a little of the other side's business culture. Their loyalty is, of course, with their employer. When an interpreter is not bicultural, his or her thoughts, feelings, and hence translation are formulated according to the interpreter's native language rather than the second language. When using an interpreter in international negotiations, a missed negative can turn an agreement into a disagreement. A poor translator can make the difference between success or failure of the negotiation.

Many U.S. business travelers expect everyone to speak English and, therefore, they do not feel compelled to get an interpreter. While people may speak English as a second language, they do not think like U.S. businesspeople unless they are bicultural. Because of this it is very easy for an interpreter to misinterpret the English being used by the U.S. businessperson and to misstate facts when translating back to English. Unless the traveler is aware of the possibility of misinterpretation and asks additional questions, the traveler could leave with the wrong conception or answer.

When using an interpreter, go over with him or her your notes, slides, presentation, or anything else you have brought with you before the meeting. The advantage of using bicultural interpreters is that you can ask them questions if you are not sure what to do next. A bicultural interpreter can also alert you to problems he or she may foresee. Interpreters should be allowed to use notes or a dictionary; allow sufficient time to clarify points. Try not to interrupt interpreters while they are translating. Use visuals to support presentations, but allow the bicultural interpreter to check them for anything that may be offensive to the other side. Remember to avoid sarcasm or innuendoes, as they are very difficult to translate. Try to state things in more than one way to be sure the point you are making is understood.

Axtell (1991) gives the following specific tips for working with interpreters:

- Get to know the interpreter in advance. Your phrasing, accent, pace, and idioms are all important to a good interpreter.
- Review technical terms in advance.
- Speak slowly and clearly.
- Don't be afraid to use gestures and show emotion.
- Watch the eyes; they are the key to comprehension.
- Insist that the interpreter translate in brief bursts, not wait until the end of a long statement.
- Be careful of humor and jokes; it is difficult to export U.S. humor.
- Use visual aids where possible. By combining the translator's words with visual messages, chances of effective communication are increased.
- Be especially careful with numbers; write out important numbers to ensure accurate communication.
- Confirm all important discussions in writing to avoid confusion and misunderstanding.

HOST LANGUAGE

If you choose to use the language of the country you are visiting, the **host language**, be especially cautious. Be sure to speak clearly and slowly and eliminate jargon, idioms, and slang. When in doubt, ask questions. Avoid using expressions or gestures that could be misinterpreted. Find out if the meaning in the host language is modified by cadence, tone, or gestures.

Learning a business partner's language can help you learn how the person thinks. Learning a foreign language and living in another cultural community will affect your view of life. You will begin to think from the other person's perspective and will reevaluate your own cultural heritage.

As has been mentioned earlier, significant differences exist when both people speak the same language in the same country. Easterners in the United States are considered by many people in other parts of the country to be direct, rude, and to the point; Southerners are considered by many to be indirect, friendly, and more likely to skirt issues. When people speak the same language but are from different countries, additional problems are encountered. For example, the English spoken in the United States is quite different from the English spoken in Australia and Great Britain. The English use a very indirect style of verbalizing, while people of the United States use a more direct style.

The best advice when using the host language is to maintain a pleasant disposition and a positive attitude toward the host language; avoid making comments that could be interpreted as criticism of their language.

THOUGHT

Thinking is universal; however, methods of classifying, categorizing, sorting, and storing information are very different.

Subjective interpretation is an interpretation placed on a message that is affected by the thought processes; it is influenced by personal judgment, state of mind, or temperament of the person. Subjective interpretation is learned through cultural contact. We perceive what is relevant to our physical and social survival and classify, categorize, sort, and store it for future use. What is important in one culture may not be important in another.

In the United States people tend to think in a very functional, pragmatic way; they like procedural knowledge (how to get from point A to point B). Europeans, however, are more abstract; they like declarative knowledge, which is descriptive. The Japanese have a different way of thinking; they like to work with precedents and rules rather than abstract probability (Borden, 1991).

Thoughts and views toward nature, for example, are culturally diverse. U.S. people view nature as something to conquer; however, Native Americans and many Asians view nature as something with which to coexist. Other cultures, such as the Colombian mestizo, consider nature to be dangerous and have a fatalistic attitude toward it and their ability to control their destiny. A culture's perception of nature can be seen in its parables and proverbs, work ethic, and religion (Condon & Yousef, 1975).

A culture's way of thinking can adversely affect its ability to make progress. People who worked with the Peace Corp, for example, found that introducing technology to a third world country could not be accomplished without a change in cultural attitudes toward technology (Condon & Yousef, 1975). Initial plans for people of the former USSR following the fall of communism in 1991 were to give them stock in businesses and housing they would own. After generations of being told what to do, however, the people had a difficult time changing their way of thinking to include taking responsibility for themselves.

In our thought processes we make associations between color and messages: *Red* is associated with *stop; green* is associated with *go*. In the United States people associate white with purity, while in China white is associated with death. Additional information related to messages conveyed through the use of color was presented in Chapter 4.

LANGUAGE AND CULTURE INTERACTION

Language can be both unifying and divisive. A common native language ties people together, yet the presence of many different native languages in a small geographic area can cause problems. Culture and language both affect each other. We have the chicken and egg dilemma—which came first, the language or the culture? The use of language/culture in creating political, social, economic, and education processes is a consequence of favoring certain ideals over others. Understanding the culture without understanding the language is difficult.

Colonialism caused many areas of the world to lose or replace their native languages with the colonial language. Because the colonies spoke the colonizers' language, the colonizers treated them from an ethnocentric view. Many areas of the world that once were colonized are now trying to reestablish their native language in an effort to regain their ethnic identity (Ferraro, 1990).

Since most U.S. Americans are immigrants and have learned English, their native languages have died. Although many U.S. citizens may not speak the languages of their ancestors, many of the thought patterns have been passed from generation to generation, such as how one shows affection for male and female friends, male and female family members, one's spouse and children, and an acquaintance. A person with a strong German background would be less likely to hug any of those group members in public; however, someone of Spanish or African descent would be much more likely to hug and show affection in public. Generally when people want to continue speaking their native language, it is because they are able to express their thoughts more clearly and maintain what is culturally comfortable.

Some U.S. African Americans speak a language called Pidgin English, which goes back to the days of slavery in the United States and communication between African Americans on various plantations. English also changes from one region of the nation to another. All these differences cause unequal power relationships to develop between people from different social and power backgrounds. Because language determines your cognition and perception, if you are removed from your linguistic environment, you no longer have the conceptual framework to explain ideas and opinions. The Sapir-Whorf hypothesis, the Bernstein hypothesis, and argot offer additional insights into language and culture interaction (Samovar & Porter, 1991; Stewart & Bennett, 1991).

Sapir-Whorf Hypothesis

The main idea of the **Sapir-Whorf Hypothesis**, named for Edward Sapir and Benjamin Lee Whorf, is that language functions as a way of shaping a person's experience, not just a device for reporting that experience. People adhere to the connections of their language to communicate effectively. Both structural and semantic aspects of a language are involved. The structural aspect includes phonetics and syntax. While the syntax aspect of language is influenced by and influences perception and categorization, the semantic aspect of language deals with meaning.

The concept of linguistic determinism is often referred to as the Sapir-Whorf Hypothesis, since the two men figured predominately in its development. **Linguistic determinism** is the assumption that a person's view of reality stems mainly from his or her language. Even though two languages may be similar, they cannot represent the same social reality; the worlds of the people who speak the two languages are different. So although languages often do have equivalencies in other languages, the social reality cannot be fully conveyed to a person who does not speak the language.

An example of the concept of linguistic determinism is the absence of a word for *snow* in Inuit, the language of the Eskimo people. The language does, however, have numerous words for types of snow, while other languages do not have the equivalent of *flaky snow* or *crusty snow*, for example. Since snow is important to the Eskimo people, they need to be able to describe it precisely (Borden, 1991; Condon & Yousef, 1975; Dodd, 1987; Ferraro, 1990; Samovar & Porter, 1991).

Argot

Each language is suited to describing and dealing with the social realities peculiar to its culture. This concept is especially true of nondominant co-cultures. Since their values and lifestyles usually differ from those of the dominant culture, they develop a language all their own that sets them apart but also permits them to convey their unique social realities with others in the culture. The term for this co-cultural language code is **argot**. Argot is a vocabulary of a particular group; it is often regional. The primary difference between argot and a foreign language is the relationship between sounds and meanings. For example, in the Spanish language the word for *house* is *casa*. Although the sounds are different, what is being referred to is the same. In argot, it is the meanings that change, while the sounds would stay the same. U.S. co-cultures that use argot are numerous; they may be subdivided by culture (French, Chinese, Spanish, African Americans) or by behavior (prostitutes, gangs, drug users, prisoners, gays). African Americans have a distinctive language sometimes referred to as **Ebonics**; for example, they use such terms as *bad* (meaning the best), *haircut* (having been robbed or cheated), and *get down* (to show enthusiasm for a particular activity), when communicating with others in the African American community. Drug users use terms such as *pipe* (large vein), *hay* (marijuana), and *heat* (police) to communicate to others in the co-culture (Dodd, 1987; Samovar & Porter, 1991). The concept of argot is important, as it provides valuable information about the lifestyles and experiences of people in a co-culture.

Bernstein Hypothesis

The **Bernstein Hypothesis** explains how social structure affects language and is an extension of the Sapir-Whorf Hypothesis. Bernstein considers culture, subculture, social context, and social system to be part of social structure.

According to the Bernstein Hypothesis, speech emerges in one of two codes—restricted or elaborated. Communication transmission channels used in the **restricted code** would be oral, nonverbal, and paralinguistic. Restricted codes would include highly predictable messages; they are for those who know you and what you are talking about quite well. These codes are similar to argot in that the communication assumes a common interest or shared experience. Because of this shared experience and identity, elaborating on the verbal message is unnecessary. You may, for example, find that your best friend sometimes finishes your sentences or knows what you are going to say before you finish speaking because of shared experiences. **Elaborated codes** are used with strangers; they involve messages that are low in predictability. You would need to give very explicit information to ensure that the message is understood. The verbal channel is important in elaborated codes, while restricted codes make use of nonverbal and paralinguistic cues (Dodd, 1987).

TERMS

Acronyms
Argot
Bernstein Hypothesis
Colloquialism
Conversation taboos
Ebonics
Elaborated codes
Euphemisms
Group Decision Support Systems
High-context
Homonyms
Host language
Jargon
Linear

Linguistic determinism
Low-context
Nonlinear
Parables
Proverbs
Repartee conversation
Restricted codes
Ritual conversation
Sapir-Whorf Hypothesis
Self-disclosure
Slang
Subjective interpretation
Verbal dueling

Exercise 6.1

Instructions: Circle the T for true or the F for false.

1. T   F   Nonverbal aspects are very important in low-context cultures.

2. T   F   The Japanese language and culture are an example of high-context communication.

3. T   F   The term *sanitation engineer* or *garbage collector* is an example of a colloquialism.

4. T   F   Politics is an appropriate topic for verbal dueling in Germany.

5. T   F   Repartee involves taking turns speaking.

6. T   F   People of the United States provide very little self-disclosure.

7. T   F   Chinese is an example of a linear language.

8. T   F   Conversation taboos in Mexico include politics and border violations.

9. T   F   The concept of linguistic determinism is related to the Sapir-Whorf Hypothesis.

10. T   F   The Bernstein Hypothesis involves restricted and elaborated codes.

—————— QUESTIONS AND CASES FOR DISCUSSION ——————

1. Explain how language differentiates us as groups.
2. Teenagers and other groups develop jargon and slang. Give examples of slang or jargon used by people with whom you associate.
3. The United States is a low-context country, and Japan is a high-context country. How would the Japanese react to a flamboyant U.S. salesperson?
4. Give examples of conversation taboos in your home or group of friends.
5. Why is a bicultural/bilingual interpreter better than a monocultural/bilingual interpreter?
6. In what worker positions would knowledge of a foreign language be more crucial for a company? Why?
7. Explain how ethnic groups in the United States participate in verbal dueling.

8. What does it mean to say two languages do not have vocabulary equivalence? To say the same language does not have vocabulary equivalence?
9. Explain what is meant by argot. Give examples from a culture with which you are familiar.
10. Explain the difference between restricted and elaborated codes in the Bernstein Hypothesis.
11. If thinking is universal across humankind, how does culture and language affect the way different groups of humans think?

Case 1   In parts of the United States, particularly in Florida where there is a large Latin American population, the suggestion has been made that Spanish should be considered the first language and English the second language and that people whose native language is Spanish should be taught in Spanish with English taught as a second language. Based on the discussion of language in this chapter, what are the advantages and disadvantages of implementing such a system? How would your argument for or against this proposed change apply to similar situations in India, Canada, or the European Economic Community?

Case 2   A U.S. production manager, Joe Sorrells, is sent to manage a manufacturing facility in Mexico. Upon arrival, his assistant production manager, Juan Lopez, suggests they go to the factory to meet the workers who have been awaiting his arrival. Joe declines Juan's offer and chooses instead to get right to work on determining why the quality and production rate of the Mexican plant are not equal to the U.S. plant. Juan stresses the importance of getting to know the workers first, but Joe lets Juan know he was sent to Mexico to straighten things out, not to form friendships with the local workers. Without further comment, Juan gets Joe the figures and records he requests. Joe made a number of changes and felt sure the plan he had prepared would improve quality and increase production. After a couple of months, no improvement has been made; Joe cannot figure out why the workers seem to resist his plans. What went wrong?

ACTIVITIES

1. Prepare a list of countries you have visited or countries in which you have worked. List one U.S. slang expression that would have a negative meaning in each country listed.
2. Quote a parable or proverb from one of the countries listed in Activity 1 and indicate how the parable or proverb characterizes some aspect of the culture.

3. List three conversation taboos in the United States and three taboos in one of the countries identified in Activity 1.

4. Write a paragraph about language problems you have encountered when communicating with students from other cultures. Include problems with tone, enunciation, pronunciation, slang, and so on.

5. Review a journal article or a chapter in a book related to use of interpreters. Prepare a one-page summary for submission to the instructor.

6. Since many books are translations from other languages, the Sapir-Whorf Hypothesis would say these translations may not preserve the exact meaning intended. This phrase from the Bible, for example, has been translated numerous times: "It is easier for a camel to go through the eye of a needle than for a rich man to enter the kingdom of God" (Mark 10:23). (One other translation is: "The eye of the needle is a narrow doorway in an ancient wall.") Give other examples of exact translations that may make understanding a book difficult.

REFERENCES

Althen, G. (1988). *American ways.* Yarmouth, ME: Intercultural Press, Inc.

Axtell, R. E. (1991). *The do's and taboos of international trade.* New York: John Wiley & Sons, Inc.

Baldrige, L. (1993). *Letitia Baldrige's new complete guide to executive manners.* New York: Rawson Associates.

Borden, G. A. (1991). *Cultural approach: An approach to understanding intercultural communication.* Englewood Cliffs, NJ: Prentice Hall.

Braganti, N. L., & Devine, E. (1992). *European customs and manners.* New York: Meadowbrook Press.

Condon, J. C., & Yousef, F. S. (1975). *Introduction to intercultural communication.* New York: Macmillan Publishing Company.

Devine, E., & Braganti, N. (1986). *The traveler's guide to Asian customs and manners.* New York: St. Martin's Press.

Devine, E., & Braganti, N. (1988). *The traveler's guide to Latin American customs and manners.* New York: St. Martin's Press.

Dodd, C. H. (1987). *Dynamics of intercultural communication.* Dubuque, IA: Wm. C. Brown Publishers.

Ferraro, G. P. (1990). *The cultural dimension of international business.* Englewood Cliffs, NJ: Prentice Hall.

Hall, E. T., & Hall, M. R. (1990). *Understanding cultural differences.* Yarmouth, ME: Intercultural Press, Inc.

Samovar, L. A., & Porter, R. E. (1991). *Intercultural communication: A reader.* Belmont, CA: Wadsworth Publishing Co.

Stewart, E. C., & Bennett, M. J. (1991). *American cultural patterns.* Yarmouth, ME: Intercultural Press.

Tsunda, Y. (1986). *Language inequality and distortion.* Philadelphia: John Benjamin Publishing Company.

7

Business and Social Etiquette

OBJECTIVES

Upon completion of this chapter, you will:

- understand cultural differences in making introductions and greeting others as well as customs related to business card exchange.

- understand how position and status affect cultural interaction.

- become familiar with cultural customs and the role protocol plays in communicating with persons of other cultures.

- understand how cultural differences in dining practices may affect intercultural communication.

- be familiar with cultural nuances of tipping.

- understand how practices of giving gifts vary from culture to culture and the role of gift giving in establishing favorable intercultural relations.

When conducting business abroad or in the United States with someone from another culture, a knowledge of certain rules of business and social etiquette is important. **Etiquette** refers to manners and behavior considered acceptable in social and business situations. Proper social behavior includes learning cultural variations in making introductions, greeting others, exchanging business cards, recognizing position and status, observing cultural customs and protocol, dining practices, tipping customs, and giving gifts.

INTRODUCTIONS AND GREETINGS

Being sensitive to cultural variations related to making introductions and greeting others will ensure that your first encounter with a person from another country will leave a positive impression. First impressions are made only once but are remembered for a long time.

The procedure for making introductions and greeting others varies from culture to culture. Persons from other cultures are struck by the informality of U.S. Americans who often say "Hi" to complete strangers. People from the United States are often perceived as insincere when they use the standard greeting of "Hi, how are you?," which does not mean that they actually want to know how you are. This outward show of friendliness is often misleading since people from the United States are in reality private and slow to make friendships. The use of "Hello, I'm pleased to meet you" is preferable as it conveys a more sincere message.

First names are used almost immediately by people from the United States and Britain. Introductions are more formal in other cultures. Titles are used when introducing people in such countries as Germany and Italy; they often indicate the person's profession or educational level. Germans always address each other as "Herr Guenther" or "Frau Kurr" in the office and out of the office, reserving first names outside the office for close friends and family.

You would address all persons with a college degree as "Doctor" in Italy. To show special respect to a man of influence and power in traditional Latin countries such as Colombia, add the title "Don" to the person's name. In Britain persons who have been knighted are addressed as "Sir" with the first name only, for example, "Sir George." The title "Doctor" is used for medical doctors in that country; other academic titles are not used (Mole, 1990).

Remember that in some cultures, such as the Chinese, the surname comes first and the given name last. Ching Lo Chang would be addressed as Mr. Ching. An example of a mistake commonly made by persons from the United States is the one made by President Clinton in a meeting in Korea. He addressed South Korean President Kim Young Sam's wife, Mrs. Sohn Myong-suk, as Mrs. Kim. He should have addressed her as Mrs. Sohn since in Korea it is the custom for women to maintain their maiden name when they marry (Kim, 1993).

Persons from Latin American countries will often add their mother's maiden name to their surname, so you would use the next to the last name when addressing them. Evelyn Rodrigues Castillo would be addressed as Señorita Rodrigues. When in doubt, ask what name is to be used. Because of such widely diverse customs in the use of titles, it is wise to research the customs of the particular culture involved (Devine & Braganti, 1988).

The handshake is an important aspect of making a favorable first impression. While a firm handshake is considered the norm in the United States, it may be considered impolite in some cultures. Thiederman (1991) presented the following summary of how various cultures differ in their idea of a proper handshake:*

Culture	Type of Handshake
U.S. American	Firm
Asian	Gentle (shaking hands is unfamiliar and uncomfortable for some; the exception is the Korean who usually has a firm handshake)
British	Soft
French	Light and quick (not offered to superiors); repeated upon arrival and departure
German	Brusk and firm; repeated upon arrival and departure
Latin American	Moderate grasp; repeated frequently
Middle Eastern	Gentle; repeated frequently

In such countries as Saudi Arabia, the handshake is accompanied with a light kiss; even males in Saudi Arabia kiss both cheeks after a handshake. In the former USSR, the "bear hug" may follow a strong, firm handshake between good male friends; neighboring Finns, on the other hand, do not hug, kiss, or have body contact with strangers. People in Latin American countries also embrace, often accompanied by a couple of slaps on the back (Figure 7.1).

Orientals, Northern Europeans, and most North Americans are uncomfortable with touching and hugging. People of Greece have no firm rules for greeting others; they may shake hands, embrace, and/or kiss a person at the first meeting or at every meeting. Bowing is the usual form of greeting in Japan. In China, bowing is also common; but a handshake is also acceptable. When conducting business with people of Japan or China, the handshake is

---

* Adapted with the permission of Lexington Books, an imprint of Macmillan, Inc., from *Bridging Cultural Barriers for Corporate Success* by Sondra Thiederman. Copyright © 1991 by Sondra Thiederman.

FIGURE 7.1   Greetings in Latin American countries are accompanied by an embrace.

FIGURE 7.2   Greetings in Japan involve bowing at the waist.

often combined with a bow so that each culture shows the other the proper respect (Baldrige, 1993). (See Figure 7.2.)

BUSINESS CARD EXCHANGE

An important aspect of business protocol is knowing the custom of exchanging business cards. Since all business contacts require a business card, the admonition of a well-known credit card company, "Don't leave home without it," applies.

Figure 7.3 Business card presentation in Japan is completed by presenting your card with both hands, positioned so that the person can read it, and bowing.

Although most U.S. businesspeople carry business cards, they do not always exchange them when meeting unless there is a reason to contact the person later. Rank, title, and profession are taken quite seriously in some cultures, so it is important to include your position and titles or degrees in addition to your company name on your card. Presentation of the card varies with the culture. The practice in the United States of glancing at the business card and promptly putting it in your pocket is considered rude in such countries as Japan. The Japanese examine the business card carefully and make some comment while accepting it. Use both hands when presenting your card in Japan or South Korea; position the card so that the person can read it (Axtell, 1993; Baldrige, 1993). (See Figure 7.3.)

In non–English-speaking countries, have the information on your card printed in English on one side and in the local language on the other side. An exchange of business cards is an expected part of all business introductions and most personal ones in Europe. Other parts of the world in which an exchange of business cards is the norm include the Middle East, the Pacific and Asia, and the Caribbean. In most of Southeast Asia, Africa, and the Middle East, with the exception of Israel, avoid presenting the card with your left hand as the left hand is reserved for taking care of bodily functions (Axtell, 1993).

POSITION AND STATUS

Position and status may have an impact on the success of intercultural communication encounters. No standard definition of social class exists that applies to all countries because people in different cultures have their own way of identifying the classes. Some cultures believe that people should occupy their proper place and that some persons are entitled to more respect than others. Most people of the United States show limited respect for rank and authority, while many other cultures are very conscious of position and power.

Although the United States is not considered a nation of classes, distinctions in position and status do exist. Because class distinctions in the United States are subtle, visitors from other cultures may be unable to spot the existence of a class structure and may believe the official propaganda of social equality. Visitors to New York, Washington, DC, and other cities, however, may see both the homeless and more affluent persons in public places. Although a system of inherited titles and ranks does not exist in the United States, certain factors distinguish between the top class, the upper middle class, and the lower middle class. Money is one factor associated with class. Further distinctions are made between those whose money is inherited but who are not currently earning money and those who have inherited money and are currently earning additional money. Style, taste, and awareness are equally important. Social class is also associated with educational opportunities and with a person's occupation or profession (Fussell, 1983).

Status is associated with education in a number of other cultures. Educational titles are used in introductions as a sign of respect and acknowledgment of the person's educational achievement. In Germany and Italy, executives and other professionals are proud of titles preceding their names, as they often reflect their education or profession. People with a college degree are entitled to be called Doctor (*Dottore* in Italian); the same rule applies to architects and lawyers. In Germany the U.S. equivalent of president or managing director of a company is called *Herr Direktor;* a medical doctor, if a woman, is called *Frau Doktor*; an engineer, if a woman, is addressed as *Frau Ingenieur*. In Mexico a lawyer is addressed as *Licenciado*, a title that is considered very important there. In England special protocol exists for addressing royalty, peers, clergy, and others. The Managing Director in a British firm is usually the top official, equivalent to a U.S. corporate president (U.S. corporate vice presidents do not carry much clout abroad) (Axtell, 1990). In some cultures, such as India, a very rigid class system exists. The society is divided into castes. The particular **caste system** a person belongs to is determined at birth; each caste has its status, rights, and duties. Although discrimination based on caste has been outlawed, in many areas, particularly rural ones, it is still a major influence on life in India. In India's rigid caste system, interaction is often limited, as it is with India's untouchables (Samovar & Porter, 1988).

Cultural differences also exist concerning the status of women in a society. Women in some cultures play a less prominent role in business than do men. The Arabs are becoming more used to women executives, and they are beginning to accept women executives from other countries. U.S. women doing business with the Arabs should understand this difference in cultural attitude and should make a special effort to conduct themselves appropriately, including dressing very modestly. In some Middle Eastern countries, men may refuse to work with women; women executives in Latin America may not receive the same respect given men executives. Women in the United States are being given increased opportunities for business travel, management positions in overseas operations, and transfers to overseas assignments. In *The International Businesswoman of the 1990s*, Rossman (1990) predicts that the progress U.S. women have made will set an example for change overseas since the United States is often a catalyst for international change.

In some cultures, such as the Chinese, people are very aware of age and hierarchy. Age is viewed as an indication of seniority. In addition to the Asian culture, the Arab world has a great respect for age. Advanced years represent wisdom and respect. Age takes precedence over rank, but rank is still important. In the Japanese society, knowing the rank of the people with whom you come in contact is important. The middle-level manager in a large company outranks a department head from a smaller company. The higher the rank of the person you are introduced to, the lower you bow. The person of lower rank bows first and lowest; a junior person stops first and bows to a senior person. Status is also shown by who goes first when entering a room or an elevator. Juniors wait for seniors to precede them. If you are the foreign guest, you may be expected to enter a room ahead of others, so if you are motioned to enter the room, do so quickly. When the Chinese or Japanese enter a room, they generally do so in protocol order with the highest ranking person entering first. They will also assume that the first member of your negotiating team is the head of your group and has the higher rank. Sitting in rank order from highest to lowest during a meeting is helpful (Axtell, 1991).

Status symbols, such as the size and location of the office, may be culturally different. U.S. businesspersons perceive a large corner office with windows and carpet located on the top floor as a status symbol. In France high-level executives sit in the middle of the work area. In the Middle East, business is conducted in small quarters rather than in the spacious offices to which U.S. citizens have become accustomed (Copeland & Griggs, 1985).

CUSTOMS AND PROTOCOL

Behavior that is considered appropriate in one culture may be considered insulting or rude in another. **Customs** are socially acceptable ways of behaving; **protocol** refers to customs and regulations having to do with diplomatic etiquette and courtesies expected in official dealings with persons in various cultures.

A business custom of people in the United States that makes little sense in other cultures is that of doing business at breakfast. The French especially do not like breakfast meetings; they prefer a leisurely breakfast with time to read the paper in the morning. The French do conduct business over lunch, however, which may last two hours or more. Another U.S. business custom that makes little sense to people in other cultures is the lengthy cocktail hour before dinner. Italians have commented that the endless rounds of cocktails before ordering a meal are exhausting, to say the least, and may result in discussions that make little sense (Baldrige, 1993). The practice in the United States of rushing to get down to business quickly and pressing for quick decisions is alien to such cultures as the Arab and the Japanese. Other customs that affect the success of intercultural business encounters that have been discussed in Chapter 4 include attitude toward punctuality, treatment of females, and use of space. People of other cultures should remember that when dealing with persons from the United States, they should keep all appointments and be punctual, treat females with the same respect given males, and stand at least an arm's length away when conversing.

A custom that has undergone close scrutiny in the past few years is bribery. **Bribery** is the giving or promising of something, often money, to influence another person's actions. U.S. managers are faced with situations that are considered illegal in their culture that are not only lawful but are an accepted part of doing business in other cultures. In some countries the bribe is considered a tip to ensure promptness or service. The public stand against bribery in recent years has resulted in U.S. legislation making the accepting of bribes illegal.

DEMEANOR/BEHAVIOR

What is considered acceptable behavior in one culture may be unacceptable in another. **Demeanor** involves one's conduct or deportment and is influenced by culture. Behavior in public places is culture specific. U.S. Americans speak louder in public than people of Germany; people from Brazil or Nigeria, however, speak louder than people of the United States. The type of public place also affects the voice volume that is considered acceptable. At sports events it is acceptable to make more noise than inside a shopping mall or health club. Good advice to follow when in a foreign country is to observe the behavior of the nationals and avoid calling attention to yourself by speaking louder than those around you.

Althen (1988) suggests the following rules for appropriate behavior in public places in the United States: keep to the right when walking in malls or on the street; wait your turn when standing in line at the post office, bank, or theater; give priority to the first person who arrives (rather than to people who are older or wealthier as is done in Asian cultures); do not block traffic; do not block someone's view at a ballgame or other public event; and be considerate of nonsmokers.

Other rules for appropriate behavior include what have been referred to as *rituals*. When greeting a colleague as you arrive at work in the morning, the appropriate ritual in the United States is: "Good morning, how are you?" The appropriate response is: "Fine, thank you. And how are you?" Some people make the mistake of failing to realize that this is only a ritual and will tell you how they are, including a detailed description of the state of their health.

Courtesy is very important in most areas of the United States. The use of "please" when you are making a request is expected; "thank you" is considered appropriate when someone has granted a request or performed a service. People of all social and educational levels are accorded equal courtesy.

Another behavior that varies with the culture is the extent of touching in public places. People in the United States usually avoid situations in which they would be touching strangers in public. They avoid getting on a crowded elevator because they are quite uncomfortable with physical contact. If they must get on a crowded elevator, they observe "elevator etiquette": refrain from speaking, face the front, and watch the floor indicator. One exception seems to be subway trains where people are often too crowded to move. People in South America, on the other hand, think nothing of squeezing onto a crowded bus or elevator and of pushing through a crowd.

DINING PRACTICES

Cultural dining practices vary widely. In many parts of the world, the main meal is at noon, while in the United States the main meal is in the evening. In Mexico lunch time is from 2 P.M. to 4 P.M. and is the main meal of the day. However, in places near the U.S.-Mexican border local businesses conform more to the U.S. lunch time of 12 P.M. to 2 P.M. The dinner hour also varies. In the United States the dinner hour varies from 5 P.M. to 7 P.M., while in such countries as Spain it may be as late as 10 P.M. In some cultures, business meals are eaten in private homes while in other cultures they are usually eaten at restaurants. When entertaining visitors from other countries, be considerate and ask whether they prefer the main meal at noon or in the evening and take them to restaurants where they would have a choice of a light or heavy meal (Devine & Braganti, 1988).

Cultural variations exist in the number of courses typically served as well as when the salad is served. A formal luncheon usually consists of two to three courses, and a formal dinner consists of three to seven courses. In some countries, including those in Latin America, even informal meals typically have numerous courses. In Italy and France, salads are often served after the main course rather than before.

A U.S. dining practice that seems unusual to people of other cultures is the serving of a glass of water with ice at most restaurants. Other countries that serve water do so without ice or serve bottled mineral water. Another dining practice that is viewed with surprise is the habit of offering coffee at the beginning of a meal; serving coffee at the end of the meal is common in most cultures. The popularity of decaffeinated coffee in the United States has not spread to other countries so visitors are often taken aback by a waiter's question of "Will you have regular coffee or decaf?" Another U.S. custom that sometimes surprises people from other cultures is that of designating certain sections in restaurants as smoking and nonsmoking.

The manner of eating is also different. The **U.S. eating style** uses the "zigzag" style: cutting the meat with the knife held in the right hand and the fork in the left, then placing the knife on the plate, shifting the fork to the right hand, and eating. Diners using the **Continental eating style** place the fork in the left hand and knife in the right; they use the knife to push food onto the back of the fork, then move the food into the mouth, with the tines of the fork down. Asians use chopsticks, especially for eating rice, but may use a spoon for soup. They appreciate foreigners' attempting to use chopsticks and are often willing to demonstrate correct usage. (See Figure 7.4.)

Other cultural variations in dining also exist. Tahitian food is eaten with the fingers. In the Middle East be prepared to eat with your fingers if your host does, but use the right hand only. In Bolivia, you are expected to clean your plate; Egyptians, however, consider it impolite to eat everything on your plate (Axtell, 1993).

FIGURE 7.4   Cultural variations in eating style.

A dining practice in France that seems unusual to persons in other cultures is the custom of bringing pet dogs into restaurants where the waiter takes the dog into the kitchen to be fed a treat. Dogs in most cultures are not allowed in public eating establishments.

Dining in Japan, especially in Japanese homes, requires sitting in a kneeling position on a tatami mat. Men keep their knees 3 or 4 inches apart; women keep their knees together. Being able to lower yourself to this position and rise from it gracefully requires practice. If you have frequent contact with the Japanese, practicing this art would be warranted (Axtell, 1993).

TIPPING

People communicate nonverbally by their tipping practices; those who are basically stingy and those who are basically generous will reveal these traits by their tipping behavior. Although it is difficult to establish definite rules for tipping, generally speaking when service has been good or when people in service positions go out of their way to do you a favor, a tip is merited. If the service is very bad, you are not expected to leave a tip but should report the situation to the manager. "Insult tipping" (leaving a few coins) shows a lack of breeding and is inappropriate regardless of how poor the service was.

Trends in tipping appear to have changed in the last few years. Although a tip of 15 percent of the bill used to be considered a generous tip in fine restaurants, 20 percent is now closer to the norm when the service is excellent.

Traveling in the United States involves numerous situations in which tipping is expected. When traveling, have a supply of $1 and $5 bills in your pocket for tipping the cab driver, the bellhop, and other service personnel who may carry your luggage, summon a cab, or perform other services, such as delivering food or small appliances to your hotel room.

Tipping in a nontipping culture can offend or insult the people of that culture. However, letters of thanks to people who have been especially helpful, including hotel managers, are very much appreciated. Tipping in Japan is also frowned upon. People in this culture consider helping you with your luggage as a gesture of hospitality and would be offended if you tipped them. If a hotel employee has performed an extra service that you wish to reward, place the yen in an envelope, since the Japanese would consider openly receiving money as embarrassing or as "losing face."

In many places, such as Europe, a service charge is added to your restaurant and hotel bill; you are usually not expected to leave an additional tip. In the absence of a service charge, leave the usual 15 to 20 percent that you would leave in the United States. Observing cultural differences in tipping can communicate nonverbally that you have researched the country and that you consider local customs to be important (Axtell, 1993).

GIFT GIVING ───────────────────────────────────────

Each country has its seasons and occasions for giving gifts. Gift giving in some cultures is an art and is considered an integral part of building intercultural professional and social relationships. The careful selection and wrapping of a gift and presenting it at the proper time with panache or style convey to others your social sensitivity and good manners.

Business gifts in the United States are very modest in price; the rule to follow, because of tax regulations, is to limit the price to $25 or less. Business gifts are sometimes given to members of your staff on such occasions as birthdays and Christmas. In addition, secretaries are generally treated to flowers and/or lunch on Secretaries' Day. Remember that business gifts to staff members should be personal; an electric pencil sharpener would be inappropriate. However, they should not be too personal; cologne or lingerie to a member of the opposite gender could be misinterpreted. Gift certificates to the person's favorite restaurant or specialty shop would be in good taste. Subordinates wait for their supervisors to set the tone on gift giving. If you are new in an office, ask what tradition is usually followed in exchanging gifts. Several years ago, when the office Christmas party was popular, colleagues often exchanged gifts as part of the occasion. The practice of exchanging gifts among colleagues, even token gifts (the office grab bag), seems to have been discontinued in many firms in favor of contributing the amount of money you would spend on such a gift to a local food bank or pooling the amount to give gifts of food or money to members of the custodial staff.

In the United States gifts are opened in front of the giver. The gift is admired, and appreciation is expressed verbally; the oral expression of thanks is followed by a written note of appreciation, unless the gift is small and is used as an advertisement (e.g., a paperweight with the company logo). Business gifts to the office or department, such as a basket of fruit or box of candy, are opened immediately and shared by all. (The manager's taking the gift home to share with his or her family is considered to be in poor taste.) The manager would write a note of thanks to the company that sent the gift and convey expressions of appreciation from staff members.

Although flowers make appropriate gifts, learn cultural taboos related to both color and variety. Red roses are associated with romance in some cultures. In some countries gladioli are a symbol of mourning. In most European countries avoid a gift of carnations, which are for cemeteries only. Chrysanthemums would be inappropriate in both Japan and Italy; they are associated with funerals and mourning. Although flowers are not expected by a Mexican host, they are appreciated; but avoid sending yellow, red, or white flowers as these colors have negative connotations for some classes of Mexicans. In some cultures the number of flowers given has a special significance (Barnum & Wolniansky, 1989). A flower shop in the host country would be the best place to get information about local customs related to giving flowers.

Gift giving is very much a part of conducting business in such countries as Japan. Japan's major gift giving times are Ochugen (July 15) and Oseibo (December). Companies give gifts to their customers as an expression of appreciation for past and future business. They also reward their employees at these times with large bonuses. U.S. companies that have ongoing business relationships with the Japanese should remember their associates with a gift at both of these times. Since Japan is the United States's second largest trading partner, knowing the nuances associated with Japanese gift giving is considered an important aspect of nonverbal business communication with people in that culture.

The Japanese are a gracious people for whom gift giving seems to be an art. The wrapping of the gift and the manner of presenting it are just as important as the gift itself. Gifts are beautifully wrapped but without the ornate bows and other decorations typically used on gifts in the United States. The color of the wrapping should be consistent with the occasion: red, gold, and white for happy events; black and purple or black and white for other occasions. The Japanese do not open a gift in front of the giver, so you would avoid opening your gift in their presence. Also avoid giving a gift when someone else is present. In the Arab countries, on the other hand, you must present a gift when others are present so it will not be interpreted as a bribe. Do not surprise your Japanese host with a gift as it might cause the person to lose face. Let your host know ahead of time by mentioning, for example, that you have found a special commemorative coin to add to his collection. Favorite gifts for the Japanese are imported liquor, consummables of high quality, and designer-made products containing such names as Gucci, Tiffany & Co., or Mark Cross. Musical tapes and CDs are also good choices. Avoid giving gifts manufactured elsewhere in Asia, as this would be an insult. Since gift giving is so important in the Japanese culture, getting advice from a Japanese colleague or from someone who has lived in Japan is recommended (Axtell, 1993; Yager, 1991).

Knowing when to present the business gift is also important. In Korea, business gifts are usually given at the beginning of formal negotiations. In Germany, however, business gifts are seldom exchanged at the beginning of negotiations but may be given at their conclusion. In the Latin American countries, present gifts only at the conclusion of negotiations.

Other gift-giving practices and guidelines in various cultures include the following:

1. When dining in a person's home in Western Europe, present your gift when you arrive so that it does not appear to be intended as payment for the meal.
2. Avoid giving gifts to the French until a personal relationship has been developed. Avoid gifts of perfume or wine; those are their specialties.
3. Gifts to Germans should not be wrapped in black, brown, or white.

4. Avoid gifts of a clock in the People's Republic of China as the clock is considered a symbol of bad luck.

5. A striped tie is not a smart gift to a British man; it may represent a British regiment other than his own.

6. Avoid gifts of a knife or handkerchief to persons in Latin America. The knife is interpreted as a desire to cut off the relationship; the handkerchief is associated with tears.

7. Avoid gifts of liquor or wine for an Arab. Since alcohol is illegal in Islamic cultures, the gift would be confiscated by customs.

8. Since the cow is sacred in India, do not give any gifts made of cowhide.

9. In Islamic countries exercise restraint in admiring personal possessions; you will probably find yourself the recipient of the object you have admired (Axtell, 1993; Stewart, 1987).

When people of the United States select business gifts for people in other countries, they should remember that the gifts should be U.S. made and utilitarian and have conversational value. Good choices include things that are typical of the United States, such as Native American art or jewelry; videotapes of U.S. movies; U.S.-made sports equipment; or food that is unique to the United States, such as candy, nuts, and California wines. Avoid gag gifts, as people of some other cultures do not appreciate them (Stewart, 1987).

COUNTRY-SPECIFIC RULES FOR BUSINESS AND SOCIAL ETIQUETTE

A summary of rules for business and social etiquette for the six countries with which the United States conducts most of its international trade follows.

Canada

Social and business etiquette in Canada is quite similar to that of the United States, but Canadians are more conservative than are people of the United States. As in the United States, shaking hands when meeting and upon departure is the usual form of greeting. Most business entertaining is done in restaurants; tipping is about the same as in the United States. Because of the strong French influence in certain parts of Canada, French cuisine is offered in many restaurants. If invited to someone's home, you would want to take flowers (but not white lilies, as they are associated with funerals) to the hostess (Axtell, 1993).

England

A soft handshake accompanied by "How do you do?" is the common greeting in England. Avoid the typical U.S. greeting of "Hi" (too informal), and avoid saying "Have a nice day" when leaving someone (the British interpret it as a command). As in the United States, first names are often used after knowing the person only a short time. When dining in England, you may wish to try some English specialties: crumpets, steak and kidney pie, or Scotch eggs, which are deep-fried hardboiled eggs that have a coating of sausage and breadcrumbs. Pubs and restaurants, rather than private homes, are used for most business entertaining. If invited to dine in a British home, a gift of flowers (except for white lilies) would be an appropriate gift for the hostess (Axtell, 1993; Braganti & Devine, 1992).

France

A light handshake when you greet someone or when you say goodbye is the usual greeting in France. Use last names unless you know the person quite well. Remember that dining can be rather lengthy as the French enjoy lively discussions while they eat. Try some French specialties, such as their pastries, wine, and cheese, and special dishes, such as quiche Lorraine (pastry filled with bacon, eggs, and cheese), crêpes (thin sweet pancakes), and pâté de foie gras (goose liver). If you try it, be prepared to finish it as the French expect you to eat everything on your plate. As in many European countries, a service charge of 10 to 15 percent is usually added to checks. The proper gift when invited to a French home for dinner, which is rare, is a box of candy or an odd number of flowers (except chrysanthemums, which suggest death, or red roses, which suggest romance). Business gifts are not expected, but gifts with aesthetic appeal, such as art work and books, are considered appropriate (Axtell, 1993; Braganti & Devine, 1992).

Germany

When greeting people in Germany, remember to use last names and a firm handshake. Status is recognized; men allow people of higher status or older women to precede them when entering a door or elevator. When dining in a restaurant, a service charge of 10 to 15 percent is generally added to the check so you do not need to leave an extra tip. Try some German specialties: beers, sausages, and potato pancakes. As in France, eating everything on your plate is considered polite. Gifts to your German host should be something simple and rather inexpensive as Germans consider expensive gifts to be in bad taste.

When invited to a German home, bring the hostess a gift of flowers (an odd number except 13; no red roses) (Braganti & Devine, 1992).

Japan

In Japan the usual form of greeting is a bow rather than a handshake; however, many Japanese who regularly associate with persons of other cultures may use both a bow and a handshake. Follow the lead of your Japanese host. The exchange of business cards is common, so be sure you have a good supply, printed on one side in English and the other side in Japanese. Remember to address your Japanese host by his last name; only family members and close friends use the first name. Most business entertaining is done in Japanese restaurants. Some Japanese specialties include sake (rice wine) and sashimi (sliced raw fish). Do not tip in restaurants; the waiter will return the money if you do. Although being invited to a Japanese home is not the norm, if invited remember to remove your shoes at the entrance of the home. A box of candy, rather than flowers, is an appropriate gift for the hostess. Since social and business etiquette is so different in Japan, do a thorough study of the culture and their customs before you go (Axtell, 1993; Devine & Braganti, 1986).

Mexico

Shaking hands is the usual greeting in Mexico; people also shake hands when saying goodbye. When introduced to a woman, a man will bow slightly and will shake hands if the woman initiates it. Address the person by his or her last name as first names are not used during initial encounters. Business cards are exchanged at a first meeting; include the Spanish translation on your cards. Be sure to indicate your position with your company and your university degrees. Deference is shown to someone whose age, social status, or position warrants it. The altitude of Mexico City may affect your digestion, so eat lightly and carefully. Always order bottled water since tap water is not considered safe. Although Mexicans will expect you to sample the fare, they will understand if you decline dishes such as tripe. Unlike many European cultures, they do not expect you to eat everything on your plate. You may wish to sample such national dishes as *mole poblano de guajolote* (turkey in a sauce of spices, herbs, and chocolate), *quesadillas* (folded tortillas filled with cheese), and *frijoles refritos* (mashed and fried cooked beans). If invited to a Mexican home, send flowers ahead of time; avoid marigolds (used to decorate cemeteries) and red flowers (used for casting spells). Appropriate gifts include gadgets, such as an electric can opener, and U.S. cigarettes; a gold cigarette lighter or pen, art books, and Scotch are also appropriate (Devine & Braganti, 1988).

A helpful rule to remember in most cultures is to follow the lead of the people in the other culture. If they shake hands, so do you. Eat what they eat and when they eat. If the other person gives you a gift, be prepared to reciprocate. Researching the country before you travel is always good advice.

_____ **TERMS** _____

Bribery   Demeanor
Caste system   Etiquette
Continental eating style   Protocol
Customs   U.S. eating style

Exercise 7.1

Intercultural Business/Social Etiquette

Instructions: Circle the T for true or the F for false.

1. T   F   In Japan, a business card should be presented with both hands.

2. T   F   When meeting after a long absence, men in Argentina hug each other.

3. T   F   The British have a firm handshake.

4. T   F   Status is associated with education in many cultures.

5. T   F   Throughout Latin America, the main meal of the day is in the evening.

6. T   F   Bolivians expect visitors to eat everything on their plate.

7. T   F   Tipping is more common in the United States than in China and Japan.

8. T   F   The practice of serving a glass of water with meals is universal.

9. T   F   In China, the gift of a clock is considered a symbol of good luck.

10. T   F   In Germany business gifts are usually exchanged at the beginning of formal negotiations.

_____ **QUESTIONS AND CASES FOR DISCUSSION** _____

1. How do introductions vary between the United States and other cultures?
2. Explain how the U.S. handshake differs from that of persons from Asia, France, Germany, and the Middle East.
3. In addition to the handshake, what other forms of greeting are used in other cultures?

4. Describe cultural variations in business card exchange.
5. Explain class distinctions in the United States and India.
6. How are gender and age related to position and status in the United States?
7. What are some U.S. business customs that people of other cultures find difficult to understand?
8. Explain how a knowledge of proper business protocol can enhance intercultural communication.
9. Explain cultural differences in what is considered acceptable behavior in public places in the United States and in other countries.
10. Identify some cultural differences in dining practices.
11. What are some guidelines for tipping appropriately? How do tipping customs vary with various cultures?
12. What are some guidelines for effective business gift giving in the United States?
13. What are some cultural differences in gift-giving practices? What gifts are considered appropriate for a person from the United States to give to someone in another culture?

Case 1   Mark was in charge of a negotiating team sent to Japan. Upon learning the importance of gift giving to a successful business relationship in this culture, prior to departure, he asked his secretary to wrap these gifts: a clock with the company logo, a leather briefcase, a country ham, and a pen and pencil set marked "made in Japan." His secretary wrapped the gifts attractively in bright red paper and with matching bows and mailed them to his Japanese hosts. What rules for appropriate gift giving in this culture have been followed? Which have been violated?

Case 2   A U.S. executive was invited to dine in the home of a Latin American businessman. The dinner invitation was for 9 P.M. The U.S. executive arrived promptly at nine bearing a gift of an unwrapped bottle of Scotch for his host and a dozen yellow and white chrysanthemums for the businessman's wife. Discuss the appropriateness of the U.S. executive's behavior.

ACTIVITIES

1. Role play to show how a business card is presented to someone from Japan.
2. Research the gift-giving practices of one of the following countries and make a brief report to the class: Japan, Taiwan, Egypt, Argentina, Germany. Include appropriate and inappropriate gifts and other related information, such as gift presentation and reciprocation.

3. Review back issues of *The Wall Street Journal* or a news magazine such as *Time* and make a copy of an article related to a cultural *faux pas* (social blunder or error in etiquette) committed by either a person from the United States when traveling abroad or by someone from another culture when visiting the United States. Share your information with the class.

4. Demonstrate the typical greeting between people in Latin American countries and Japan.

5. Demonstrate the proper handshake in the United States, France, and Germany.

6. Research the dining practices of such countries as Zimbabwe, Samoa, and Tanzania; write a one-page summary in which you identify major differences between dining practices in the United States and these countries.

7. Practice introducing your U.S. manager to each of the following:
    a. An Italian manager, John Giovanni, with a college degree.
    b. Chung Lo Wang, a manager from China.
    c. María Comerlato Velasquez, a business associate from Brazil.
    d. Thomas Edward Peacock, a British associate who has been knighted.

REFERENCES

Althen, G. (1988). *American ways*. Yarmouth, ME: Intercultural Press, Inc.

Axtell, R. E. (1990). *Do's and taboos of hosting international visitors*. New York: John Wiley & Sons, Inc.

Axtell, R. E. (1991). *Gestures: The do's and taboos of body language around the world*. New York: John Wiley & Sons, Inc.

Axtell, R. E. (1993). *Do's and taboos around the world*. New York: John Wiley & Sons, Inc.

Baldrige, L. (1993). *Letitia Baldrige's new complete guide to executive manners*. New York: Rawson Associates.

Barnum, C., & Wolniansky, N. (1989, April). Glitches in global gift giving. *Management Review*, pp. 61–63.

Braganti, N. L., & Devine, E. (1992). *European customs and manners*. New York: Meadowbrook Press.

Copeland, L., & Griggs, L. (1985). *Going international*. New York: Random House.

Devine, E., & Briganti, N. L. (1986). *The travelers' guide to Asian customs and manners*. New York: St. Martin's Press.

Devine, E., & Briganti, N. L. (1988). *The travelers' guide to Latin American customs and manners*. New York: St. Martin's Press.

Fussell, P. (1983). *Class*. New York: Ballantine Books.

Kim, J. Y. (1993, July 11). Clinton couldn't get protocol right to save his Seoul. *The Commercial Appeal*, p. A5.

Mole, J. (1990). *When in Rome. . . .* New York: AMACOM.

Rossman, M. L. (1990). *The international businesswoman of the 1990s*. New York: Praeger.

Samovar, L. A., & Porter, R. E. (1988). *Intercultural communication: A reader*. Belmont, CA: Wadsworth Publishing Company.

Stewart, M. Y. (1987). *The new etiquette*. New York: St. Martin's Press, Inc.

Thiederman, S. (1991). *Bridging cultural barriers for corporate success*. New York: Lexington Books.

Yager, J. (1991). *Business protocol: How to survive & succeed in business*. New York: John Wiley & Sons, Inc.

8

Country-Specific Information

OBJECTIVES

Upon completion of this chapter, you will:

- understand the role that dress and appearance play in interacting with persons from other countries.

- understand the importance of a knowledge of basic geography, selected history, and notable personalities to successful intercultural communication.

- know how a knowledge of the economy of specific countries can enhance the intercultural communication process.

- understand the importance of knowing about the holidays and holy days of the country in which you are traveling or conducting business.

- be able to identify special foods considered typical of various cultures and respect consumption taboos of other countries.

Country-specific information that would prove useful when doing business in another country or hosting visitors from other cultures includes knowledge of the country's dress and appearance, basic geography, selected history, notable personalities, language, economy, current events, holidays and holy days, and special foods and consumption taboos.

Since a comprehensive examination of many countries is not possible here, emphasis will be placed on the six countries with which the United States does most of its international business: Canada, England, France, Germany, Japan, and Mexico. To obtain information about other countries, consult such sources as Brigham Young University's *Culturgrams* (David M. Kennedy Center for International Studies, 280 HRCB, Brigham Young University, Provo, UT 84602). The 1994 edition contains briefings on over 100 countries. Other sources include the embassy of the individual country in Washington, DC, and, of course, your school or public library.

DRESS AND APPEARANCE

What you wear sends a nonverbal message about you and your company. Clothes can enhance your credibility or destroy it. According to Axtell (1993), the general rule everywhere is that for business you should be "buttoned up": conservative suit and tie for men, dress or skirted suit for women.

Business dress in Canada, England, France, Germany, Japan, and Mexico is similar to that worn in the United States with slight differences. In Canada people dress more conservatively and formally than people in the United States. The French are very fashion conscious since France is considered a leader in fashion. When conducting business in Europe, remember that dress is very formal; coats and ties are required. Jackets stay on in the office and restaurants even when the weather is hot. Dress in Japan is also formal. Japanese women dress very conservatively and wear muted colors to the office. Care should be exercised in wearing very casual attire in public in these countries, as this practice is considered inappropriate (Devine & Braganti, 1986).

More casual attire is, however, appropriate in certain cultures. In the Philippines, men wear the barong, a loose, white or cream-colored shirt with tails out, no jacket or tie. In Indonesia, batiks (brightly patterned shirts worn without tie or jacket) are worn (Axtell, 1993).

Although Western business dress has been widely adopted in other cultures, you may wish to learn cultural distinctions in what is considered appropriate business attire. When visiting Saudi Arabia, for example, the Saudi might wear the traditional Arabic white, flowing robe and headcloth. You would not, however, attempt to dress in a like manner. You would dress in the same manner as you would for an important meeting in your U.S. office.

Color of clothing is also a consideration because in some cultures color is associated with such things as grief and royalty. Do not wear black, purple, or solid white in Thailand. Avoid wearing all white in the People's Republic of China as white is the symbol of mourning. In the United States black is typically worn at funerals but has no special significance in business situations.

Shoes are considered inappropriate in certain situations in various cultures. They should not be worn within Islamic mosques and Buddhist temples. Shoes should also be removed when entering most Asian homes or restaurants. Place them neatly together facing the door you entered. Following the host's lead is good advice; if the host goes without shoes, so do you. Remember that in the Arab culture the soles of the feet should not be shown, so keep both feet on the floor or the bottoms of your feet covered.

Women who conduct business abroad should be especially careful to conform to local customs concerning what constitutes appropriate attire. Women conducting business in the Arab countries, for example, should avoid wearing pants and should wear clothes that cover most of the body, such as long-sleeved dresses and dress/skirt lengths below the knees. In Europe women do not wear pants to the office or to fine restaurants. Ask before you go; consult a colleague who is familiar with the culture (Axtell, 1993; Devine & Braganti, 1986, 1988).

BASIC GEOGRAPHY

A knowledge of basic geography in some countries can be essential to your health and well-being. Visitors to La Paz, Bolivia, for example, should understand the impact that the city's elevation of 12,500 feet above sea level may have on their health and performance. Mexico City, with an elevation of 8,000 feet above sea level, has also caused discomfort. In addition to altitude, other physical features of the land to research include topographical features of the terrain and proximity to famous geographic landmarks.

Another aspect of basic geography that would be important to research is the climate. Find out if your visit to a country coincides with the rainy season; make inquiries concerning humidity and temperature particularly if you are going to the tropics. This knowledge will enable you to dress more appropriately.

Information concerning plants and animals that are indigenous to the country could prove useful, particularly if finding a scorpion in your bed or shoes would not be considered great cause for alarm by local inhabitants.

Knowing the correct geographical terms used in the area is also helpful. In the Middle East, for example, the Arabian Gulf is not referred to as the Persian Gulf. In Scotland, the people are called Scots, not Scotch (a whiskey). Before traveling to such countries as the former USSR and Germany, determine what cautions should be taken when referring to certain geographical areas and the people who inhabit the areas. Axtell (1990) offers these "geographical nuggets" to govern your conversations with persons of other cultures:

- Taiwan is officially called the "Republic of China" and should not be confused with the "People's Republic of China." Taiwan was originally called Formosa.
- Two distinct Irelands exist: the Republic of Ireland (the largest portion of the island with Dublin as the capital) and Northern Ireland (part of the United Kingdom, with Belfast as the capital).
- Belgium has two major groups: the Flemish in the north (who speak a language related to both German and Dutch) and the Walloons in the south and southeast (who speak French).
- Two distinct Koreas exist: North and South Korea. The People's Democratic Republic of Korea is the official name in the north; the Republic of Korea is the official name in the south.
- The name Great Britain refers to the island that contains England, Scotland, and Wales. The United Kingdom includes Northern Ireland.
- Moslems (or Muslims) are people who practice the Islamic religion (referring to the religion as *Mohammedanism*, though technically correct, is impolite).
- Canadians dislike being referred to as *Americans*.
- The correct name of Mexico is *The United States of Mexico*.
- The terms *Scandinavian* and *Nordic* should not be used as synonyms. Swedes, Norwegians, and Danes accept being referred to as Scandinavians; Nordic refers to a subdivision of the Caucasoid ethnic group predominant in Scandinavia.

A knowledge of the geography of the host culture can prove to be useful when communicating with people in that culture. In the near future, keeping abreast of changing names of Central European countries will be made possible with CD-ROMs. Currently, companies desiring to stay current on changes in the United States can purchase De Lorme Mappings *Street Atlas USA*, which allows viewing to one-tenth of a mile (CD-Rom Trends, 1992).

SELECTED HISTORY AND NOTABLE PERSONALITIES

When conducting business in another country, it is helpful to learn something of the history of the culture and to learn the names of some of its important people. Since people in such countries as Mexico and Japan spend much time getting to know the person with whom they are negotiating, numerous opportunities exist for "small talk." A knowledge of the country's history and names of notable personalities would probably be useful during the initial stages of negotiation when the emphasis is on topics other than the business to be transacted. Historical information to research might include significant events that have resulted in special holidays or commemorative occasions. A list of notable personalities would undoubtedly include the names of the president or other head of state, sports heroes, dancers, artists, movie and television stars, prominent state or community leaders, and, of course, prominent persons in the organization with which you are conducting business. Know the names of major newspapers and their political positions. Some successful negotiators have recommended arriving at least a day before the appointed meeting to become familiar with the local history and with names of important persons; others suggest that those who know the language secure copies of the local newspapers at least a month prior to departure to obtain information about the local culture. Learn the people who are considered the country's heroes. Visiting some of the countries in South America without knowing who Simon Bolivar is would be comparable to visiting the United States without knowing who George Washington is.

Short summaries of the history of the United States and the six countries with which the United States conducts most of its international trade follow.

United States

The people who call themselves "Americans" in the United States are quite varied. People indigenous to the United States are the Native American Indians and the Inuits. Since the seventeenth century, the indigenous people have been displaced by Europeans, Africans, Asians, Latin Americans, and Middle Easterners. The American Revolution in 1776 resulted in independence from England. The Civil War in 1861 divided the states in the North against those in the South over such issues as state's rights, slavery, and economic problems. International conflicts in which the United States was involved include World War I, World War II, the Korean War, the Vietnam conflict, and the Gulf War.

Canada

Canada also had indigenous populations of Inuits and Native American Indians. The French were the first to settle in Canada during the 1600s followed by British immigration and control. The British captured Quebec in 1759 and Montréal in 1760. In 1867, the British North American Act created the Dominion of Canada. Canada still considers the British monarch to be the titled head of state although England has no control over Canada. In 1931 the Statute of Westminster gave Canada sovereignty. Quebec still maintains the French language and culture.

England

England has a long history dating back to 55 B.C. when the Romans incorporated the country into the Roman empire. Subsequently, various groups invaded and occupied the country, including Angles, Saxons, Jutes, and Norsemen. After the battle with the Spanish Armada in 1588, the British became a great power due to the strength of their Navy. British rule expanded around the globe with colonies and commonwealths. After World War I, expansion ceased; many colonies were given independence after World War II. England is a participant in the European Economic Community.

France

Since history is important to the French, it is necessary to know some of their heroes: Clovis, Hugh Capet, Philippe August, Saint Louis, Henry IV, Louis XIV, Jeanne d'Arc, Jean Baptiste Colbert, Napoleon, and Charles de Gaulle. During the reign of Louis XIV in the late 1600s, France was a European power; however, Napoleon's reign changed France's dominant position. Later, France lost much of its world power after World War I (Hall & Hall, 1990).

Germany

Due to the number of wars Germany has been involved in, the borders of Germany have changed significantly over the years. Germany was completely torn apart by the Thirty Years' War (1618–1648). Under the eighteenth-century King Frederick the Great, the Prussian dominance grew. Territory was added in 1815 by the Congress of Vienna, and Austria was lost in the Seven Weeks' War of 1866. Germany became a powerful nation between 1864 and 1870 following the three wars engineered by Prussian leader Otto von Bismarck. World War I cost the German Empire large expanses of European territory. After World War II, and the reign of Adolf Hitler, Germany was split into East and West Germany. In 1989 the Berlin Wall was dismantled, and Germany was reunited as one country (Hall & Hall, 1990).

Japan

For many years the Japanese were isolated from world events. Japan has had many emperors in the last 2000 years. Shoguns (feudal lords) played a significant role in Japanese politics between the twelfth and late nineteenth centuries. Following the loss of power of the shoguns in the 1860s, emperors maintained political control. To this day, no one can be a Japanese citizen who is not ethnically Japanese. The Russo-Japanese War and World War I made Japan a military power. Losing in World War II cost the Japanese their military power. After World War II, the collectivistic attitude of the Japanese allowed them to accept defeat and rebuild. They have become one of the top economic powers today (Moran & Stripp, 1991).

Mexico

The indigenous Indian population was inbred with the Spanish conquerors to form the majority of the Mexican population. While there are still a few ethnically pure Indians and Spaniards, most Mexicans are a mixture of both cultures. Mexico became independent from Spain in 1821. After losing Texas in 1836, additional territory was lost in Mexico's war with the United States, from 1846 to 1848. The result of this war was the loss of a great deal of what is now the southwestern United States. In 1861, France invaded Mexico and named Maximilian the dictator. Dictatorships continued until 1910 when the Mexican people revolted against them. Since the 1940s, Mexico has had a stable government (Ruch, 1989).

LANGUAGE

Successful communication with someone from another culture involves understanding a common language. Without this shared language, communication problems may occur when a third party, the translator or interpreter, attempts to convey both the verbal and nonverbal intent of your message.

Although Chinese is the language spoken by the largest number of native speakers with English ranking second, English is considered the language of international business. So you can expect your foreign hosts to speak and understand at least some English in most intercultural business encounters. Because so many variations in the English language exist, however, messages are often misunderstood when both parties speak this language with its many accents, dialects, and regional peculiarities. Unfamiliar accents may present barriers to effective communication.

People who speak English as a second language retain much of their foreign accent. Those for whom Spanish is a first language and English the second language, for example, often pronounce vowels as they are pronounced in the Spanish language, for example, "ē" is pronounced as "ā" and "ī" is pronounced as "ē." They may also pronounce certain consonants as they would in Spanish, such as "j" is pronounced as "h" (Hoolian for Julian). When the wrong syllable is accented (such as dév-eloped rather than de-vél-oped), understanding is difficult. Regional variations in pronunciation and word usage can exist within a nation and between nations. In the United States the word "fixin'" is used in many parts of the South to mean "ready" or "preparing," as in "I'm fixin' to leave" or "He's fixin' breakfast." U.S. English has numerous slang expressions and jargon that complicate comprehending what another person is saying. The literal translation of such terms as *red tape, bottom line,* and *ball park figure* give no clue as to the intended meaning of the message. England's English is not the same as U.S. English. To the English, an *elevator* is a *lift*; a *car hood* is a *bonnet*; an *international call* is a *trunk call.* Being able to recognize regional expressions is important since the comprehension of the message may be affected.

Sociolinguistics refers to the effects of social and cultural differences upon a language. People reveal class differences by their accent, phrasing, and word usage. According to Fussell (1983), U.S. people with good educational backgrounds and with relatively high incomes speak in a similar manner regardless of the part of the country they live in. People who use such terms as *ain't, reckon* (suppose), and *afeared* (afraid) are considered uneducated and/or from lower-class backgrounds. Since people in other cultures also reveal their class level by their accent, pronunciation, and word usage, when you select an interpreter be sure to determine if the person is experienced in the regional and sociolinguistic groups with which you are dealing.

Although you are not expected to learn the language of every country with which you may conduct business, if you plan an extended relationship with a particular culture, learning to speak the language is important since you may have to communicate with persons who do not speak your language. Make an effort to at least learn how to say such basic expressions as *please* and *thank you,* greetings, and other terms commonly used by people in the culture. Examples of such terms in French, German, and Spanish appear in the accompanying table.

English	*French*	*German*	*Spanish*
Good day	Bonjour (bawn-JHOOR)	Guten Tag (GOO-tun TAHK)	Buenos días (Bway-nos Dee-ahs)
Goodbye	Au revoir (o reh-VWAHR)	Auf Wiedersehen (owf VEE-der-zeyn)	Adiós (ah-DYOS)
Please	S'il vous plait (seel-voo-PLEH)	Bitte (BIT-teh)	Por favor (POR fah-vor)
Thank you	Merci (mehr-See)	Danke (DUNK-uh)	Gracias (GRAH-see-ahs)
Good evening	Bonsoir (bawn-SWAHR)	Guten Abend (GOO-tun AH-bent)	Buenas noches (BWAY-nahs NO-chase)
Excuse me	Excusez-moi (ex-kyou-zay MWAH)	Verzeihung (fare-TSY-oong)	Perdóneme (per-DOH-nay-may)

ECONOMY

When conducting business with persons in other cultures, a knowledge of the country's economy, including **imports** (goods brought into the country) and **exports** (goods sent out of the country), can promote an understanding of the people and their culture and may prove useful in the negotiation process. A brief description of the economies of the six countries with which the United States conducts most of its international business is given in the following sections. Additional information related to economic systems was included in Chapter 2.

United States

The economy in the United States is the largest in the world, with an average annual **gross national product (GNP)** per capita of US$21,700. (GNP is the value of goods and services earned per capita.) The United States is the major world financial center. Its exports include capital goods, cars, consumer goods, food, and machinery. Tourism is important to many state economies.

The United States is part of the North American Free Trade Agreement (NAFTA) that will make expanding markets, services, and manufacturing between the United States, Canada, and Mexico easier. The unit of currency is the U.S. dollar.

Canada

Canada, which has one of the world's strongest economies, has an average annual gross national product (GNP) per capita of US$21,418.

Canada is ranked second in the world in the production of gold and uranium; it ranks third in silver and fourth in copper. Canada is a major supplier of wood pulp and other timber-related products. Tourism is an important source of revenue in recent years. Canada exports wheat, barley, oats, and other agricultural products. Canada exports more to the United States than it imports. The unit of currency is the Canadian dollar.

England

England is part of Great Britain. Some of England's economic problems were eased by privatization of some industries in the 1980s. The average annual gross national product per capita is US$16,070.

Exports include manufactured goods, machinery, fuels, transport equipment, and chemicals. England's natural resources include coal, oil, natural gas, tin, iron ore, and salt. England exports slightly less to the United States than it imports. The pound sterling is the unit of currency.

France

France has a mature economy, and the standard of living is quite high with an average annual GNP per capita of US$19,480. France is a major producer of such products as wine, milk, butter, cheese, barley, and wheat. France has a higher level of debt than other European countries, but the economy usually grows at about 2 percent.

The principal exports are machinery and transport equipment, iron and steel products, and agricultural products. France exports less to the United States than it imports. The French franc is the unit of currency.

Germany

Germany, one of the five top economic powers in the world, has an average annual GNP per capita of US$22,730 in the 11 western states and US$14,000 in the eastern states. With the unification of Germany, the eastern economy is being revived with money from the western states.

Germany's main exports include cars, steel, aluminum, televisions and other manufactured goods. Germany imports less from the United States than it exports. Principal crops include sugar beets, wheat, barley, and potatoes. The German deutsche mark is the unit of currency.

Japan

Japan's economy is growing at an annual rate of about 1 percent. The average annual GNP per capita is US$25,430.

Japan imports almost half of its food supply since much of the land is unsuitable for cultivation. Japan is one of the world's leading fish producers. Machinery, electronics, engineering, textiles, and chemicals are major industries in Japan. Japan exports much more to the United States than it imports. This trade imbalance is a source of friction between Japan and the United States. The yen, Japan's currency, is one of the strongest currencies in the world.

Mexico

Mexico's economic growth has been hampered by low world oil prices, high debt and inflation, and unemployment. The earthquake in Mexico City in 1985, which claimed the lives of thousands of people, has also had an impact on Mexico's economy.

The current average annual gross national product per capita is about US$3,200. U.S. companies, such as General Motors, Sam's Wholesale Clubs, Hunter Fan, and Blockbuster Video, have shown their faith in Mexico's economic stability by investing billions of dollars there.

Mexico no longer depends heavily on oil revenues; business has diversified. The new privatization of state industries has forced them to become competitive and profitable. Mexico's wealth, once concentrated in 5 percent of the population, is now becoming more widely distributed. Over half of the population have money to purchase discretionary consumer goods.

About 26 percent of Mexico's labor force is employed in agriculture. Corn, cotton, coffee, oilseed, sorghum, sugar cane, vegetables, and wheat are major crops. Rubber, cocoa, and chicle, used in making chewing gum, are also produced. Mexico considers tourism important in providing employment for many people. Mexico is also a major supplier of marijuana, despite government attempts to curb the drug trade. Although mining and petroleum are the two most important industries, they employ less than 2 percent of the workforce. Mexico exports agricultural products, cotton, shrimp, and engines. Mexico's main trading partner is the United States. The unit of currency, the peso, underwent devaluation in the 1980s, which caused additional economic problems.

HOLIDAYS AND HOLY DAYS

An awareness of the holidays and holy days of other cultures is important so that telephone calls and business trips can be scheduled around them.

Holidays may celebrate a prominent person's birthday (Washington's Birthday) or a historic event (Independence Day) or pay homage to a group (Veterans' Day and Memorial Day). Holy days are associated with religious observances (Ramaden, Christmas, Easter, and Yom Kippur). Since business may not be conducted on some of these special days, you will want to consider this information when planning a trip abroad.

People who travel to the United States, for example, should understand that business is not conducted on Christmas Day or Thanksgiving. Business is rarely conducted when Independence Day is observed (July 4). The holiday is generally celebrated with fireworks, picnics, parades, and parties. In the United States, most businesses are closed on Sunday, which is the Sabbath for many religions. The Sabbath in Israel, on the other hand, is observed on Saturday, while the Arabs observe the Sabbath on Friday.

In some countries, holidays are similar to those celebrated in the United States. Some Catholic countries, such as Germany, have a carnival season similar to the New Orleans Mardi Gras, which is not a good time for conducting business. Many countries celebrate the New Year; the nature, duration, and time of the year of the celebration may vary.

The holidays observed in the United States and those observed by the six countries with which the United States conducts most of its international business follow (Beach, Hinojosa, & Tedford, 1991; Casady, 1993).

United States

New Year's Day
Martin Luther King Jr.'s Birthday (third Monday in January)
President's Day (third Monday in February)
Memorial Day (last Monday in May)
Independence Day (July 4)
Labor Day (first Monday in September)
Columbus Day (second Monday in October)
Veteran's Day (November 11)
Thanksgiving (fourth Thursday in November)
Christmas Day

Canada

New Year's Day
Easter Sunday and Monday
Labor Day (May 1)
Victoria Day (third Monday in May)
Canada Day (July 1)
Thanksgiving Day (second Monday in October)
All Saints Day (November 1)
Remembrance Day (November 11)
Christmas
Boxing Day (December 26)

Quebec has two additional holidays: The Carnival de Quebec (February) and St. Jean-Baptist Day (June 24).

England

New Year's Day
Good Friday (April 9)*
May Day (May 3)*
Easter Sunday and Monday
Spring Bank Holiday (May 31)*
Summer Bank Holiday (August 2)*
Late Summer Holiday (August 30)*
Christmas
Boxing Day (December 26)

France

New Year's Day
Mardi Gras (Shrove Tuesday in February)
Easter Sunday and Monday
Labor Day (May 1)
Liberation Day (May 8)
Ascension (May 20)*
Whit Monday (May 31)*
Bastille Day (July 14)
Pentecost
Assumption (August 15)
All Saints Day (November 1)
World War I Armistice Day (November 11)*
Christmas

Germany

New Year's Day
Good Friday (April 9)*
Easter Sunday and Monday
Labor Day (May 1)
Ascension (May 20)*
Whit Monday (May 31)*
Day of German Unity (October 3)
All Saints Day (November 1)
Day of Prayer and Repentance (November 17)*
Christmas

Japan

New Year's Day (January 1)
Coming of Age Day (January 15)
National Foundation Day (February 11)
Vernal Equinox (March 21)
Greenery Day (April 29)
Constitution Day (May 3)

Bon Festival (August 15)
Respect for the Aged Day (September 15)
Autumnal Equinox (September 23)
Sports Day (October 10)
Culture Day (November 3)
Labor Thanksgiving Day (November 23)
Emperor Akihito's Birthday (December 23)

Mexico

New Year's Day
St. Anthony's Day (January 17)
Constitution Day (February 5)
Carnival Week
Birthday of Benito Juarez (March 21)
Easter (April 9–12)*
Labor Day (May 1)
Cinco de Mayo (May 5)
Corpus Christi (May or June)
Assumption (August 15)
President's Annual Message (September 1)
Independence Day (September 16)
Columbus Day (October 12)
All Saints Day (November 1)
All Souls Day (November 2)
Revolution Day (November 20)
Day of the Virgin Guadalupe (December 12)
Christmas

In addition to their holidays, some countries have other times during which business is curtailed. Do not expect to conduct business in Europe during August as this is considered the vacation month, and many people close their businesses. In addition to the Sabbath, little business is conducted with the Arabs during Ramadan, the Islamic fasting season, which lasts a month. In Japan many companies close from April 29 to May 5.

---

* Dates vary; those shown are for 1993.

SPECIAL FOODS AND CONSUMPTION TABOOS _____

Most cultures have unusual foods that are looked upon with surprise or even disdain by persons in other cultures. Foods that are common in the United States that people in other cultures find unusual include corn-on-the-cob (in other countries considered a food for animals only), grits, popcorn, marshmallows, and crawfish (Althen, 1988; Axtell, 1991). (See Figure 8.1.)

Foods in other cultures that some U.S. Americans have a problem with include Japanese sushi (raw fish), dog meat in South Korea, and sheep's eyeballs in Saudi Arabia. In parts of Mexico, chicken soup may contain the chicken's feet; in China, you may be served duck's feet and raw monkey brains. (See Figure 8.2.)

Since you are expected to eat what you are served in other countries, you may find it advisable to swallow quickly, avoid asking what it is, or pretend to eat by moving the food around so that it changes form. People who are experienced travelers also advise cutting the food into very thin slices and imagining that the unusual food, such as snake or gorilla, looks or tastes like something palatable such as chicken.

Knowing consumption taboos of the host culture is important. People in the United States, for example, do not knowingly eat horse meat although there is no religious taboo associated with this practice. Strict Muslims do not consume pork (or any animal that is a scavenger) or alcohol. Orthodox Jews eat neither pork nor shellfish. They also observe such rules as not serving meat and milk together and requiring that cattle or fowl must be ritually slaugh-

FIGURE 8.1 Popcorn (*a*), crawfish (*b*), and corn-on-the-cob (*c*) are considered unusual U.S. foods.

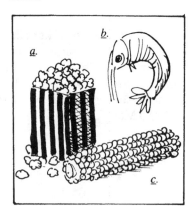

FIGURE 8.2 Sheep's eyeballs (*a*), monkey brains (*b*), and chicken soup containing the feet (*c*) are foods in other countries considered unusual by U.S. standards.

tered so that it is "kosher"; strict Muslims also observe ritual slaughtering. Hindus do not eat any beef; the cow is considered sacred. People from such countries as India are often vegetarians because of personal or religious beliefs (Axtell, 1993).

Since business encounters are often conducted in social settings, you will want to become familiar with special foods associated with the host culture as well as consumption taboos so that your lack of knowledge of cultural eating habits will not negatively affect the communication process. Special foods and consumption practices and taboos associated with the United States and with the six countries with which the United States conducts the majority of its international trade are identified in the following section.

United States

The majority of U.S. people eat the meat of animals except for certain parts of the animal, such as the feet and eyes. Most U.S. people do not feel comfortable eating something if they cannot easily identify what it is. Meats that are consumed are beef, pork, and fowl, as well as fish and shellfish. Fresh vegetables and fruits are enjoyed and easily obtained year round.

U.S. Americans are great supporters of the fast-food industry; they frequent such restaurants as McDonald's, Wendy's, Kentucky Fried Chicken, and Hardee's. In metropolitan areas, ethnic and international cuisine is readily available.

Canada

Although the majority of Canadian people eat many of the same foods as people in the United States, the French influence is apparent in restaurants in many parts of Canada. The Atlantic Canadians maintain a diet of seafood including lobster and seaweed. Pacific Canadians are partial to smoked salmon. The Canadians in the interior of Canada eat more grain products and red meats. As in the United States, ethnic and international cuisine is readily available in the metropolitan areas.

England

Although similarities exist between consumption practices of the United States and England, differences are numerous. Kippers (smoked herring) and kidneys are often served at breakfast, while in the United States a typical breakfast would be cereal or bacon and eggs. Another difference is the serving of tea every afternoon from 3:30 to 4:30, which might include small sandwiches of cucumber, watercress, and egg, as well as cookies and cakes. English food tends to include a lot of meat and potatoes. Meats that are popular include beef, mutton, and fish. Sauces and fancy preparations are not considered necessary. Cooked vegetables are also an important part of the meal. Tea and beer are popular drinks. Mixed drinks, as in much of Europe, are served with no ice or with one ice cube (Braganti & Devine, 1992).

France

Foods typical of certain regions of France that are considered somewhat unusual by U.S. standards include *tripes à la mode de Caen* (a stew of tripe, cider, and vegetables), *escargots à la bourguignonne* (snails served in garlic butter), and *lamproie à la bordelaise* (eels cooked in red wine). The French are renowned for their fine wines and cuisine. Eating is an art in France, and the presentation of the meal is as important as the food. French sauces, soups, breads, and pastries have been the measure of fine cooking in the Western world since the Middle Ages (Braganti & Devine, 1992).

Germany

Germany, like England, tends to have a cuisine that is "meat and potatoes" oriented. Since many cuts of meat tend to be tough in texture, most foods are cooked for a long time or cut up and served with sauces. Foods considered unusual by U.S. standards include *Eisbein* (pig's knuckle), *Schavelfleish* (raw hamburger), and *Hasenpfeffer* (rabbit stew). The serving of beer, wine, and soft drinks warm, common in Germany, is uncommon in the United States (Braganti & Devine, 1992).

Japan

Some foods considered usual in Japan are considered unusual in the United States. Dried squid, a food symbolic of happiness that is served at New Year's, is an example of a food a U.S. person would consider unusual. Another unusual food is *fugu*, blowfish or glowfish, which requires special preparation as the liver and ovaries contain a dangerous poison. The Japanese diet, consisting of very little meat and a lot of rice and vegetables, is unusual by U.S. standards. Coffee has surpassed tea as the preferred drink. Food presentation is an important part of the meal (Devine & Braganti, 1986).

Mexico

Typical Mexican cuisine includes tortillas, beans, and various unusual soups, such as *sopa de lima* (chicken and lime soup). An hors d'oeuvres people of the United States find unusual is *chicharrón* (pork crackling served with a piquant sauce). In some parts of Mexico, a favorite dish is *pollo borracho* (chicken flavored with a tequila sauce). Other unusual foods include *ceviche* (raw fish with onions, tomatoes, lime juice, and chiles) and *huevos motuleños* (corn tortillas with black beans, ham, fried eggs, and tomato sauce). Many foods are highly spiced; bland foods, such as breads and rice, are used to temper the hot seasonings (Devine & Braganti, 1988).

_____ **TERMS** _____

Exports   Imports
Gross national product (GNP)   Sociolinguistics

Exercise 8.1

Matching

Instructions: Match the currencies on the right with their country on the left.

___ 1. Australia	A. dollar
___ 2. England	B. drachma
	C. franc
___ 3. France	D. krone
___ 4. Hong Kong	E. lira
	F. mark
___ 5. Japan	G. peso
___ 6. Mexico	H. pound
	I. ruble
___ 7. Norway	J. rupee
___ 8. Former USSR	K. yen
	L. yuan
___ 9. Taiwan	
___10. Germany	

Exercise 8.2

Instructions: Circle the T for true or the F for false.

1. T   F   Business dress in Canada is similar to that in the United States.

2. T   F   When conducting business in another country, wear what the people in that country typically wear.

3. T   F   In Europe pants are not considered appropriate business attire for women.

4. T   F   People in Mexico do not waste time with "small talk"; they get right down to business.

5. T   F   "I am going to carry my daughter to the doctor" is an example of a regional expression.

6. T   F   Pronunciation and enunciation are associated with differences in educational background and social class.

7. T   F   Japan imports more from the United States then it exports to the United States.

8. T   F   Mexico's major problems have included unemployment and inflation.

9. T   F   All cultures celebrate Christmas and Easter.

10. T   F   Corn-on-the-cob, a U.S. food, is considered by most cultures to be food for animals only.

―――― QUESTIONS AND CASES FOR DISCUSSION ――――

1. What are some sources for obtaining information about specific countries?
2. In what countries is business dress similar to that worn in the United States?
3. Identify cultures in which business dress may be different from that worn in the United States.
4. What guidelines for business dress should women observe when conducting business in other cultures?
5. Explain how a knowledge of geography of a country can be useful when visiting the country.

6. Give examples of how variations in the English language exist within regions of the United States.
7. How do you say "Good day" in French, German, and Spanish?
8. Compare the economies of Canada, England, and Mexico in terms of GNP, inflation, and unemployment.
9. Discuss the import–export balance between the United States and France, the United States and Japan, and the United States and Germany.
10. How is a knowledge of holidays and holy days helpful when conducting business with another culture?
11. What U.S. foods do people of other cultures find unusual? What foods of other cultures do people of the United States consider unusual?
12. List some consumption taboos of people in various cultures.

Case 1   Your organization is having a large party in the United States for all of its distributors worldwide. Since there will be people from all over the world, what would you serve so as not to offend anyone?

Case 2   You have unknowingly arrived in Mexico during Carnival Week. Because people are busy partying and celebrating, they are not interested in meeting with you to discuss business. However, since you are here, they have invited you to join in their activities. Should you accept or reject their invitation?

ACTIVITIES

1. Research appropriate business and social dress in one of the following countries: India, Israel, Thailand, or Saudi Arabia.
2. List some religious taboos associated with food consumption in a subculture of the United States or a culture of your choice.
3. Write a paragraph summarizing your experience in trying a U.S. American dish for the first time and a food in another culture.
4. Research the economy of a country other than the six included in the chapter. Write a one-page summary including such information as imports/exports, GNP, unemployment rate, and other aspects of the economy.
5. Practice saying the following in French, German, and Spanish: please, thank you, goodbye, and excuse me.
6. Research geographic features of a country you would like to visit. Include such features as climate, altitude, population, and notable landmarks.

REFERENCES

Althen, G. (1988). *American ways.* Yarmouth, ME: Intercultural Press, Inc.

Axtell, R. E. (1990). *Do's and taboos of hosting international visitors.* New York: John Wiley & Sons, Inc.

Axtell, R. E. (1993). *Do's and taboos around the world.* New York: John Wiley & Sons, Inc.

Beach, L., Hinojosa, B. L., & Tedford, A. K. (1991, November/December). Holiday express. *Instructor,* pp. 25–34.

Braganti, N. L., & Devine, E. (1992). *European customs and manners.* New York: Meadowbrook Press.

CD-Rom Trends. (1992, October 19). *Fortune,* p. 18.

Casady, M. J. (1993). Strategies for teaching international concepts in business courses. *Instructional strategies: An applied research series, 9*(2), 1–6.

Culturgram '94. (1994). Provo, UT: Brigham Young University's David M. Kennedy Center for International Studies.

Devine, E., & Braganti, N. L. (1986). *The travelers' guide to Asian customs and manners.* New York: St. Martin's Press.

Devine, E., & Braganti, N. L. (1988). *The travelers' guide to Latin American customs and manners.* New York: St. Martin's Press.

Fussell, P. (1983). *Class.* New York: Ballantine Books.

Hall, E. T., & Hall, M. R. (1990). *Understanding cultural differences.* Yarmouth, ME: Intercultural Press, Inc.

Moran, R. T., & Stripp, W. G. (1991). *Dynamics of successful international business negotiations.* Houston, TX: Gulf Publishing Company.

Ruch, W. V. (1989). *International handbook of corporate communication.* Jefferson, NC: McFarland & Company Inc., Publishers.

9

Cultural Shock

OBJECTIVES

Upon completion of this chapter, you will:

- understand the nature of cultural shock and its relationship to success in overseas assignments.

- be able to identify the typical stages of cultural shock.

- know ways to alleviate cultural shock, including careful selection of persons for overseas assignments and predeparture training.

- understand the role of cultural stress, social alienation, social class and poverty–wealth extremes, financial matters, and relationships in dealing with cultural shock.

- understand how differences between the extent to which persons in the host and home cultures reveal their private selves may contribute to cultural shock.

Cultural shock (commonly called culture shock) is the trauma you experience when you move into a culture different from your home culture. Cultural shock is basically a communication problem that involves the frustrations that accompany a lack of understanding of the verbal and nonverbal communication of the host culture and its customs and value systems. Frustrations may include lack of food, unacceptable standards of cleanliness, different bathroom facilities (see Figure 9.1), and fear for personal safety. In a survey of 188 students from two mid-South universities who had traveled or lived abroad, the greatest degree of cultural shock was reported in the areas of lack of modern conveniences and standards of cleanliness. Other areas in which cultural shock showed statistical significance included attitudes toward women, nonverbal communication, clothing/business dress, family and marriage practices, housing, climate, educational system, financial problems, and values and ethical standards (Chaney & Martin, 1993). The absence of conveniences taken for granted in the United States, such as telephones that work, running water available 24 hours a day, or buses that run on time, is an additional source of frustration. People with strong religious ties may feel spiritually adrift without a church of their faith. Without the bounty of U.S. shopping malls, supermarkets, and multiple television sets, depression may result. In addition to depression, people who experience cultural shock can become homesick, eat or drink compulsively, and even develop physical ailments.

Cultural shock has received increased attention by researchers only in the past two decades. However, Jack London, in his story "In a Far Country" published in 1900, stressed that a visitor to another culture should be prepared to acquire new customs and abandon old ideals. He suggested that sojourners should find pleasure in the unfamiliar because those who could not fit into the new culture would either return home or "die" of both psychological and physical ailments. London's advice is still sound almost a hundred years later (Lewis & Jungman, 1986).

A special kind of cultural shock experienced by U.S. people has been identified by Engholm (1991). He terms it *AsiaShock*. Engholm identifies these five progressive stages of AsiaShock:*

- Frustration with the culture, which includes the language, the food, and an exasperation with local customs.
- Unwillingness to understand the rationale behind the local ways of doing things; people of the United States quickly label a cultural behavior as backward and inefficient without trying to understand the rational basis for the behavior.

---

*Engholm, C. (1991). *When Business East Meets Business West*. Copyright © 1991 by John Wiley & Sons, Inc. Reprinted by permission of John Wiley & Sons, Inc.

- Ethnocentricity; people of the United States often label Asians as dishonest because they seem to say one thing and do another, failing to realize that Asians consider their behavior to be face-saving rather than dishonest.
- Racism, including the unflattering labeling of all Asians into such groups as *Japs* and *Coolies*.
- Avoidance of the culture; people of the United States tend to form their own clubs at which they commiserate about the difficulty of doing business in Asia rather than intermingling with the people of the culture.

Cultural shock can be costly to a firm, since it often results in the premature return of U.S. people working overseas. Ferraro (1990) quotes research that shows employees sent to work in foreign countries fail not because they lack technical or professional competence but because of their inability to understand and adapt to another culture's way of life. Estimates on early return of U.S. expatriate managers range from 45 to 85 percent (Ferraro, 1990). When companies implement measures to combat cultural shock, such as conducting training programs for sojourners (people who visit or reside temporarily in another country), the early return rate drops to less than 2 percent.

Some companies have used short-term stays of two to three months to determine the employee's potential for tolerating the culture. Sometimes these short-term projects are designed to prepare the person for a longer stay later. On other occasions, these brief trips are simply ways to utilize the talents of technical professionals who would be unwilling to go in the first place if it meant disrupting the professional advancement of a career-oriented spouse. Short trips are also cost effective, as the need to move the family is reduced or

FIGURE 9.1   Cultural shock can result from bathrooms with different fixtures or arrangements.

eliminated. While the degree and type of cultural shock experienced by people who travel to another country for a short stay may be similar to the shock experienced by those who plan an extended visit, the strategies for coping during the short-term visit may differ. Brislin (1981) identifies five strategies used for coping with the new culture during short visits:

1. One strategy is *nonacceptance* of the host culture; the traveler simply behaves as he or she would in the home culture. No effort is made to learn the language or the customs of the host culture.
2. A second strategy is known as *substitution.* The traveler learns the appropriate responses or behaviors in the host culture and substitutes these responses or behaviors for the ones he or she would ordinarily use in the home culture.
3. A third strategy is known as *addition.* The person adds the behavior of the host culture when in the presence of the nationals but maintains the home culture behavior with others of the same culture.
4. A fourth strategy is known as *synthesis.* This strategy integrates or combines elements of the two cultures, such as combining the dress of the United States and the Philippines.
5. The final strategy is referred to as *resynthesis,* the integration of ideas not found in either culture. An example of this strategy would be a U.S. traveler to China who chooses to eat neither American nor Chinese food, but prefers Italian food.

STAGES OF CULTURAL SHOCK

Cultural shock generally goes through five stages: excitement or initial euphoria, crisis or disenchantment, adjustment, acceptance, and reentry.

The first stage is excitement and fascination with the new culture, which can last for only a few days or for several months. During this time, everything is new and different; you are fascinated with the food and the people. Sometimes this stage is referred to as the "honeymoon" stage during which your enthusiasm for the new culture causes you to overlook minor problems, such as having to drink bottled water and the absence of central heating or air conditioning.

During the second stage, the crisis or disenchantment period, the "honeymoon" is over; your excitement has turned to disappointment as you encounter more and more differences between your own culture and the new culture. Problems with transportation, unfamiliar foods, and people who do not speak English now seem overwhelming. The practice of bargaining over the purchase price of everything that you originally found amusing is now a constant source of irritation. People in this stage often cope with the situation by making disparaging remarks about the culture; it is sometimes referred to as the "fight back" technique. Others deal with this stage by leaving, either physically or psychologically. Those who remain may withdraw from people in the culture, refuse to learn the language, and develop coping behaviors of excessive drinking or drug use. Some individuals actually deny differences and will speak in glowing terms of the new culture.

In the third stage, the adjustment phase, you begin to accept the new culture. You try new foods and make adjustments in behavior to accommodate the shopping lines and the long waits for public transportation. You begin to see the humor in situations and realize that a change in attitude toward the host culture will make the stay abroad more rewarding.

In the fourth phase, the acceptance or adaptation phase, you feel at home in the new culture, become involved in activities of the culture, cultivate friendships among the nationals, and feel comfortable in social situations with people from the host culture. You learn the language and may adopt the new culture's style of doing things. You even learn to enjoy some customs, such as afternoon tea and the mid-day siesta, that you will miss when you return to the home country.

The final phase is reentry shock, which can be almost as traumatic as the initial adjustment to a new culture, particularly after an extended stay abroad. **Reentry shock** is experienced upon returning to the home country and may follow the stages identified earlier: initial euphoria, crisis or disenchantment, adjustment, and acceptance or adaptation. You would at first be happy to be back in your own country, then become disenchanted as you realize that your friends are not really interested in hearing about your experiences abroad, your standard of living goes down, and you are unable to use such skills as a foreign language or bargaining in the market. You then move into the adjustment stage as you become familiar with new technology and view with appreciation such things as the abundance and variety of foods and clothing and the improved standards of cleanliness. You finally move into the acceptance stage when you feel comfortable with the mores in the home culture and find yourself returning to many of your earlier views and behaviors.

Although reentry shock typically occurs for a shorter period of time than the first four stages of cultural shock, expatriates who have made a good adjustment to the host culture may go through a rather long period of adjustment, lasting six months or more, when they are confronted with the changes that have taken place in their absence. Some of these changes are work related; expatriates may feel "demoted" when they return to middle-management positions without the bonuses, perks, and professional contacts they enjoyed abroad. In other situations, changes have taken place in the home country, including in politics and styles of clothing, that require readjustment. In research conducted by Chaney and Martin (1993), the four areas in which reentry shock was experienced by college students who had traveled abroad that were statistically significant were readjusting to lifestyle, change in social life, change in standard of living, and reestablishing friendships.

Some reentry problems are personal in nature. Many repatriates have changed; they have acquired a broadened view of the world and have undergone changes in values and attitudes. Personal problems may include unsuccessful attempts to renew personal and professional relationships as the realization sets in that their former friends do not share their enthusiasm for their overseas experiences and accomplishments. They must then make new friends who share this common experience. Children of expatriates encounter similar readjustment problems as their former friends have made new ones and they find that the education they received abroad is sufficiently different to cause problems when returning to schools in the United States.

Since reentry shock is a natural part of cultural shock, multinational corporations must provide training for expatriates to assure that the transition to the home culture is a positive experience. In the absence of such training, you can do much to counteract reentry shock by sharing your feelings (not your experiences) with sympathetic family members and friends, particularly those who have lived abroad. Correspond regularly with members of the home culture; ask questions concerning changes that are taking place. Subscribe to the home newspaper to stay abreast of current happenings. Keep in touch with professional organizations and other groups with which you may want to affiliate. Many repatriates have found that maintaining ties with the home culture cushions the shock associated with reentry (Dodd, 1987; Dodd & Montalvo, 1987; Khols, 1984; Klopf, 1991).

ALLEVIATING CULTURAL SHOCK

Many multinational firms find that cultural shock can be alleviated by selecting employees for overseas assignments who possess certain personal and professional qualifications. Another method of easing cultural shock is to conduct training programs for employees prior to overseas deployment (Krapels, 1993).

Selection of Overseas Personnel

Careful selection of persons for overseas assignments is important to enhance chances for a successful sojourn. Personal qualifications needed when working in an unfamiliar culture include adaptability, flexibility, empathy, and tolerance of ambiguity. Good interpersonal skills and high self-esteem have also been found to be important.

The ability to react to different and often unpredictable situations with little apparent irritation shows a tolerance for ambiguity. Ambiguities are inherent in intercultural communication; many people, situations, rules, and attitudes do not make much sense. A lot of confusion results from being in another culture, so maintaining a high degree of tolerance and flexibility is essential. Some companies spend a lot of time in college recruiting because they are looking for candidates who already have such qualifications as language proficiency and overseas experience, during which time the person has learned how to adapt to another culture. Many recruiters believe that tolerance can be developed but that adaptability is difficult to develop; they prefer, therefore, to hire persons who have already acquired this trait through living abroad (Geber, 1992; McEnery & DesHarnais, 1990). Adaptability screening reduces costly turnover. Harvey (1985) suggests the use of the following questions to determine a candidate's adaptability:

- Is the person cooperative, able to compromise, and sensitive to others?
- Is the candidate open to the opinions of others?
- How does the person react to new situations and what effort does he or she make to understand and appreciate differences?
- Does the candidate understand his or her own culturally derived values?
- Is the candidate sensitive and aware of values in other cultures?
- How does the person react to criticism?
- How well does the candidate understand the U.S. government system?
- Will the candidate be able to make and develop contacts with counterparts in the foreign culture?
- Is the candidate patient when dealing with problem situations?
- Is the candidate resilient when faced with adverse situations?

By using such questions as these, interviewers are better able to determine a candidate's suitability for the overseas assignment as well as the person's motivation for wanting to work abroad.

The ability to see the environment from the perspective of the host nationals is an indication of empathy. Bennett's concept of empathy recommends replacing the Golden Rule (do unto others as you would have them do unto you) with the **Platinum Rule** (do unto others as they would have done unto them). You can still maintain your own cultural identity but be able to interpret the new culture through the eyes of the national (Broome, 1991).

Professional qualifications include a knowledge of business practices in the host culture and technical competence. Language skills are considered crucial by some companies. When the destination is the Orient, many companies believe some language training prior to departure is needed. When the use of English is pervasive in a country, proficiency in the host language may not be necessary. In any case, language knowledge seems to give an expatriate an extra chance of succeeding in the host culture. In addition to language knowledge, understanding the educational, political, economic, and social systems of a country is considered important (Tung, 1981).

Predeparture Training for Host Country

Because of the reported lack of intercultural training by U.S. multinationals, acculturation problems have affected the overall success rate of businesspersons in foreign countries. Research conducted by Krapels (1993) involving 102 international businesspersons representing 35 international mid-South companies determined that 46 percent of the firms participating offered some type of predeparture training; however, only one firm had a formal training program in place. Since early return rates drop significantly when training programs are implemented, many multinational firms are now experimenting with a variety of training programs. Some companies are trying to boost tolerance of another culture by including trainees from overseas locations in their U.S.-based training programs. Other firms conduct training sessions overseas and send U.S. managers to these courses to provide training in the host culture at the same time that some exposure to the culture occurs. Still other companies incorporate cross-cultural awareness into their regular management training courses.

Approaches to intercultural training may be grouped as follows:

1. **Information or fact-oriented training,** in which participants are given facts about the host country using a variety of instructional methods, such as lectures, group discussions, and videotapes.
2. **Attribution training,** which focuses on explanations of behavior from the point of view of a person in the host country.
3. **Cultural awareness approach,** which includes a comparison of values and behaviors of people in the home country and the host country.
4. **Cognitive-behavior modification approach,** which applies principles of learning to specific adjustment problems in other cultures.
5. **Experiential learning approach,** which affords participants an opportunity to actively experience the culture through field trips or such simulations as Bafa, Bafa, in which participants are divided into two cultures, Alpha and Beta, learn the rules of their culture, and interact with members of the other culture.
6. **Interaction approach,** in which participants interact with people in the host country, either nationals or U.S. persons who have been in the host country for some time.*

* From *Managing Cultural Differences* by Philip R. Harris and Robert T. Moran. Copyright © 1991 by Gulf Publishing Company, Houston, TX. Used with permission. All rights reserved.

Advances in communication technology are now being used in intercultural training. Global videoconferencing has been used by a major international firm to train employees and their families at more than 200 sites around the world. Global educational networks with various universities are being developed to train executives who are going abroad. Computers are being used to enhance training effectiveness. According to Harris and Moran (1991), computer-aided training or learning has immense potential for multicultural education because it cuts across traditional language barriers. Research indicates that such instruction not only encourages one-to-one learning, but can save 30 percent of the time of more traditional methods. Regardless of the type of training offered, companies realize that success is limited to the extent that there is no substitute for actually living in another culture.

ASPECTS OF CULTURAL SHOCK

Aspects of cultural shock include cultural stress, social alienation, social class and poverty–wealth extremes, financial matters, and relationships and family considerations. In addition, differences between the extent to which persons in the host and home cultures reveal their private selves may cause acculturation problems, particularly in communication.

Cultural Stress

Entering an unfamiliar culture is stressful; in fact, transitions of any type are both psychologically and physically stressful. The stress of getting ready for the move, of unpacking and getting settled upon arrival, and of adjusting to new foods can be so stressful that people become physically ill. Problems with housing, climate, services, or communication in another language bring additional stress.

Expatriates learn to utilize a variety of coping skills to alleviate stress. Unfortunately, some coping behaviors are negative. Taking drugs or drinking alcohol may provide a temporary superficial relief to the stressful situation but avoids dealing with the real source of stress. Another negative coping method, using food to alleviate stress, may create weight gain problems. Positive techniques include diversions such as taking up a hobby or learning a new skill, planning family events, sharing problems with friends and family members, and changing one's mental outlook. Physical coping mechanisms, such as exercise and meditation, are useful in alleviating stress, as well as spiritual techniques, such as volunteering to help others and religious worship.

Some companies have found that providing prospective expatriates with a mentor who has worked in the host country can help to reduce anxiety about adjustments that may be necessary in the new culture. Providing a second mentor located in the host country can reduce stress associated with learning acceptable behavior in the new culture and will help avoid serious business and social blunders.

To alleviate culture stress, prepare for the second culture by reading up on the country, studying the language, and becoming aware of customs and traditions in the culture. Maintaining a sense of humor is very important in dealing with cultural stress.

Social Alienation

An aspect of cultural shock that can have adverse effects upon the newcomer to a culture is social alienation and the feelings of loneliness that are associated with being isolated from friends and the home culture.

Feelings of alienation may be delayed somewhat, since concern over such basic matters as housing, transportation, and work may buffer these feelings initially. As the months pass, however, you may feel more isolated as you experience numerous cultural differences, such as what is considered an appropriate topic of social conversation. The concern of people in the United States with fitness, exercise, and healthful eating is not shared by persons of many cultures and is, therefore, an inappropriate topic of conversation. You also may feel uncomfortable during political discussions as persons of other cultures cannot understand the logic behind such decisions as voting for a person for president who is inexperienced in the international arena rather than for a seasoned politician who is respected in the international community.

Making an effort to become familiar with the nuances of the culture and cultivating friendships with persons from the home culture and the host culture can alleviate feelings of alienation. Enrolling in language classes and including host nationals in social events can cushion the shock of the new culture and pave the way toward a better understanding and appreciation of the people and their culture.

Social Class and Poverty–Wealth Extremes

In many developing countries, no "middle class" exists. Social classes and extremes in poverty and wealth are readily apparent.

The mention of social class in the United States is greeted with uncertain responses since many U.S. citizens prefer to believe that no social classes exist in the United States. According to Fussell (1983), class distinctions do exist in the United States but are so complicated and subtle that visitors from other countries often miss the nuances and even the existence of a class structure. So the official propaganda of social equality is basically a myth. According to people in the lower stratum, class is related to the amount of money you have. People in the middle stratum acknowledge that money has something to do with it but believe that the kind of work you do and your education are almost as important. People in the top stratum believe that your tastes, values, style, and behavior indicate your class, regardless of your education, occupation, or money (Fussell, 1983). Since U.S. personnel are accustomed to perpetuating this "fable of equality," the obvious existence of social class in other societies may make U.S. Americans quite uncomfortable. In cultures with virtually no middle class, U.S. persons are usually forced into the upper class of the host culture and may, at least temporarily, feel quite ill at ease in a social role in which numerous servants are the norm and distinctions are made between acceptable and unacceptable friends.

The informality of U.S. Americans, such as greeting strangers on the street with "Hi!" and calling people they scarcely know by their first name, is a source of cultural shock for many visitors to the United States. In many cultures, starting a conversation with a stranger in a shop or on a bus is considered unacceptable; in the United States, this behavior is commonplace. Another source of shock to foreigners is the discovery that not all U.S. Americans are wealthy and well educated—that we have large numbers of homeless persons and people who have not graduated from high school.

The poverty of the lower class in other cultures often makes U.S. Americans so uncomfortable that they feel compelled to help but may do so in socially unacceptable ways, such as paying a gardener twice the usual rate simply because the person is poor. Mentors in the host culture can be very helpful in advising U.S. persons regarding acceptable ways of dealing with poverty–wealth extremes and with gaining an insight into the class structure of the culture (Althen, 1988).

Financial Matters

Because adapting to a new culture and reentering the home culture involve financial adjustments, companies should provide financial counseling both to expatriates and repatriates. Although the focus would be a little different, the primary consideration would be the same: optimum utilization of the financial resources available.

Financial counseling for expatriates would include such information as cost and availability of housing, banking practices (including exchange rates), use of credit cards and checks, and costs of schooling for employees with families. Since substantial salary increases are often related to an employee's willingness to relocate, these increases should be discussed in terms of real purchasing power. Expenses related to a higher standard of living, which many expatriates enjoy, would include hiring domestic help and investing in appropriate formal attire. Customs in purchasing, such as bargaining in the market, should be addressed as well as the additional marketing expenses, which may include paying someone to guard your car while you shop, someone else to carry parcels, and another person to find fresh eggs or meat that is available only on the black market. Buying goods in grams, rather than pounds, is an additional purchasing consideration. Added expenses of securing goods, such as the cost of tailor-made clothes in the absence of locally available clothing, is another appropriate topic to include.

By providing counseling before reentry, the company is acknowledging that financial problems will occur and is demonstrating a willingness to help with these problems. One financial problem relates to the loss of buying power; upon returning to the United States the decrease can be about 30 percent in net disposable income (Clague & Krupp, 1980). The focus of financial counseling for repatriates would include costs involved in relocating in a stateside home and accompanying adjustments to a lower salary and a loss of perquisites. Since the loss of elite status is often difficult to accept, counseling should include the positive side, such as the fact that less money will be spent on clothes. To ease the transition financially, some companies provide a relocation pay supplement. Others grant annual leave in advance of the return to allow time for house hunting and related problems. Another expense that is receiving increased attention is the cost of providing counseling for family members, particularly children whose adolescence is delayed. Since repatriated children are usually three to four years retarded socially, counseling is often needed to help them work through this transition of readjusting to the home culture (Bird & Dunbar, 1991).

Relationships and Family Considerations

Problems with relationships, such as failure of the spouse and other family members to adapt to the new culture, are a major factor in the early return of expatriates. Family and personal issues can be disruptive to acculturation, especially for families with children ages 3 to 5 and 14 to 16 (Harvey, 1985). The 3- to 5-year-olds often have emotional problems from being uprooted from familiar surroundings; the 14- to 16-year-olds may have problems from adapting socially as well as making adjustments to a different educational system. Adolescents in particular need social continuity and often feel resentment toward their parents for uprooting them. Care must be taken to prepare children for the move by discussing openly their anxieties and fears and by providing them with information concerning expected changes in their lives. Being separated from family members and friends in the United States may cause loneliness for all involved. In addition, the spouse is experiencing his or her own problems in adjusting to an alien work environment and is unable to provide the time and emotional support needed during this difficult period of adjustment. Two-career families, in which one spouse, usually the wife, gives up a career to accompany the relocated spouse, pose special adjustment problems. Job opportunities in the new culture may be nonexistent, and resentment and boredom may lead to family conflict. Adding unhappy children and an unhappy spouse to the stress of the new job in a foreign culture increases the probability of an early return to the home culture (Harvey, 1985).

Companies that provide training for employees prior to departure rarely include the family in such training. Since adjustment problems often involve the family, difficulties could be avoided in many cases by including family members in predeparture training.

PUBLIC AND PRIVATE SELF

People in various cultures differ with respect to how much of the inner self is shared with others. A way of looking at a person's inner world is through the **Johari Window**, which includes "panes" that represent the self that is known and unknown to oneself and the self that is known and unknown to others. The Johari Window (Luft, 1984), named for its creators, **Jo**seph and **Harring**ton, is shown in Figure 9.2.

The first window pane is information that is shared; it includes what is known both to oneself and to others. This information may be limited to a few facts that the person chooses to share, such as occupation or telephone number, or it may include numerous facts and opinions that are shared with a large audience. The second pane represents what is known to others but not to one-

FIGURE 9.2   The Johari Window.

(Reprinted from *Group Processes: An Introduction to Group Dynamics* by Joseph Luft, by permission of Mayfield Publishing Company. Copyright © 1963, 1970, 1984 by Joseph Luft.)

	Things I Know	Things I Don't Know
Things Others Know	Arena	Blind Spot
Things Others Don't Know	Hidden	Unknown

self; it represents the person's blind area. This may include motives that others are able to discern but that the person cannot see. The third pane represents what is known to oneself but is unknown to others. Things that a person chooses to keep from others may range from a past indiscretion to aspects of one's family life, such as marital status, that the person does not wish to disclose. The fourth pane is that aspect of one's inner self that is unknown both to others and to oneself. This may be information that is deeply embedded in the subconscious to the extent that neither the person nor others know of its existence.

The major dimensions of the Johari Window, what is known to self and to others, can be translated into one's public self and private self. The public self may include information about work, family, interests, or opinions on political and social issues. In some cultures, such as the Japanese, the public self is relatively small, while the private self is relatively large. People of the United States use a style of communication that includes a larger public self with the private self being relatively small. U.S. citizens readily express their opinions and reveal their attitudes and feelings to a larger extent than do persons from the Asian culture. U.S. people use a variety of communication channels, including greater verbalization and greater use of nonverbal communication, such as touch. They conceal less than the Japanese and communicate on a wide range of topics. The Japanese offer fewer opinions and feelings and have fewer physical contacts. People of the United States have less rigid boundaries between the public and private selves; they use more spontaneous forms of communication and fewer ritualized ones. Because of this larger public self, U.S. Americans are sometimes criticized by persons of other cultures as being too outgoing and friendly, too explicit, and too analytical (Barnlund, 1975).

Obstacles to effective communication may be overcome to some degree by becoming knowledgeable about the communication styles of other cultures and by compromising between the two styles. When communicating with the Japanese, for example, U.S. Americans should avoid prying questions, observe formalities and rituals, respect the use of silence, maintain harmony, and understand that evasiveness is a natural part of their communication process.

Cultural shock is a reality that must be addressed by firms doing business abroad. The subject must be openly explained and understood. By admitting the existence of cultural shock and explaining how it may affect individuals, the shock loses some of its intensity, and adapting to the new culture is less traumatic.

The length of cultural shock/reentry shock will depend on such factors as personal resiliency, the length of the assignment, and the effort you put forth prior to departure to learn about the host culture.

Exercise 9.1
Cultural Shock

Instructions: Circle the appropriate number to indicate the types and degree of cultural shock (either positive or negative) you experienced when entering a foreign culture or a subculture of the United States.

Type of Cultural Shock	High Degree			Low Degree		None
1. Attitudes toward time	5	4	3	2	1	0
2. Attitudes toward women	5	4	3	2	1	0
3. Gestures, eye contact, and other nonverbal messages	5	4	3	2	1	0
4. Climate	5	4	3	2	1	0
5. Clothing/business dress	5	4	3	2	1	0
6. Customs, traditions, and beliefs	5	4	3	2	1	0
7. Educational system	5	4	3	2	1	0
8. Family and marriage practices	5	4	3	2	1	0
9. Financial problems	5	4	3	2	1	0
10. Food and diet	5	4	3	2	1	0
11. Housing	5	4	3	2	1	0
12. Lack of modern conveniences	5	4	3	2	1	0
13. Social class/poverty–wealth extremes	5	4	3	2	1	0
14. Social alienation (absence of people of same culture)	5	4	3	2	1	0
15. Standards of cleanliness	5	4	3	2	1	0
16. Transportation	5	4	3	2	1	0
17. Values and ethical standards	5	4	3	2	1	0
18. Work habits and practices	5	4	3	2	1	0

Exercise 9.2

Instructions: Circle the T for true or the F for false.

1. T   F   During the second stage of cultural shock, many sojourners develop such coping behaviors as drug and alcohol abuse.

2. T   F   Cultural shock can be alleviated by careful selection of employees for overseas assignments.

3. T   F   The Platinum Rule states: "Do unto others before they do unto you."

4. T   F   The experiential learning approach to intercultural training is basically fact-oriented training.

5. T   F   Cultural stress can have both psychological and physical consequences.

6. T   F   A source of shock to foreigners is the discovery that not all U.S. citizens are well educated.

7. T   F   A source of cultural shock for many U.S. persons living abroad is the financial burden of the required higher standard of living.

8. T   F   A major factor in the early return of expatriates is family problems.

9. T   F   The Johari Window represents how you see the world.

10. T   F   Children of expatriates experience less reentry shock than do adults.

TERMS

Attribution training
Cognitive-behavior modification
    approach
Cultural shock
Experiential learning approach

Information or fact-oriented training
Interaction approach
Johari Window
Platinum Rule
Reentry shock

────────── QUESTIONS AND CASES FOR DISCUSSION ──────────

1. Explain what is meant by the term *cultural shock.*
2. Identify and discuss the stages of cultural shock.
3. How can multinational firms alleviate cultural shock?
4. Identify and describe the approaches to intercultural training offered by multinational firms.
5. Identify types of cultural stress that may confront persons who are living abroad.
6. Identify positive coping skills that may be used to alleviate stress.
7. How can social class and poverty–wealth extremes be sources of cultural shock for U.S. Americans in overseas assignments?
8. What types of financial adjustments may be associated with cultural shock?
9. Explain how the Johari Window is related to cultural shock.
10. What types of reentry problems are often encountered by persons returning to the home culture? How can reentry shock be alleviated?

Case 1   Larry was sent to Japan to represent his company and wanted to make a good impression on his Japanese hosts. He immediately asked them to call him by his first name and told several humorous stories intended to break the ice. He brought along gifts containing his company's logo and asked about the state of the Japanese economy. Larry got the impression that things were not going well and that he may have behaved inappropriately. What advice would you give him?

Case 2   Karl, his wife, and five-year-old son were completing a three-year assignment in Brazil and were scheduled to return to the United States in a month where Karl would work in the home office in Chicago. What should Karl and his family do to lessen the shock of returning to their home culture?

────────── ACTIVITIES ──────────

1. For persons who have traveled or lived in a foreign country for a time, discuss the degree of reentry shock experienced upon returning to the home country in the following areas:
   a. Reestablishing friendships
   b. Readjusting to lifestyle
   c. Readjustment to job
   d. Change in social life
   e. Change in standard of living

2. Assume that you have just been made manager of your company's plants in Egypt. Prepare a list of the types of cultural shock you would expect to encounter.

3. After a year in Kenya, you are being returned to your U.S. office. List the types of reentry shock you would expect to experience.

4. You are reviewing applications of persons in your firm who have expressed an interest in an overseas assignment. List the special qualifications you would look for in deciding which three to interview.

5. Conduct a library search to determine what training films or materials are available for predeparture intercultural training of businesspersons.

REFERENCES

Althen, G. (1988). *American ways*. Yarmouth, ME: Intercultural Press, Inc.

Barnlund, D. C. (1975). *Public and private self in Japan and the United States*. Yarmouth, ME: Intercultural Press, Inc.

Bird, A., & Dunbar, R. (1991, Spring). Getting the job done over there: Improving expatriate productivity. *National Productivity Review*, pp. 145–156.

Brislin, R. W. (1981). *Cross-cultural encounters: Face-to-face interaction*. New York: Pergamon.

Broome, B. J. (1991). Building shared meaning: Implications of a relational approach to empathy for teaching intercultural communication. *Communication Education, 40*(7), 236–249.

Chaney, L. H., & Martin, J. S. (1993, October). *Cultural shock: An intercultural communication problem*. Paper presented at the Annual Convention of the Association for Business Communication, Montréal, Quebec, Canada.

Clague, L., & Krupp, N. B. (1980, Spring). International personnel: The repatriation problem. *The Bridge*, pp. 11–14.

Dodd, C. H. (1987). *Dynamics of intercultural communication*. Dubuque, IA: Wm. C. Brown Publishers.

Dodd, C. H., & Montalvo, F. F. (Eds.). (1987). *Intercultural skills for multicultural societies* (pp. 70–80). Washington, DC: Sietar International.

Engholm, C. (1991). *When business East meets business West*. New York: John Wiley & Sons, Inc.

Ferraro, G. P. (1990). *The cultural dimension of international business*. Englewood Cliffs, NJ: Prentice Hall.

Fussell, P. (1983). *Class*. New York: Ballantine Books.

Geber, B. (1992, July). The care and breeding of global managers. *Training*, pp. 33–37.

Harris, P. R., & Moran, R. T. (1991). *Managing cultural differences*. Houston: Gulf Publishing Company.

Harvey, M. G. (1985, Spring). The executive family: An overlooked variable in international assignments. *Columbia Journal of World Business*, pp. 84–92.

Khols, R. L. (1984). *Survival kit for overseas living*. Yarmouth, ME: Intercultural Press, Inc.

Klopf, D. W. (1991). *Intercultural encounters*. Englewood, CO: Morton Publishing Company.

Krapels, R. H. (1993). *Predeparture intercultural communication preparation provided international business managers and professionals and perceived characteristics of intercultural training needs*. Doctoral dissertation, Memphis State University, Memphis, TN.

Lewis, T. J., & Jungman, R. E. (Eds.). (1986). *On being foreign; culture shock in short fiction*. Yarmouth, ME: Intercultural Press.

Luft, J. (1984). *Group processes: An introduction to group dynamics*. Palo Alto, CA: Mayfield Publishing Company.

McEnery, J., & DesHarnais, G. (1990, April). Culture shock. *Training and Development Journal*, pp. 43–47.

Tung, R. (1981, Spring). Selection and training of personnel for overseas assignments. *Columbia Journal of World Business*, pp. 68–78.

10

Intercultural Negotiation Process

OBJECTIVES

Upon completion of this chapter, you will:

- be able to define the intercultural negotiation process.

- be able to distinguish between negotiation models.

- understand different cultural conflict perspectives.

- understand conflict resolution in intercultural negotiations.

- be able to decide if alternatives to negotiation are justified.

The increasing globalization of industries will necessitate an increase in strategic alliances and hence intercultural negotiations. **Intercultural negotiation** involves discussions of common and conflicting interests between persons of different cultural backgrounds who work to reach an agreement of mutual benefit (Moran & Stripp, 1991). Some of the reasons global joint ventures and strategic alliances are on the increase include economic deregulation, rapid technological changes, large capital requirements, government-supported industries, economic maturation, and improved communications.

CHARACTERISTICS OF EFFECTIVE NEGOTIATORS

Effective negotiators are observant, patient, adaptable, and good listeners. They appreciate the humor in a situation but are careful to use humor only when appropriate. Good negotiators are mentally sharp; they think before they speak; and they are careful to speak in an agreeable, civil manner. They do their homework on the countries with which they are negotiating and become knowledgeable about their history, customs, values, and beliefs. Effective negotiators know that in many cultures history is revered, and displaying a knowledge of the country's past can do much to pave the way to smooth negotiations. Good negotiators praise what is praiseworthy and refrain from criticizing anything about the negotiators or their countries. They keep their promises and always negotiate in good faith (Moran & Stripp, 1991).

Negotiators, however, cannot escape their own cultural mindset. Even professional training cannot erase the deep-seated perceptions from childhood (Cohen, 1991). These perceptions must not be vocalized, though, because nothing is to be gained by denouncing the behavior or customs of others simply because they do not fit your cultural mindset. Since such factors as social skills, gender, age, experience in intercultural relations, and background may be important in a specific culture, considering these factors when selecting negotiators is recommended.

CROSS-CULTURAL NEGOTIATION CONSIDERATIONS

Fisher (1980) identifies five considerations that should be addressed before negotiating with persons from another culture: the players and the situation, decision-making styles, national character, cultural noise, and use of interpreters and translators.

The Players and the Situation

According to Fisher (1980), you should find out how negotiators and negotiating teams are selected. Try to determine something of the background of the players to anticipate the opponent's behavior. Determine the expectations of the other negotiators, their negotiating style, and the role they have played in past negotiations. Attempt to provide an environment that is free of tension and conducive to an exchange of ideas and problem resolution.

Decision-Making Styles

The way members of the negotiating team reach a decision, as well as individual negotiating styles, must be taken into consideration. Although negotiators usually reflect the mindset of their particular culture, this may not always be the case. For example, negotiators from the United States are by nature very individualistic; their attitude on making a decision on exports would be "anything is permitted unless it is restricted by the state." In another culture the attitude might be "nothing is permitted unless it is initiated by the state" (Vernon, 1974).

National Character

According to Fisher (1980, p. 37), "patterns of personality do exist for groups that share a common culture." The question then becomes: How much does this idea of national character affect the negotiation process? The answer is: a great deal. As has been mentioned in earlier chapters, people of the United States value time; punctuality is very important. They also believe they determine their fate to a large degree. The people of the Latin American countries, on the other hand, are less concerned with time and stoically accept their fate. While numerous other differences exist between the values of the two cultures, these two attitudes could hamper negotiations considerably, regardless of the attractiveness of the terms offered.

Cultural Noise

Cultural noise includes anything that would distract or interfere with the message being communicated. Nonverbal messages, such as body language, space, and gift giving, can impede or expedite negotiations. Here is an example of cultural noise or "getting off on the wrong foot": when introducing the Japanese to its airline and new air routes between the two countries, a U.S. airline invited a group of Japanese corporate executive officers to a reception that included a tour of its planes; one of the gifts presented to each visitor was a white chrysanthemum boutonniere (that flower is associated with death in the Japanese culture).

Use of Interpreters and Translators

Using interpreters and translators can affect the negotiation process both positively and negatively. On the positive side, you have more time to think about your next statement while your previous statement is being translated. Because of the time it takes to translate, you are also more careful to state the message succinctly. On the negative side, since language and culture are intertwined, translators may not convey the intended message because of the nuances of the languages involved. Additional suggestions for using interpreters and translators were given in Chapter 6.

VARIABLES AFFECTING INTERCULTURAL NEGOTIATION

According to Moran and Stripp (1991, p. 92), four components, divided into 12 variables, affect the outcome of intercultural negotiations*:

1. Policy	—Basic Concept of Negotiation
	—Selection of Negotiators
	—Role of Individual Aspirations
	—Concern with Protocol
	—Significance of Type of Issue
2. Interaction	—Complexity of Languagae
	—Nature of Persuasive Argument
	—Value of Time
3. Deliberation	—Bases of Trust
	—Risk-Taking Propensity
	—Internal Decision-Making Systems
4. Outcome	—Form of Satisfactory Agreement

Utilizing these 12 variables can help negotiators develop a profile of their counterpart's philosophy that will be useful in the negotiation process.
For negotiations to proceed expeditiously, examining the negotiation process, which involves defining, observing, analyzing, and evaluating what happens between negotiators, is important.

DEFINING THE PROCESS

In defining the negotiation process, you will choose where the meeting will be held. If a meeting is held on your turf, you of course have more power; but you

---

also have more responsibility for seeing to your opponent's comforts. If the meeting is held on your opponent's turf, he or she has the power and responsibilities. If it is held at a neutral location, you are each responsible for your own comforts. In intercultural negotiations you also need to consider the differences in tactics, strategies, power, social expectations, conflict perspectives, and conflict resolution that may be used during the negotiation by your opponents.

Distinguishing the opponents' interests in the negotiation from the issues on which positions are taken is important. Issues are points of conflict (Sebenius, 1992).

OBSERVING, ANALYZING, AND EVALUATING

As negotiations proceed, you will have to be very observant of changes from your initial expectations, carefully analyze the differences, and adapt your negotiation strategy accordingly. Constant evaluation of verbal, nonverbal, and group interaction will be necessary if you are to negotiate from the best position possible.

In order for negotiations to be successful, they must allow for both parties to gain something—a win–win situation—though the parties probably will not gain equally.

Analysis involves defining the problem by separating and subjectively assessing probabilities, values, risk attitudes, time preferences, structuring and sequencing of the opponents' choices, and the unknown (Sebenius, 1992). In addition, the people who are involved in the negotiation, their style of negotiating, the national culture, the differences in the two cultures, and the interpreters and translators need to be analyzed and evaluated. The developmental process of observing, analyzing, and evaluating is completed for each of the following eight steps in negotiation (Moran & Stripp, 1991):

1. Physical location of the negotiations
2. Agenda or issues in the negotiation
3. Preliminary statements and limitations
4. Solution of some issues and identification of the issues of no agreement
5. Preliminaries to final negotiations
6. Final negotiations
7. Contract or confirmation of agreement
8. Implementation of the agreement

Intercultural negotiation assumes the parties are from different cultures and because of this may not share the same values, beliefs, needs, and thought patterns. During the interaction periods of the negotiation, the values, beliefs, needs, and thought patterns that are not shared by both groups can cause many unanticipated problems. As a negotiator, one needs to become adept, through continual observation, analysis, and evaluation, at catching the problems and adapting the negotiation strategy accordingly. The following list shows factors that must be considered when negotiating interculturally (Casse & Deol, 1991, pp. 3–4).

Negotiation is...	*Intercultural implications*
• A situation	• Appreciation of cultural differences is essential in cross-cultural situations
• Mutual understanding	• A conscious endeavor to manage cultural differences is required
• Communication	• Both parties must be in a position to communicate clearly and overcome cultural barriers to effective communication
• Need satisfaction	• Ascertain expectations and then work for their achievement
• Compromise or settlement	• Narrow down differences and emphasize commonalities of interest
• A deal	• Both written and unwritten aspects of negotiation are important
• A bargaining process	• Prepare to give and take
• Anticipation	• Familiarize yourself with management styles and assumptions of others to anticipate their moves
• Persuasion	• Establish your credibility, be soft while not losing your grip on the problem
• Achieving consensus	• Reduce differences to reach an agreement
• Practicing empathy	• Appreciate problems and limitations of your "opponents"
• Searching for alternatives	• Be systematic and simple (don't try to impress with complex models)
• Conflict management	• It is possible to manage conflicting interests
• Winning	• It can create problems and generate bad feelings

- A means of getting what you want from others
- Gaining the favor of people from whom you want things manner
- Managing power and information

- Time and opportunity management

- More of an art than a science

- Selling
- Least troublesome method of settling disputes

- It also means giving what others expect of you
- It is easier gaining favors when acting in a genuine and rational
- Know in advance the limitations of your power; gain information while managing the process of negotiation
- Timely actions based on opportunity analysis provide the needed edge in highly competitive situations
- Be natural; don't play on others' sensibilities
- Create the need first
- Use of intercultural negotiating styles, modes, and skills is important

INTERCULTURAL NEGOTIATION MODELS

The model you choose to use when negotiating interculturally will depend on the people you are negotiating with as well as your own personal biases. Since research has shown that social, cultural, political, and legal issues; timing of delivery; payment; terms of payment; role of consultants; and authority to make binding decisions take up most of the negotiation time, researching a particular company and culture could greatly reduce the time spent in negotiation (Ghauri, 1983).

People tend to negotiate interculturally as they do intraculturally unless they realize they need to adapt to another culture. The effect of culture in intercultural negotiation is one of relative, not absolute, values. The negotiations will proceed as smoothly as the abilities of all participants to be empathetic and to adapt to each other's cultural constraints. For example, Russian negotiating tactics include a need for authority, a need to avoid risk, and a need to control. Negotiating style is not neutral; it is culturally based and somewhat subconscious. A clash of negotiating styles can lead to a breakdown in the negotiation (Cohen, 1991).

Socio-Psychological Model

The **socio-psychological model** has five parts: the goals the parties want to reach, the communication and actions leading to the negotiations, the expected outcomes for each, the preexisting relationship and cultural factors of both parties, and the conditions under which the negotiations are conducted. The model assumes a certain amount of ethnocentrism due to the fact that the national character of the negotiators cannot be overcome and may lead to certain negative interpretations being made incorrectly by each side (Ghauri, 1983).

Principles Model

The **principles model**, also known as the *comparative model*, has two assumptions with four parts. The assumptions are that the negotiators are problem solvers and that the negotiators share a goal that they wish to reach efficiently and amicably. The four parts are (1) the people are separate from the problem, (2) the focus is on interests, (3) the options have mutual gains, and (4) the criteria used to judge the gains are objective. The model assumes both parties would prefer to negotiate in this manner and there would be no use of power or other negative tactics; the long-term relationship would be stressed because this negotiation model does not give enough attention to the power/dependence characteristic in negotiations. The model assumes the negotiators have knowledge of each other's behaviors. (Ghauri, 1983).

Directional Model

The **directional model** is based on the prediction that tough or soft moves will be followed by similar moves by the other negotiating party. The parties using this model have fallen into a pattern of reciprocal moves from which they do not seem to be able to escape. The directional model has been used extensively in the past in intercultural negotiations when foreign buyers had few alternatives and U.S.-made products sold themselves even though they may not have entirely met the needs of the users (Ghauri, 1983).

Interaction Model

The **interaction model** includes four aspects: environment, atmosphere, parties, and process. The environment includes political, social, and cultural variables that regulate the negotiation process. Atmosphere includes distance (the space between their positions that will need to be bridged), conflict, cooperation, power, dependence, and expectations. The corporate and national cultures of the parties to the negotiations affect the negotiations. The process includes the history and preconceived ideas of the negotiators (Ghauri, 1983).

Package Deal Model

The **package deal model** has four parts: background factors, process, atmosphere, and outcome. Background factors include the objectives, environment, market position, third parties, culture, and negotiators. The process includes time, issues, and contacts. Atmosphere includes cooperation/conflict, distance power/dependence, and expectations. Outcome allows for win–win, lose–lose, or continued negotiations. The model includes cultural factors and background research before beginning the negotiation process (Ghauri, 1983).

PERSPECTIVE CONFLICTS

Being able to identify the conflict in which you are involved is important. Issues form out of substantive and relationship-based differences. The substantive issues include use and control of resources. The relationship-based issues center on the long-term friendship or partnership, and it is important that negotiations be conducted in such a way as to protect future relations.

The conflict may be seen from both negotiators' points of view or may only be seen by one of the negotiators. The conflict may involve a deadlock, behavior difference, lack of a common goal, communication problems, poor translators, misunderstandings, secrets, lack of feedback, or unfamiliar tactics. Some of these factors may be due the negotiators' perceptions of reality and their unconscious ability to block out information that is inconsistent with their cultural beliefs. Negotiation breakdown or deadlock may be identified by the negotiators' repeating themselves by using the same arguments; the negotiators may not be saying anything (allowing the passage of time), or non-negotiation tactics may be used to try to change the attitudes of the other side (Fells, 1989).

Cognitive dissonance, logic and reasoning differences normally due to cultural differences, is often the focus of such conflicts because your perspectives are based upon your cultural training, and your oppositions' perspectives are based on their cultural training. Cognitive dissonance may generate the following emotions and actions: frustration, regression, fixation, resignation, repression, projection, and aggression (Cohen, 1991). If you are aware of the possible cultural shocks before entering negotiations with individuals from another culture, it will be easier to adapt your negotiation style to accommodate both your own and others' ethnocentrism and maintain your patience while dealing with the differences. Part of negotiation is being able to figure out what is going on mentally with the negotiators on the other side of the table. By studying the psychological predisposition of the other culture and your own culture, you will be familiar with at least some of the variations between the two cultures. Communicating adequately is difficult when the cultural programming of the negotiators differs. Normally within a culture there is an internal consistency to the beliefs and values of that culture when negotiating intraculturally. In intercultural negotiation, people need to be cognizant of not projecting their own cultural thinking onto the other side. Be sure to discuss everything and not attribute motives to the other side that may in fact be nonexistent. The conceptualization of information, how the information is used, and how causes and effects are associated do change from culture to culture.

Interpreters and translators, if not well versed in both cultures, may, unintentionally (though well intended), translate your communications inaccurately. Care should be exercised in selecting interpreters and translators so that they enhance rather than impede the negotiation process (Cohen, 1991).

Because lifestyles within cultures vary, so does the vocabulary that develops to explain the culture. When cultures are extremely different, the words that develop will also be different. The subjective meaning of the translation can be very important. The United States is an individual-oriented society; however, the Japanese equivalent of the word for individual has a negative connotation because the Japanese are a group-oriented culture. Education in the United States means academic achievement and is associated with school attendance; however, in the Spanish language, education includes being polite, well-bred, and sensitive as well as school attendance and academic achievement. The idea of "fair play" is an example of a concept that does not exist in any other language yet is used in U.S. business, sports, and other aspects of life all the time. Since fair play is a culturally bound phrase, other cultures cannot be expected to understand its meaning. Gestures, tone of voice, and cadence further complicate the translation situation (Cohen, 1991).

CONFLICT RESOLUTION

Negotiator selection is an important aspect of conflict resolution. Negotiators should be chosen because their background (technical or social), emotional makeup, values, and viewpoints are the best for the negotiations that are going to take place. Some important areas to be considered are gender, age, political affiliation, social class, cooperativeness, authoritarianism, and risk-taking propensity. Evaluating the negotiators from the other side as to why they were chosen will be helpful in selecting or adapting your strategy (Cohen, 1991).

Evaluating yourself as an intercultural negotiator within the constraints of the situation is important. Be sure you clearly perceive your objectives, know the facts, and have chosen your strategies and tactics carefully. Negotiation is essentially communication with an encoder and a decoder. To the extent that the encoder and decoder share the same perceptions is the degree to which their communications will be sent and received as intended. Communicating successfully with someone in your own society is often difficult; when you add different cultural meanings, different experiences, and different languages, the possibility for miscommunication increases (Cohen, 1991).

In decoding and encoding messages, the careful choice of ideas, words, or descriptions is crucial to all parties drawing matching semantic assumptions. Negotiators from different cultural backgrounds cannot rely on shared experiences or word meanings. For example, the U.S. and Korean meanings for the word "corruption" are negative for both cultures. However, in the United States corruption carries a connotation of being morally wrong while for the Koreans it implies being socially unfortunate. If you consider these factors consciously as you are negotiating, then you will be better prepared to resolve the conflicts that arise (Cohen, 1991).

Learning the social system and cultural values of the other negotiators will help you identify the signs of conflict or prevent the conflict from forming. Knowing whether to develop a personal relationship, being conscious of rank and position, having an understanding of the thought patterns of other negotiators, and knowing how to develop trust are essential to successful conflict resolution. Because of culture differences, negotiators may focus on different aspects of the negotiations as being more important. A U.S. negotiator, for example, may focus on legal and financial agreements while the Mexican or Japanese negotiator may emphasize the personal relationship (Herbig & Kramer, 1991).

If you have done your homework and are still having conflicts that defy resolution, you may wish to turn to a third party, a consultant, or apologize to the other negotiators and ask them to explain what the problem seems to be. When you are in another culture, it is very important to live as its members live. Practicing cultural relativism is part of the empathy that needs to be utilized in intercultural negotiations. Judge people in a culture by their standards and realize that for their geographical, historical, and social context the cultural views are valid (Moran & Stripp, 1991).

The best way to avoid conflicts is to prepare, plan, and respect the culture with which you are negotiating before negotiations commence. Be sure you know and respect the customs of the other negotiator's culture and be careful of gestures, nuances in meanings, and taboos of the other culture. Avoid using jargon, idioms, or slang. Realize that even if you are using a bicultural interpreter, quite often equivalent concepts do not exist between different languages. Many times a picture will help with explanations; therefore, you may wish to bring photographs, drawings, overhead transparencies, samples, or anything that can assist in the other side's understanding your presentation.

According to Lewicki, Litterer, Saunders, and Minton (1993), a mediator can sometimes productively solve disputes. The first thing a mediator would do is stabilize the setting, including such things as greeting the participants, designating seating, identifying each person, stating the purpose of the mediation, and confirming his or her neutrality. After setting this stage, the mediator would get a commitment from the participants to proceed in a businesslike manner.

The second step is helping the parties to communicate in an orderly fashion. The mediator would decide who is to speak first and would provide a rationale to the group. As each participant speaks, the mediator would take notes, actively restate, be a calming influence, and focus on the issues. Then, the mediator would summarize, asking the speakers for their agreement. Next, the mediator would help the participants set priorities.

Step three would be to assist the parties to solve their disagreements. The negotiator would ask everyone to list alternative possibilities for settlement and a workable alternative, increase understanding of the alternatives, and rephrase them if necessary.

Finally, step four involves clarifying the agreement, checking to be sure both sides are in agreement and understand the terms, establishing a time for follow-up, emphasizing that the agreement belongs to the parties not the mediator, and congratulating the negotiators on their resolution.

Additional training and education in the art of intercultural negotiation will be needed for many managers and their management teams. Learning techniques, including language classes, cultural assimilator sessions, and other cultural training, are part of becoming an effective intercultural negotiator able to deal with shared decision making, outsiders' ideas, and building long-term relationships.

STEREOTYPES THAT AFFECT INTERCULTURAL NEGOTIATIONS

The way people of a culture view themselves and the way they are actually viewed by persons of other cultures often has an impact on intercultural negotiations. (A discussion of stereotypes of persons of selected cultures was included in Chapter 1.)

According to Ruch (1989, p. 37), a disparity exists between the way U.S. people think of themselves and the way they are viewed by foreigners:

U.S. Persons' Views	*Foreigners' Views of U.S. Persons*
Informal, friendly, casual	Undisciplined, too personal, familiar
Egalitarian	Insensitive to status
Direct, aggressive	Blunt, rude, oppressive
Efficient	Obsessed with time, opportunistic
Goal/achievement oriented	Promise more than they deliver
Profit oriented	Materialistic
Resourceful, ingenious	Work-oriented; deals more important than people
Individualistic, progressive	Self-absorbed, equating the "new" with "best"
Dynamic, find identity in work	Driven
Enthusiastic; prefer hard-sell	Deceptive, fearsome
Open	Weak, untrustworthy

Negotiators from the U.S. should, therefore, take into consideration this disparity in viewpoints and should make a concerted effort to change some of the negative stereotypes, such as being rude and obsessed with time, when interacting during negotiations.

Intercultural negotiators need to be selected very carefully. Because people can negotiate well in their own culture does not mean they can be successful interculturally. Intercultural negotiators need to be able to ascertain where their opposition "is coming from." The negotiator must be able to grasp the situation and be able to answer such questions as: Are the opposition's negotiators bound by their culture or do they take on some of your cultural characteristics? Being able to discern role behavior and know the proper deference is important in intercultural negotiations (Moran & Stripp, 1991).

CULTURE-SPECIFIC NEGOTIATION INFORMATION

A brief comparison of the negotiation styles of different cultures follows (Elashmawi & Harris, 1993; Ruch, 1989):

Element	U.S. Americans	Japanese	Arabians	Mexicans
Group composition	Marketing oriented	Function oriented	Committee of specialists	Friendship oriented
Number involved	2–3	4–7	4–6	2–3
Space orientation	Confrontational; competitive	Display harmonious relationship	Status	Close, friendly
Establishing rapport	Short period; direct to task	Longer period; until harmony	Long period; until trusted	Longer period; discuss family
Exchange of information	Documented; step-by-step; multimedia	Extensive; concentrate on receiving side	Less emphasis on technology, more on relationship	Less emphasis on technology, more on relationship
Persuasion tools	Time pressure; loss of saving/ making money	Maintain relationship references; intergroup connections	Go-between; hospitality	Emphasis on family and on social concerns, goodwill measured in generations

Element	U.S. Americans	Japanese	Arabians	Mexicans
Use of language	Open/direct; sense of urgency	Indirect; appreciative; cooperative	Flattery; emotional; religious	Respectful; graciousness
First offer	Fair +/− 5 to 10%	+/− 10 to 20%	+/− 20 to 50%	Fair
Second offer	Add to package; sweeten the deal	−5%	-10%	Add and incentive
Final offer package	Total package	Makes no further concessions	−25%	Total
Decision-making process	Top management team	Collective	Team makes recommendation	Senior manager and secretary
Decision maker	Top management team	Middle line with team consensus	Senior manager	Senior manager
Risk taking	Calculated; personal responsibility	Low group responsibility	Religion based	Personally responsible

The following summary of the negotiating styles of the United States and other selected countries is not intended to be all inclusive. Individual differences exist in other cultures just as they do in the U.S. culture.

United States

According to Graham and Herberger (1983), the following statements are characteristic of the U.S. style of negotiating:

- "I can handle this by myself" (to express individualism).
- "Please call me Steve" (to make people feel relaxed by being informal).
- "Pardon my French" (to excuse profanity).

- "Let's get to the point" (to speed up decisions).
- "Speak up; what do you think?" (to avoid silence).
- "Let's put our cards on the table" (to convey the expectation of honesty).
- "A deal is a deal" (to indicate an expectation that the agreement will be honored).

In addition, Ruch (1989) emphasized that the space requirements in the United States have a direct bearing on negotiations. Entering the intimate space (up to 18 inches) of a person from the United States causes great discomfort. Another consideration when negotiating with people of the United States is related to their attitude toward saving face. Since people of the United States are not as concerned with saving face as people of other cultures, they may be quick with "constructive criticism" that may be a source of humiliation or discomfort for persons in other cultures.

Canada

Recently, a large group of Hong Kong businesspeople immigrated to Canada in fear of the takeover of Hong Kong by the People's Republic of China; this move has introduced another culture into the country (Harris & Moran, 1991). Canada is a bilingual country with French as the primary language in the province of Quebec and English in the other provinces. The English spoken is closer to British English than U.S. English. Canadians appear to be open and friendly, yet they are reserved, conservative, and very formal. They are also patriotic and lawful and observe strict rules of etiquette. Canadians are not and do not like being considered the same as U.S. people or that their country is part of the United States. Canadians tend to be individualistic and speak a mixture of British/Scottish English. Respect the fact that the Canadians are proud of their heritage and that they did not fight for independence from England. Otherwise, negotiation practices are similar to those in the United States.

China

The Chinese have the largest population in the world. The Chinese are reserved and known for their hospitality and good manners. China has been very ethnocentric due to its chosen isolation behind the Great Wall for some 2,300 years. Westerners have had difficulty doing business with the Chinese because of a lack of understanding of the Chinese culture. The Chinese believe they are the center of human civilization and as such should be revered. Protocol that should be followed during the negotiation process would include giving small, inexpensive presents. As the Chinese do not like to be touched, a short bow and brief handshake will be used during introductions. Last names are used in conversation and printed first when written. Business cards may or may not be used by the Chinese. Alcoholic beverages are not consumed during meals until the host proposes a toast; the guest should toast the other people at the table throughout the meal. In China it is proper for the guest of honor to leave first; this should be shortly after the meal is finished. The Chinese consider mutual relationships and trust very important. Therefore, in the beginning time will be spent enjoying tea and social talk. However, they are some of the toughest negotiators in the world. Technical competence of the negotiators is necessary, and a noncondescending attitude is important because the Chinese research their opponents thoroughly to gain a competitive advantage during negotiation. Nothing is final until it is signed; they prefer to use an intermediary. The Chinese delegation will be large. They rarely use lawyers, and interpreters may have inadequate language skills and experience. While Chinese negotiators imply that there is no compromise or third choice, in reality there is ample room for compromise (Axtell, 1993; Cohen, 1991; Moran & Stripp, 1991).

England

The English consider British English superior to U.S. English. English negotiators reflect their cultural characteristics; they are very formal and polite and place great importance on proper protocol. They are also concerned with proper etiquette. However, the English are not as casual and fast to make friends as U.S. persons are nor is this considered necessary for conducting any business in England. The English can be tough and ruthless; they excel at intelligence gathering and political blackmail. Because they sometimes appear quaint and eccentric, negotiators from other cultures may underestimate their skill. As U.S. law is based on English law, understanding the meaning of a British contract is relatively easy (Cohen, 1991; Harris & Moran, 1991).

France

France was the largest country in Western Europe until the reunification of Germany. Needless to say, this change has not added to French self-esteem. The French expect everyone to behave as they do when doing business, including speaking their language. They are very much individualists and have a sense of pride that is sometimes interpreted as supremacy. The French enjoy conversation for the sake of conversation, but they are also very pragmatic about details of the proposed agreement during negotiations. During conversations, keep in mind that the French are world leaders in fashion, art, literature, cuisine, and diplomacy. The French follow their own logic, referred to as "Cartesian" logic, when negotiating. Their logic is based on principles previously established; it proceeds from what is known, in point-by-point fashion, until agreement is reached.

Protocol, manners, status, education, family, and individual accomplishments are keys to success when dealing with the French (Moran & Stripp,

1991). Trust has to be earned; they are impressed by results. The French prefer detailed, firm contracts.

Germany

With the dismantling of the Berlin Wall in late 1989, there is now one unified Germany. In business, Germans are typically group oriented; however, as people they are rather individualistic.

Protocol is important and formal. Dress is conservative; correct posture and manners are required. Germans tend to use a handshake at the beginning and end of meetings. Remember to use titles when addressing members of the negotiating team and to use *please* and *thank you* freely. Since Germans believe friendships and personal relationships can complicate negotiations, they prefer to keep a distance between themselves and the other team of negotiators. German is the official language of Germany; however, most Germans speak several languages.

Since Germans tend to be detail oriented, having technical people as part of the negotiation team is important. Being punctual is expected. Contracts are firm guidelines to be followed exactly. The society is quite paternalistic. Corporate decisions are made at the top but with a great deal of detail from workers. Quality is important, and decisions are pondered and carefully scrutinized to be sure such quality exists in any projects they undertake. To a U.S. person, Germans may seem pessimistic due to their ability to entertain every perceivable negative point possible. Once they accept a project, however, they give 100 percent to its successful implementation (Moran & Stripp, 1991).

India

India is the second most populous country and tenth most industrialized country in the world. India has been influenced by Britain, which ruled India until 1947. While the educated people speak English, Hindi is spoken by 30 percent of the population. Besides English and Hindi, there are 14 other Indian languages. Indians are family oriented and religious.

Business is conducted in a formal yet relaxed manner. Bribery is common, and having connections is important. Remember to avoid using the left hand in greetings and eating; request permission before smoking, entering, or sitting (Moran & Stripp, 1991). Building relationships is important; an introduction is necessary. Use titles to convey respect. A knowledge of local affairs is considered important to people of India.

Intermediaries are commonly used. Since people of India place importance on building relationships, the negotiation process can be rather long by U.S. standards. Indian management is paternalistic toward subordinates. Due to status differences, group orientations are generally not used by the Indians. Indians, in an effort to maintain harmony, may tell the other party what it would like to hear. People of India do not approve of displays of emotion, and negotiators must use patience and allow the Indians to take the lead in the negotiations (Moran & Stripp, 1991).

Japan

The Japanese people are the most homogeneous culture on the globe and consider themselves to be very ethnocentric. The Japanese business culture is very different from that in the United States. The Japanese wish to maintain harmony and group consensus in all aspects of business. The importance of the individual has been suppressed; however, signs that this may be changing in Japan include the position women are taking in business and the trend toward changing jobs between companies rather than staying with one company for a lifetime.

Business etiquette is extremely important in Japan. A business meeting should be arranged by an intermediary who has a relationship with both parties. Negotiating parties normally consist of five people. Business cards are exchanged ritualistically at the first formal meeting. The business cards should be printed in Japanese on one side and English on the other side. The Japanese are addressed by their titles or last names. Last names are printed in front of first names unless they have westernized their cards. The senior negotiator sits in the middle of the team on one side of the table, and the other negotiating team sits on the other side of the table.

Social meetings are important to building a relationship of trust and friendship. Eventually the real negotiations will go on behind the scenes at such social meetings, allowing everyone to retain face in the formal negotiation meetings. The development of a relationship based on trust is important to good business negotiations. Completing a deal quickly is not important to the Japanese. Unless the U.S. negotiators view the negotiations as part of a long-term commitment, the Japanese are not interested in negotiating or becoming involved with the U.S. company. The Japanese are interested in fairness and will offer a proposal that they believe is correct and reasonable.

The negotiating practices of the Japanese companies are based on the keiretsu systems. A **keiretsu system** is a company group formed by the principal company and the partner companies that supply parts, equipment, financial support, or distribution of the final products. In Japan, every company in the keiretsu works to provide the customer the best product for the lowest price while maintaining an acceptable return on investment. A keiretsu group is viewed as a long-term commitment (Yonekura, 1991).

Communication is very complex with the Japanese. In order to avoid having someone lose face, lose the group harmony, or disappoint another person, the Japanese use very subtle and complex verbal and nonverbal cues. You need to read between the lines in order to interpret what has been said. Although their nonverbal cues are very subtle, you will need to use more silence and less eye contact than is considered normal for U.S. Americans. Because the Japanese do not use the word "no" and have such subtle cues, ask plenty of questions in order to be sure you understand the intent of what is being communicated (March, 1989).

Silence is an important Japanese nonverbal communication and should not be interrupted. Standing at the table, slouching, doodling, crossing the legs, or other informal behavior by sellers is considered disrespectful (Engholm, 1991).

Even after a written agreement is signed, if a problem is found, the Japanese will resolve the difference through mutual agreement with the other party, as they always consider contracts flexible instruments. Since Japan has very few business lawyers by U.S. standards, the Japanese will be very suspicious of a negotiating team that includes lawyers (March, 1989).

Latin America

Latin America includes Mexico and Central and South America. The people are from Spanish, Aztec, and Mayan descent with German, Italian, Portuguese, English, African, ancient Polynesian, and Japanese influences in given geographic areas. The people are significantly different from the United States in the manner in which they conduct business. Developing a warm relationship or friendship is necessary to a successful negotiation process, which can be lengthy.

Since Latin Americans may believe that U.S. Americans have taken advantage of them, a negotiator must be careful to maintain the self-esteem of the Latins. If your trust is questionable or lost, the opportunity to negotiate will probably be lost. Relationships are important because of the need to have contacts. Since bribery is common, the contacts can help you determine who to approach in order to get the business moving. The government is very involved in business.

Latins emphasize general principles more than problem solving. A story told by a U.S. businessman illustrates the difference in approaches. The U.S. businessman was invited by a Guatemalan to supply equipment for a cereal factory the Guatemalan was planning to open in his country. The U.S. supplier focused on the financing of the purchases, the Guatemalan's credit rating, and how the Guatemalan was going to pay the supplying company. A German contractor, who eventually got the production line order, concentrated on how the production line was going to operate and meet the Guatemalan's needs. The Germans even sent a representative of the company to live on site for the first three months of production. The U.S. interest in the financial aspects of the contract was a turnoff to the Guatemalan (Axtell, 1991).

Negotiators will be chosen based on their family connections, political influence, education, and gender. Female negotiators should be in the background rather than the foreground of the negotiation. Latins are very individualistic in business; however, they are very group oriented concerning family and friends.

Social competence is paramount in Latin business. Handshaking and asking about the health and well-being of business contacts and their families are expected. In business, people are addressed by their titles and maternal and paternal surnames. Business cards are exchanged and should include the negotiator's academic degrees.

Since most agreements are consummated over lunch, suitable, informal luncheon accommodations are important. Many meetings will be held in order to allow for a personal relationship to develop. The negotiations will begin with social and personal conversation that is sensitive but formal. Numerous meetings will be the norm, and time is not seen as important. Latins are people oriented rather than task oriented. Since body language is important and different from that in the United States, research nonverbal messages of the Latins; such behavior as putting your hands in your pockets should be avoided. Another gesture that should be avoided is placing the hands on the hips, which is a sign of a challenge; hands should be on the top of the table. As you become more friendly with Latins, you may be treated more as a member of the cultural family. Latins tend to stand and sit close together when talking; they touch one another, and often place a hand on another's shoulder.

As Mexico and Central and South America cover a large geographical area, important negotiating differences exist between countries within this area. Negotiators need to find out as much specific information as possible about the particular country, company, and people with whom they will be negotiating (Harris & Moran, 1991).

Nigeria

The Nigerian people have been strongly influenced by being a tribal society, by the British, and by the Islamic and Christian religions. Although more than 250 different languages and their dialects are spoken, many Nigerians are educated in English; the official language of the country is English.

Negotiation in the form of bargaining in the marketplace is practiced by all Nigerians from childhood, and they are very skillful at it. Since they are an individualistic society, negotiations are viewed as a competitive process. Since age is equated with wisdom, it is an important criterion when selecting negotiators. Gender, cultural background, and educational credentials are also important considerations.

Tribal loyalties are very strong, and it is best not to mix tribes. Nepotism is practiced because of the responsibility to support family and tribe members. Developing a personal relationship is important to the success of the negotiations. Time is not particularly important; therefore, negotiations will take a while to complete. Titles and last names are used in business. An intermediary should make the initial introductions. Being well dressed is important, and conscious demonstration of courtesy and consideration is expected. A successful negotiation is completed when the parties reach a verbal understanding. Contracts are considered flexible; they may be oral or written. A bribe in the form of a mobilization fee may be required to expedite business (Stripp & Moran, 1991).

Russia

The former USSR is now divided into 15 republics with 130 languages although Russian is the official language. Ethnic groups include Eastern Slav, Turk, Baltic, Mongolian, and Eskimo. In 1991, the government and production facilities were decentralized.

Political and economic changes have happened rapidly. The Russians want to learn and take part in Western management practices. Currently there is a lot of opportunity for joint ventures that include industrial modernization. Russia has had no business schools. People were formerly trained as specialists (in engineering or the sciences) rather than as generalists.

Some negotiation tactics may remain the same; however, many tactics will probably change as other management practices are learned. In the past, negotiation sessions with the Russians have been long, with the Russians controlling the agenda. Russians seem to be concerned with age, rank, and protocol. Russians are addressed by their full name and tend to be somewhat formal. Like U.S. people, Russians see time as money; friendships are not crucial to business. Russians are not concerned with equality between business partners but are concerned with maximizing their own profits. Contracts are interpreted rigidly (Elashmawi & Harris, 1993; Moran & Stripp, 1991).

As Moran and Stripp (1991, p. 1) emphasize: "Negotiating on a global scale can present tremendous opportunities." Corporations can expand their markets, increase their profits and productivity, and lower their costs by negotiating globally.

TERMS

Cultural noise	Keiretsu system
Directional model	Package deal model
Interaction model	Principles model
Intercultural negotiation	Socio-psychological model

Exercise 10.1

Instructions: Circle the T for true or the F for false.

1. T   F   In intercultural negotiation the meeting location is associated with power and responsibilities.
2. T   F   Russian negotiating strategies include a need to control.
3. T   F   The socio-psychological negotiation model assumes no use of power or negative tactics.
4. T   F   The principles negotiation model assumes a certain amount of ethnocentrism.
5. T   F   The interaction negotiation model involves environment, atmosphere, parties, and process.
6. T   F   Social class is unimportant in negotiator selection.
7. T   F   Gender is important when negotiating in the Latin American countries.
8. T   F   The Japanese prefer negotiating teams, rather than a single negotiator.
9. T   F   Bribery is a common part of conducting business in India.
10. T   F   Protocol is very important when dealing with the French.

QUESTIONS AND CASES FOR DISCUSSION

1. Intercultural negotiations have many implications. Discuss how two of these implications would affect negotiations between a U.S. negotiation team and a Japanese negotiation team. Discuss how two of these implications would affect negotiations between a Japanese negotiation team and a Mexican negotiation team.
2. Explain why following the saying, "When in Rome, do as the Romans do," is appropriate to the negotiation process.
3. Are most negotiation conflicts culturally based?
4. How can you prepare for cultural shock in negotiations?
5. What are the issues you need to consider when choosing a negotiation process model?
6. List the three ways you may recognize a negotiation deadlock.

7. What does the intercultural negotiation process involve?
8. Give three reasons why global joint ventures and strategic alliances are increasing.
9. When analyzing a negotiation problem, what are the factors to consider?
10. Which negotiation model would you choose when negotiating with Canadians?

Case 1   A U.S. corporation has sent four people to meet with a group from a Russian organization. As the groups have had previous negotiations and contact, the U.S. group is hoping to go home with an agreement. The first meeting lasts 12 hours and ends in a deadlock. After agreeing to meet the next day, one of the U.S. negotiators notices the Russians leaving for an evening on the town. The next morning the meeting is a repeat of the first morning except that it is cut short so that the Russian negotiators can play golf; all agree to meet the next morning. The U.S. lead negotiator asks his company for time to wait out the Russians. Three weeks later after many repeat meetings with no concessions, the Russians begin to make concessions. What do you know of the Russian culture that could explain what happened? Did the U.S. negotiator make the right move or would pressure have made the Russians move faster?

Case 2   A U.S. salesman is in Spain negotiating a contract with a Spanish company. He has expressed to his Spanish colleagues an interest in going to a bullfight, so they invite him to one. As the first bull is released, the salesman jokingly says, "So who's going to win? I'll put my money on the bull." The Spaniards remained silent. The salesman felt very uncomfortable during the rest of the bullfight. Explain what the salesman's *faux pas* was and the negative effects it may have on his progress. If the salesman had not taken time to research bullfighting, how might he have better handled the situation?

ACTIVITIES

1. Invite three or four businesspersons who have had experience in international negotiation to serve as a panel to discuss "Negotiating with the Japanese" (or another culture of your choice).
2. Prepare a "negotiation profile" for a person who will be negotiating with representatives of a manufacturing firm in Mexico. Include verbal and nonverbal "Do's and Don'ts."
3. Select a recent book containing information on international negotiation, such as Dean Allen Foster's *Bargaining Across Borders* or Roger E. Axtell's

The Do's and Taboos of International Trade, and prepare a one-page summary of nonverbal aspects of negotiating with persons of a culture of your choice.

4. Review recent issues of a business journal or news magazine for an article related to international negotiation to be used as a basis for class discussion.

5. Prepare a list of possible problems U.S. businesswomen might encounter when negotiating with Asians.

———— **REFERENCES** ————————————————————————

Axtell, R. E. (1991). *The do's and taboos of international trade.* New York: John Wiley & Sons, Inc.

Axtell, R. E. (1993). *Do's and taboos around the world.* New York: John Wiley & Sons, Inc.

Casse, P., & Deol, S. (1991). *Managing intercultural negotiations.* Washington, DC: Sietar.

Cohen, R. (1991). *Negotiating across cultures.* Washington, DC: United States Institute of Peace Press.

Elashmawi, F., & Harris, P. (1993). *Multicultural management, new skills for global success.* Houston: Gulf Publishing Company.

Engholm, C. (1991). *When business East meets business West.* New York: John Wiley & Sons, Inc.

Fells, R. (1989). Managing deadlocks in negotiation. *Management Decision, 27*(4), 32–38.

Fisher, G. (1980). *International negotiation.* Yarmouth, ME: Intercultural Press.

Ghauri, P. N. (1983). *Negotiating international package deals.* Doctoral dissertation, Acta Universitatis Upsaliensis Studia Oeconomiae Negotiorum.

Graham, J., & Herberger, R. (1983). Negotiators abroad—Don't shoot from the hip. *Harvard Business Review, 61,* 160–169.

Harris, P. R., & Moran, R. T. (1991). *Managing cultural differences.* Houston: Gulf Publishing Company.

Herbig, P. A., and Kramer, H. E. (1991). Cross-cultural negotiations: Success through understanding. *Management Decision, 29*(8), 19–31.

Lewicki, R. J., Litterer, J. A., Saunders, D. M., & Minton, J. W. (1993). *Negotiation.* Homewood, IL: Irwin.

March, R. M. (1989). No-nos in negotiating with the Japanese. *Across the Board, 26*(4), 44–51.

Moran, R. T., & Stripp, W. G. (1991). *Dynamics of successful international business negotiations.* Houston: Gulf Publishing.

Ruch, W. V. (1989). *International handbook of corporate communication.* Jefferson, NC: McFarland & Company, Inc., Publishers.

Sebenius, J. K. (1992). Negotiation analysis: A characterization and review. *Management Science, 38*(1), 18–38.

Vernon, R. (1974). Apparatchiks and entrepreneurs: U.S.-Soviet economic relations. *Foreign Affairs, 52*(2), 249–262.

Yonekura, S. (1991). *What's the "keiretsu"?* Paper written at Hitotubashi University, Japan.

11

Intercultural Negotiation Strategies

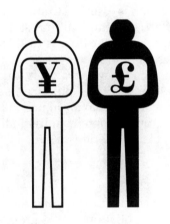

OBJECTIVES

Upon completion of this chapter, you will:

- be able to differentiate between negotiation strategies.

- understand the effects of different personal constructs.

- recognize and use successful intercultural negotiation guidelines.

- understand various trade agreements that affect intercultural negotiation.

Intercultural negotiation requires choosing the appropriate communication channels. As you learned earlier in the text, a knowledge of protocol for communicating effectively in your culture is important. When you negotiate in another culture, the protocol will probably change. Differences to consider include the chain of command, organizational decision making, nonverbal communication, the proper place to negotiate, gender of negotiators, and the effects different strategies may have on different cultures. The greater the difference between cultures, the greater the likelihood that miscommunication that could result in negative outcomes will occur.

STRATEGIES

Negotiation strategies are plans organized to achieve a desired objective. Because strategies are used to elicit desired responses, negotiations can take many forms. Predicting how the opponent will respond is essential to strategic planning. Intercultural negotiation strategies differ from intracultural styles for most cultures. U.S. Americans tend to make fewer adjustments to their opponent's behavior, and they change their negotiation strategy less than other cultures when dealing interculturally. This tendency is partially due to the fact that the world has wanted what the United States produces, so U.S. persons lacked sufficient motivation to change their behavior in negotiation encounters. Negotiation strategies include group-oriented, individual-oriented, media, and face-to-face approaches (Copeland & Griggs, 1985).

Group Oriented

Group orientation ideally results in a solution that is good for everyone, since all points of view are supposedly considered. Negotiations with group-oriented negotiators would be detail oriented in order to determine the proper solution. Your identity belongs to the group of which you are a part. The group would have to reach a consensus on any and all decisions, and this probably would not be done during the negotiation sessions. The individuals in the group would avoid making an individual decision. Individuals who are not group oriented may believe that group-oriented negotiators appear to stall, are not interested in the negotiations, and give ambiguous statements. Group-oriented cultures tend to view contracts as flexible (Hofstede, 1991).

The Japanese are the most group-oriented culture in our world due to the number of years they were physically secluded from other cultures. Although the Japanese culture is particularly different from that in the United States, Japan and the United States do have a common work ethic—hard work is applauded by both. Even though the management styles were very different originally, as joint ventures and U.S. subsidiaries of Japanese companies become part of the U.S. economy, U.S. corporations are beginning to use some of the Japanese management concepts, and both cultures are gaining an understanding of their differences and are learning to cope. Other cultures that are also group oriented are the Chinese, Polynesians, native American Indians, and Africans (Hofstede, 1991). This group approach assumes that the action taken is conservative and well thought out and that all options were considered in the decision (Foster, 1992).

Individual Oriented

If you are individually oriented, you will be concerned with the best contract for your company and may not be concerned about whether the agreement is good for the other company. If there is more than one negotiator on your team, one person will probably control the negotiations and make the final decision concerning the various issues being discussed. Usually much individual sparring has taken place with members of the other team before the negotiation meeting. The individually oriented person would tend to interpret the contract very rigidly.

The United States is probably the most individualistic culture in the world. Another individualistic culture is that of Latin Americans. According to Foster (1992), a Latin negotiation is frequently an internal contest of individual will battling for position and power. Other cultures that are also individualistic include England, France, Australia, and Canada (Hofstede, 1991).

Face-to-Face

Face-to-face strategies are concerned with negotiating in person rather than through the mail, fax, telephone, telegraph, or through lawyers or other intermediaries. People in many cultures will only negotiate on a face-to-face basis. The Japanese, in particular, do not like to make commitments over the telephone or in writing until after numerous face-to-face meetings have taken place. In many European countries, as well as India and Japan, contracts are considered an insult to the trust of the partners. They place great importance on face-to-face encounters and oral agreements (Prosser, 1985).

ROLE OF THE MEDIA

Representatives of the media—TV, radio, and newspapers—have a unique position in creating multicultural understanding and misunderstanding. Most of the views you have of other cultures have been gained through the media window. The media have been used in various ways, including supporting and tearing down political candidates and officeholders and explaining and distorting numerous messages. Media people also represent a culture and have cultural biases. The media tend to have a stereotypical view of business.

Media members have generally presented other cultures through the bias of the U.S. perceptual grid.

Advertisers make up the largest group of negotiators in the world—they all compete for consumers' dollars. Advertisers use media extensively and have learned that differences in culture necessitate different delivery and content if the ad is to successfully promote the product (Prosser, 1985).

An example of media influence in the world today is the CNN (Cable News Network) broadcasts during Operation Desert Storm. CNN coverage was watched by the antagonists and protagonists in the battle and practically everyone else in the world who had access to satellite television broadcasts. Another example of media influence is the number of teenagers worldwide who wear jeans and listen to the same music and watch the same movies. Movies are big promoters of stereotypes. Many times the wrong perception of a culture is gained from the subject matter presented in movies or a television series that is broadcast in foreign countries. Many of the stereotypes foreigners have of U.S. Americans, such as that they all carry guns, are due to movies and television series. Likewise, U.S. Americans hold views of other cultures, such as the belief that all followers of Islam do not drink alcoholic beverages, based on movie and television messages. Since perceptions of other cultures are often acquired through the media and may be brought to the negotiation table, an awareness of the media's role is important.

PERSONAL CONSTRUCTS

Personal constructs refer to individual belief systems and attitudes. The individual belief system, attitudes, or personal constructs differ from culture to culture and many times from person to person within a given culture. What you expect to happen cognitively is based on all the experiences of your life. No two people in the world have the same set of life experiences. Cultural stereotypes are dangerous even though they provide clues to the behavior of the average person in the culture.

The reason the phrase "Birds of a feather flock together" is such a powerful adage is that we like to spend time with those who are like us. This is one of the reasons people say, "They're in America; they should act like Americans." The "Americans" who make these statements, however, do not understand that they need to reciprocate and adopt certain foreign behaviors when they visit another country. Of course, without a lot of time and willingness, it would be very difficult "to do as the Romans do." However, it is possible to learn about the culture, customs, and traditions and to be sensitive to them. Everyone is ethnocentric to a great degree. Because losing ethnocentrism means changing, it is a very powerful construct. Resistance to change is a uni versal construct (Copeland & Griggs, 1985; Herbig & Kramer, 1991). Negotiations take place within the political, economic, social, and cultural systems of the countries involved; these are the environmental issues of negotiation.

The cultural systems involved in the negotiation may be similar or divergent. Negotiations take place within the context of the four Cs: common interest, conflicting interests, compromise, and criteria (Moran & Stripp, 1991).

Common interest considers the fact that both parties in the negotiation share, have, or want something that the other party has or does. Without a common goal, there would be no need for negotiation. Areas of conflicting interests would include payment, distribution, profits, contractual responsibilities, and quality. Compromise involves resolving areas of disagreement. Although a win–win negotiated settlement would be best for both parties, the compromises that are negotiated may not produce that result. The criteria include the conditions under which the negotiations take place.

Communication is plagued with misinterpretations. When perspectives, environment, the four Cs, and the negotiation situation are all considered together, the possibility of misinterpretations is magnified. For example, ethics and ethical behavior, which are always near the surface, can confound negotiations if the two cultures have very differing views on proper business ethics. For example, the Japanese consider a contract to be an adaptive tool rather than a rigid legal document as most U.S. Americans would interpret it. Nigerians, Mexicans, and the Chinese find bribes placed in the proper places help business run smoothly; such behavior is considered unethical in the United States.

If friendship and trust are important, it may be necessary to plan a number of social activities to build personal relationships before negotiations begin or a solution can be reached in the negotiations. In many cultures business is conducted with family and friends, and personal relationships are considered important for the long run. In other cultures friendships are not important to business relationships.

Environment

The environment in which the negotiations take place is particularly important for intercultural negotiations. If meetings are held at the office of one of the parties, then that party has control and responsibility as host to the other party. When negotiators are in their home territory, they are likely to be more assertive than when they are in the host's territory. Reasons for this include the fact that we have been conditioned to believe that it is rude to be impolite to someone when in his or her home or office. The host negotiators may also have a feeling of superiority since the other team is coming to them. In addition, if the negotiators have traveled a considerable distance, they will probably suffer from jet lag (Lewicki & Litterer, 1985).

One way to avoid this competitiveness is to choose a neutral site that does not belong to either side in the negotiation. The neutrality of the site eliminates the psychological advantage of the home ground.

The actual room where the negotiations will take place could be important if the room makes one of the negotiating teams feel comfortable and the other team uncomfortable. Cultural differences need to be considered when choosing the site. Things to consider include the physical arrangement of the room, the distance between people and teams, and whether the room has a formal or informal atmosphere.

Power and Authority

Power is the ability to influence others; **authority** is the power to give commands and make final decisions. With the ability to influence comes the responsibility for the action taken. Power has the ability to make people and companies dependent or independent. Power can be an advantage or a disadvantage depending on how it is used. Power must be used within the bounds of moral and ethical behavior (Lewicki & Litterer, 1985).

In order for power to be meaningful, it has to be accepted. When you accept power, you are giving it the authority to exist to the extent that it is acceptable to you. The personal constructs of the receiver of the power determine the strength of the power exerted.

An example of the use of power and authority would occur in a meeting between the Chinese, who do not believe in a time schedule for negotiations, and impatient U.S. Americans, who do have a time schedule. The Chinese would have the power of time on their side and possibly could make the U.S. Americans feel pressured to make compromises. Japanese negotiators have stated that they can make U.S. negotiators agree to concessions because they can "outwait" the impatient Americans (Figure 11.1).

FIGURE 11.1   The negotiation waiting game.

Perception

The process by which individuals ascribe meaning to their environment is strongly affected by their culture. The stress of negotiation can cause misperception; however, more often in intercultural conflicts it will be due to the verbal and nonverbal cues having different meanings in the cultures involved. An example of misinterpreted nonverbal messages would be U.S. Americans talking with their hands to clarify or exaggerate a particular point during negotiations with a German negotiating team; the Germans could incorrectly interpret the motions as spontaneous emotional displays, which are considered impolite. In addition, if a company were to send only one person to negotiate with the Japanese, they would assume the company was not serious about negotiating an agreement (Lewicki & Litterer, 1985).

Stimuli have both a physical size and a socioenvironmental meaning that can be different for each individual within and across cultures. Our experiences determine to what stimuli we are sensitive or insensitive. While it is obvious to the Japanese and U.S. people that the two cultures are very different, it may not be so obvious that U.S. people and Canadians also have many cultural differences. Sometimes the more alike we think we are can be more dangerous than knowing we are different and therefore being careful of our verbal and nonverbal behaviors.

Tactics

Tactics are maneuvers used for gaining advantage or success. Tactics used to communicate a point can be so distracting that the receiver has a distorted perception due to the attributes the receiver attaches to the tactic used. Jokes often used by people of the United States to "break the ice" are examples of such tactics. Although these work well when the negotiations are between U.S. companies, jokes generally do not translate well to other cultures. Generally, jokes are derogatory toward someone and in group-oriented cultures may be considered offensive (Moran & Stripp, 1991).

Distracting tactics can be detrimental to the negotiation process. Allowing insufficient time for the negotiations is typical of cultures that want to get right to business. By doing so, the other negotiating team may believe you really are not interested in a long-term relationship and, consequently, they are not interested in what your team may have to say.

Whether the climate during negotiations is supportive or defensive depends on how the cultures negotiating view each other. What one culture considers defensive, dominating, retaliatory, and threatening may be considered normal by the other culture. However, if a negotiator is perceived as defensive or supportive, whether or not that is the perception the negotiator wants the other team to have, the other team will respond according to its perceptions and not according to what was intended. Climate is an important area to research so that you do not read your opponents incorrectly too often. One way to avoid being defensive is to ask questions and find out what your opponent is thinking. Clarify or restate what you understand to have been said and ask if that is correct or incorrect. Try to follow the other side as it explores the issues rather than always taking the lead. Use role reversal to put yourself in the other culture's position and argue from its perspective. Role reversal helps to understand and appreciate the other side's position.

Courtesy

Courtesy that is used to allow someone to save face or clarify a misinterpretation is valued in some cultures. Knowing the correct etiquette may be more important than knowing the facts in some countries. The Japanese above all else wish to maintain harmony with everyone at all times. Therefore, the Japanese will progress very slowly through negotiations in order to be sure they completely understand what is being communicated. If you were to ask them for a direct *yes* or *no* answer, they would say *yes* because saying *no* directly in their culture is impolite. The manner in which the *yes* is stated implies whether the answer is actually *yes* or *no*. An example is when the Japanese use the word *difficult* as an answer. *Difficult* means that what you ask is not possible. Saying *no* through a mediator is much easier for the Japanese (Moran & Stripp, 1991).

Mediation

Mediation is the use of a third party to settle differences between negotiating teams to bring them to common agreement. Mediation may be the fastest road to discovering exactly what the barriers to negotiation may be. If you are dealing with members of a culture who do not like confrontation, who are afraid of losing face or causing you to lose face, using a mediator may be the best path to follow (Moran & Stripp, 1991).

Many times it will be necessary to have a common friendship, business relationship, or other contact in order to obtain an appointment for business. Even if the other negotiating team speaks your language, it is a good idea to take along your own interpreter and translator. Because languages do not translate word for word, you need to have someone you can depend on for translation quality. Remember that in many countries lawyers are not involved in the negotiation sessions, and your foreign hosts may feel intimidated or distrustful if you bring a lawyer with you (Casse & Deol, 1991).

Gender

Although women have made significant strides in the U.S. business world, there are still many parts of the world where women are not welcome in business. In some countries where you do find women, they are in support functions or are simply "window dressing" for the firm. Women are considered as equals at the negotiation table in the United States, Israel, England, France, Switzerland, and India and are beginning to gain equality in other parts of the world.

INTERCULTURAL NEGOTIATION GUIDELINES

Effective negotiators will generally be successful in their negotiation attempts, and their ideas will be feasible to implement. Skilled negotiators consider a number of alternatives, are not as concerned about the sequence of the items to be negotiated, emphasize areas of agreement, and consider the long-term consequences of their agreements.

Copeland and Griggs (1985) have developed 20 rules for intercultural negotiation.* The rules are a beginning point for negotiators; other points will probably be added with experience.

Before the Negotiation

Rule 1: Determine that the negotiation is feasible.

Rule 2: Define what you want from the negotiation.

Rule 3: Research your facts, such as culture-specific information and business style.

Rule 4: Decide on your strategy.

Rule 5: Send the proper team, including your own interpreter; if consultants are proper, include them. Do not change negotiators.

Rule 6: Allow plenty of time; do not, however, tell the other side your time table.

Beginning the Negotiation

Rule 7: Make sure the environment is correct; be familiar with the agenda, physical arrangements, and the area where the negotiations will take place.

Hard Bargaining

Rule 8: Control the information you give your opponents.

Rule 9: Watch your use of idioms, slang, and other verbal and nonverbal communication.

* From *Going International* by Lennie Copeland and Lewis Griggs. Copyright © 1985 by Lennie Copeland and Lewis Griggs. Reprinted by permission of Random House, Inc.

Rule 10: Put your thought processes on the same plane as your opponents. Remember that they are not U.S. Americans and that your persuasion techniques need to be flexible.

Rule 11: Adjust to the way of life in the host culture. Remember the well-known adage, "While in Rome, do as the Romans do."

Rule 12: Talk informally away from the pressure.

Rule 13: Remember to save face for everyone.

Rule 14: Avoid a deadlock; neither side wins and both sides lose.

Rule 15: Do not agree to a bad deal; be prepared to walk away.

Rule 16: Make sure the agreement is signed before you leave.

Rule 17: Be sure both parties understand the meaning of what they signed.

Rule 18: Be flexible in your view of what a contract is.

Beyond the Contract

Rule 19: Discuss differences and come to agreements rather than legal settlements.

Rule 20: Maintain a good relationship with the other side.
By using these guidelines, planning properly, treating people individually rather than stereotyping them, and learning from your mistakes, you will have made a good start to becoming a successful intercultural negotiator.

U.S. Americans, in particular, need to be aware of their shortcomings, which are well known to many of their opponents. To people of many cultures, people in the United States always seem to be in a hurry. It is generally known that U.S. negotiators are often in a rush and may not be as completely prepared as the other side.

During negotiation orientations, U.S. Americans need to learn to take advantage of the opportunity to learn more about the personalities of their opponents. U.S. Americans tend to rush through this stage or treat it as if it is unimportant. The orientation allows each side to gain valuable information about the opponents.

Due to the self-imposed time constraints of U.S. Americans, concessions are often made before they need to be; and many times the size of the concession is larger than would have been necessary had more time been taken. If a concession is made too soon, or too large a concession is made, the opponent is not as likely to see the concession as much of a gain. The Russians and the Chinese are very good at making such concessions work for them.

The United States also looks at negotiations from a legal point of view. Most cultures are not as concerned with the legal view but are concerned with having a good agreement and a shared perception and trusting the other side (Moran & Stripp, 1991).

Points that need to be considered in distributor agreements and can be handled ahead of time include the following, identified by Axtell (1991):

1. Effective dates of the agreement
2. Options at the end of the agreement
3. Place of jurisdiction
4. Terms of termination before agreement ends
5. Arbitration
6. Geographical boundaries of agreement
7. Degree of exclusivity
8. Description of products being distributed
9. Agreed-upon sales quotas
10. Responsibility for import duty, freight, and insurance
11. Responsibility for warehousing, inventory control, and accounting
12. Information that must be reported to the sourcing company
13. Payment currency to be used
14. Terms of payment
15. Provisions for secrecy
16. Competitive products that can or cannot be carried
17. Responsibility for warranty and repairs
18. Responsibility for advertising, merchandising, and public relations
19. Protection of patents and trademarks
20. Responsibility for drop-shipping
21. Payment provisions of commissions and bonuses
22. Responsibility for taxes
23. Responsibility for indemnifications
24. Responsibility for translation
25. Consideration of legal assignment, waivers, force majeure, notices, severability, Foreign Corrupt Practices Act
26. Responsibility for setting prices
27. Responsibility for payment of drop-shipments

Many of the preceding items would be controlled by lawyers during the negotiations between U.S. firms. However, when you are dealing interculturally and multinationally, the preceding points need to be addressed so that everyone understands both the letter and intent of the contract.

TRADE AGREEMENTS

Trade agreements are the laws under which U.S. businesses must function when exporting. All exports are controlled by the U.S. government. The two types of trade agreement licenses are general and validated. Because the general license is never actually issued, many firms do not realize they are operating under such a license. The validated license is very specific, and the Department of Commerce will assist you with the regulations that apply. The validated license allows an exporter to export specific products to specific places. To find out more about validated licenses, get a copy of *Export Administration Regulations* from the Department of Commerce.

Some other books from the Department of Commerce that will prove useful to the overseas negotiator are *Basic Guide to Exporting, Exporters' Guide to Federal Resources for Small Business, Government Periodicals and Subscription Services*, and a nongovernment magazine titled *Export Today* (write to P.O. Box 28189, Washington, DC 20038).

Free trade zones are zones of international commerce where foreign or domestic merchandise may enter without formal customs entry or custom duties. The North American Free Trade Agreement (NAFTA) is an expansion of the free trade zone (FTZ) concept as is the European Economic Community (EEC).

The **NAFTA** agreement between the United States, Canada, and Mexico was ratified in 1993 (Figure 11.2). NAFTA deals with trade in goods, technical barriers to trade, government procurement, investment, services and related matters, intellectual property, and administrative and institutional provisions. The objectives of NAFTA are to

1. Eliminate barriers to trade and facilitate cross-border movement of goods and services
2. Promote fair competition
3. Increase investment opportunities
4. Provide adequate and effective protection for intellectual property

FIGURE 11.2   Before and after NAFTA.

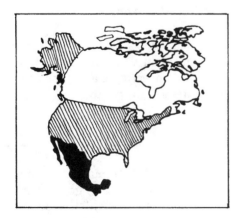 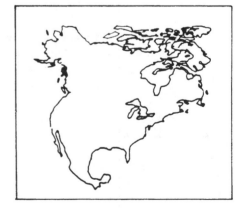

5. Develop effective procedures to handle disputes

6. Expand cooperation and increase benefits to the three countries (NAFTA, 1992).

Many different products are covered by NAFTA, and tariff implementation varies from 1993 to 2006. The EEC is still working out problems mainly due to the breakdown of the communist block countries. Other regional trade associations include one in each of the following regions: Central America, Southeast Asia, and Latin America.

The **General Agreement of Tariffs and Trade (GATT)** is a multinational trade agreement of which the United States is a member. The problem with this agreement is that all the nations with which the United States currently does business are not members. For example, China and Taiwan account for 24.3 percent of the clothing and textiles imported into the United States, yet they are not members of GATT. GATT provisions are continually being negotiated or renegotiated. Many stalemates have occurred as countries vie to protect specific industries or commodities. GATT deals with intellectual property, services, national treatment for services (members must treat other nation members equal to or better than service suppliers in their own nation), market access for services, foreign investment, antidumping, subsidies, textiles, agriculture, market access, dispute settlement, and telecommunications. Small modifications to a product can change its classification as far as tariffs are concerned.

The **European Economic Community (EEC)** is a free trade zone involving 12 countries: Belgium, Germany, France, Italy, Luxembourg, Netherlands, Denmark, Ireland, United Kingdom, Greece, Spain, and Portugal. The popularity of the EEC is expected to grow in the future. As of 1987 the number of active trade agreements entered into by the United States with other countries for specific products was 512. The trade agreements are indexed in the *UST Cumulative Index*, which is a cumulative index to the U.S. slip treaties (loose paper treaties before binding) and agreements.

The U.S. **antiboycott regulation** prohibits U.S. firms or their employees from refusing to do business with friendly nations or in any way responding to a boycott. If a company is approached to boycott a country, it is required by law to notify the Department of Commerce or be subject to large fines.

TERMS

Antiboycott regulation
Authority
European Economic Community (EEC)
Free trade zones
GATT (General Agreement of Tariffs and Trade)
Mediation

NAFTA (North American Free Trade Agreement)
Negotiation strategies
Personal constructs
Power
Tactics
Trade agreements

Exercise 11.1

Your negotiating team has just finished telling the Japanese negotiating team about the technological lead your company has on the competition and what the new technology will cost the Japanese. In response to the proposal, the Japanese say "yes" and become silent. You should

a. Take this to mean agreement and acceptance of these additional costs by the Japanese.
b. Take this as a negative response to your proposal.
c. Interpret this as neither positive nor negative.

Exercise 11.2

Instructions: Circle the T for true or the F for false.

1. T   F   Protocol changes when negotiating with another culture.

2. T   F   U.S. Americans tend to make more adjustments in their negotiation strategies than their opponents.

3. T   F   Group-oriented negotiations are generally positive for both sides.

4. T   F   Some cultures adjust more easily to negotiation differences.

5. T   F   The room environment, including the physical arrangement, distance between people and teams, and the formality of the room, is important to negotiations.

6. T   F   If the United States were to send only one person to negotiate with the Japanese, they would assume the U. S. company was serious.

7. T   F   Mediation may be the best way to find out what the negotiation barriers may be.

8. T   F   A woman can negotiate as well in Japan, Saudi Arabia, and France as she can in the United States.

9. T   F   During negotiations it is a good idea to have informal talks away from the negotiation site.

10. T   F   Trade agreements are laws that affect business functioning within the United States.

——————— **QUESTIONS AND CASES FOR DISCUSSION** ———————

1. Describe your strategy for negotiating with people whose culture believes that to win is everything. How would your strategy change if you believe that if you trust people they will take advantage of you?

2. Discuss differences in negotiating with people who are group oriented versus those who are individual oriented. Give examples of cultures that are group oriented and those that are individual oriented.

3. Explain how media affect intercultural communication. Give examples of media-induced stereotypes.

4. Explain what is meant by personal constructs and how they affect the negotiation process.

5. How can misperceptions and cultural tactics negatively affect the negotiation process?

6. Discuss how courtesy is an important element in negotiation. How do perceptions of courtesy differ in various cultures?

7. What role does mediation play in the negotiation process?

8. Explain how gender can have an impact on successful negotiation. Identify cultures in which women are treated as equals at the negotiation table and cultures in which they are not.

9. Identify guidelines to effective negotiation.

10. Describe your strategy for negotiating with people whose culture believes no one should lose face, negotiation is an ongoing process, and consensus is the only way to reach an agreement.

11. Describe your strategy for negotiating with people whose culture believes that being emotional in a negotiating setting is good, that it is not important to know facts or details, and that status is important.

12. How can the negotiation situation and environment affect the participants in the negotiation if it is held in the home country, the opponent's country, or a neutral country?

13. Identify three personal constructs you hold that would differentiate you from most of your country's people, and explain how these may confuse a negotiator who has a stereotype in his or her mind about your country's culture.

14. Would it be easier for a U.S. American to negotiate with a Canadian, Mexican, or Japanese? What support can you give for your answer?

15. Regional free trade zones are becoming popular. What are the negative and positive points of such trade zones? How will they help or hinder global organizations?

16. What is NAFTA? What is GATT? Explain their relationship to intercultural negotiation.

Case 1   Your instructor will separate the class into negotiation teams. One team is from the United States; the other team is from Mexico. You are to respond from the cultural perspective of your country (either the United States or Mexico). The U.S. corporation desires to lower its cost of production and believes it can do so by manufacturing in Mexico. However, since the U.S. firm does not have experience manufacturing in Mexico, it wishes to negotiate with Agua Manufacturing in Mexico. The management of Agua Manufacturing is eager to do the production for the U.S. corporation because it has excess capacity. The negotiations will take place in Mexico so that the U.S. representatives will be able to see and evaluate the facilities. Answer the following questions from the point of view of the Mexican negotiation team and the U.S. negotiation team. You will probably need to research the cultural background of Mexico and the United States. Remember that even if you were born and reared in the United States, it is sometimes difficult to see yourself as others see you.

   a. Explain what the negotiation perspective, environment, and negotiation situation would be.
   b. Where would you expect to find common interests, conflicting interests, and compromise? What would be the criteria for achievement?
   c. What would your negotiation strategy be? Your tactics?
   d. How important is culture in this situation?

Case 2   A U.S. American woman executive is sent to negotiate a contract with a corporation in Saudi Arabia. She dresses conservatively in a dark business suit and completes her makeup and hair as she would in the United States. She finds the Arabs to be aloof. She is asked when her boss will be arriving and is basically feeling ignored. What mistakes have been made? What can be done to correct such a situation?

Case 3   Your company has chosen to use an Export Management Company that will handle all the sales and financial transactions for your products overseas. In what way could this be an advantage, and how could it be a disadvantage? Does the size of the firm matter?

─────── **ACTIVITIES** ──────────────────────────────

   1. Write a paragraph on the role that holidays and religion might play when negotiating in Saudi Arabia.
   2. Consult a book on etiquette, such as Letitia Baldrige's New Complete Guide to Executive Manners, which contains a chapter on International

Business Manners, and write a one-page summary on the role that gift giving plays when negotiating with the Japanese.

3. Consult a book on nonverbal communication, such as Roger E. Axtell's *Gestures: The Do's and Taboos of Body Language Around the World*, and prepare a one-page summary of the role that nonverbal communication plays when negotiating with persons in a South American country of your choice.

4. From recent issues of *The Wall Street Journal* or your local newspaper, find an article related to trade agreements between the United States and another country. Make a short oral report summarizing the article.

5. Be prepared to discuss the role that bargaining plays when negotiating with persons in different cultures.

6. Underline unacceptable behavior in the following scenario:

> The ABC Corporation's negotiating team has been invited to dine with the Mexican team at a Mexican restaurant. Some of the team members do not care for Mexican food. At the restaurant, Tom is uncomfortable and hot, and before sitting down takes his jacket off and loosens his tie. He now feels comfortable and starts talking with two of the Mexican team members. As Juan refers to him as Dr. Ross, Tom stops him and tells him to please call him Tom. Tom asks the Mexican team leader if there is some way in which they can compromise over an issue discussed during the day. The first course is served. It is chicken soup with the chicken's feet in the dish. Tom winces as he sees the chicken's feet and pushes the bowl to the side.

7. The following is a self-assessment exercise you may take; the interpretation of the results follows.

Negotiation Skills Self-Assessment Exercise*

Please respond to this list of questions in terms of what you believe you do when interacting with others. Base your answers on your typical day-to-day activities. Be as frank as you can. For each statement, please enter on the Score Sheet the number corresponding to your choice of the five possible responses given below:

1. If you have never (or very rarely) observed yourself doing what is described in the statement.

2. If you have observed yourself doing what is described in the statement occa-

*Adapted by Pierre Casse from Interactive Style Questionnaire Situation Management Systems, Inc., in Training for the Cross-Cultural Mind, SIETAR, Washington, DC, 1979.

sionally, but infrequently: that is, less often than most other people who are involved in similar situations.

3. If you have observed yourself doing what is described in the statement about an average amount: that is, about as often as most other people who are involved in similar situations.

4. If you have observed yourself doing what is described in the statement fairly frequently: that is, somewhat more often than most other people who are involved in similar situations.

5. If you have observed yourself doing what is described in the statement very frequently: that is, considerably more than most other people who are involved in similar situations.

Please answer each question.

1. I focus on the entire situation or problem.
2. I evaluate the facts according to a set of personal values.
3. I am relatively unemotional.
4. I think that the facts speak for themselves in most situations.
5. I enjoy working on new problems.
6. I focus on what is going on between people when interacting.
7. I tend to analyze things very carefully.
8. I am neutral when arguing.
9. I work in bursts of energy with slack periods in between.
10. I am sensitive to other people's needs and feelings.
11. I hurt people's feelings without knowing it.
12. I am good at keeping track of what has been said in a discussion.
13. I put two and two together quickly.
14. I look for common ground and compromise.
15. I use logic to solve problems.
16. I know most of the details when discussing an issue.
17. I follow my inspirations of the moment.
18. I take strong stands on matters of principle.
19. I am good at using a step-by-step approach.
20. I clarify information for others.
21. I get my facts a bit wrong.
22. I try to please people.
23. I am very systematic when making a point.
24. I relate facts to experience.
25. I am good at pinpointing essentials.
26. I enjoy harmony.

27. I weigh the pros and cons.
28. I am patient.
29. I project myself into the future.
30. I let my decisions be influenced by my personal likes and wishes.
31. I look for cause and effect.
32. I focus on what needs attention now.
33. When others become uncertain or discouraged, my enthusiasm carries them along.
34. I am sensitive to praise.
35. I make logical statements.
36. I rely on well-tested ways to solve problems.
37. I keep switching from one idea to another.
38. I offer bargains.
39. I have my ideas very well thought out.
40. I am precise in my arguments.
41. I bring others to see the exciting possibilities in a situation.
42. I appeal to emotions and feelings to reach a "fair" deal.
43. I present well-articulated arguments for the proposals I favor.
44. I do not trust inspiration.
45. I speak in a way which conveys a sense of excitement to others.
46. I communicate what I am willing to give in return for what I get.
47. I put forward proposals or suggestions which make sense even if they are unpopular.
48. I am pragmatic.
49. I am imaginative and creative in analyzing a situation.
50. I put together very well-reasoned arguments.
51. I actively solicit others' opinions and suggestions.
52. I document my statements.
53. My enthusiasm is contagious.
54. I build upon others' ideas.
55. My proposals command the attention of others.
56. I like to use the inductive method (from facts to theories).
57. I can be emotional at times.
58. I use veiled or open threats to get others to comply.
59. When I disagree with someone, I skillfully point out the flaws in the other's arguments.
60. I am low key in my reactions.
61. In trying to persuade others, I appeal to their need for sensation and novelty.

62. I make other people feel that they have something of value to contribute.
63. I put forth ideas which are incisive.
64. I face difficulties with realism.
65. I point out the positive potential in discouraging or difficult situations.
66. I show tolerance and understanding of others' feelings.
67. I use arguments relevant to the problem at hand.
68. I am perceived as a down-to-earth person.
69. I go beyond the facts.
70. I give people credit for their ideas and contributions.
71. I like to organize and plan.
72. I am skillful at bringing up pertinent facts.
73. I have a charismatic tone.
74. When disputes arise, I search for the areas of agreement.
75. I am consistent in my reactions.
76. I quickly notice what needs attention.
77. I withdraw when the excitement is over.
78. I appeal for harmony and cooperation.
79. I am cool when negotiating.
80. I work all the way through to reach a conclusion.

Score Sheet

Enter the score you assigned each question (1, 2, 3, 4, or 5) in the space provided. (Note: The item numbers progress across the page from left to right.) When you have recorded all your scores, add them up vertically to attain four totals. Insert a "3" in any numbered space left blank.

1._____	2._____	3._____	4._____
5._____	6._____	7._____	8._____
9._____	10._____	11._____	12._____
13._____	14._____	15._____	16._____
17._____	18._____	19._____	20._____
21._____	22._____	23._____	24._____
25._____	26._____	27._____	28._____

29._____   30._____   31._____   32._____

33._____   34._____   35._____   36._____

37._____   38._____   39._____   40._____

41._____   42._____   43._____   44._____

45._____   46._____   47._____   48._____

49._____   50._____   51._____   52._____

53._____   54._____   55._____   56._____

57._____   58._____   59._____   60._____

61._____   62._____   63._____   64._____

65._____   66._____   67._____   68._____

69._____   70._____   71._____   72._____

73._____   74._____   75._____   76._____

77._____   78._____   79._____   80._____

IN:_____   **NR:**_____   **AN:**_____   **FA:**_____

Negotiation Style Profile

Now enter your four scores on the bar chart that follows. Construct your profile by connecting the four data points.

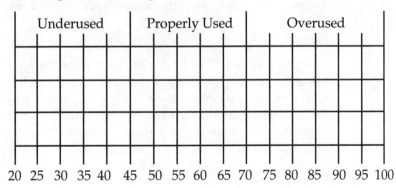

Intuitive

Basic Assumption: "Imagination can solve any problem."

Behavior: Making warm and enthusiastic statements, focusing on the entire situation or problem, pinpointing essentials, making projections, being imaginative and creative in analyzing the situation, switching from one subject to another, going beyond the facts, coming up with new ideas all the time, pushing and withdrawing from time to time, putting two and two together quickly, getting the facts a bit wrong sometimes, being deductive.

Key Words: Principles, essential, tomorrow, creative, idea.

Normative

Basic Assumption: "Negotiating is bargaining."

Behavior: Judging, assessing, and evaluating the facts according to a set of personal values, approving and disapproving, agreeing and disagreeing, using loaded words, offering bargains, proposing rewards, incentives, appealing to feelings and emotions to reach a "fair" deal, demanding, requiring, threatening, involving power, using status, authority, correlating, looking for compromise, making effective statements, focusing on people and their reactions, judging, attention to communication and group processes.

Key Words: Wrong, right, good, bad, like.

Analytical

Basic Assumption: "Logic leads to the right conclusions."

Behavior: Forming reasons, drawing conclusions and applying them to the case in negotiation, arguing in favor or against one's own or others' position, directing, breaking down, dividing, analyzing each situation for cause and effect, identifying relationships of the parts, putting things into logical order, organizing, weighing the pros and cons thoroughly, making identical statements, using linear reckoning.

Key Words: Because, then, consequently, therefore, in order to.

Factual

Basic Assumption: "The facts speak for themselves."

Behavior: Pointing out facts in neutral way, keeping track of what has been said, reminding people of their statements, knowing most of the details of the discussed issue and sharing them with others, clarifying, relating facts to experience, being low key in their reactions, looking for proof, documenting their statements.

Key Words: Meaning, define, explain, clarify, facts.

Guidelines for Negotiating with People Having Different Styles

1. Negotiating with someone having a factual style

   Be precise in presenting your facts.

   Refer to the past (what has already been tried out, what has worked, what has been shown from past experiences).

   Be indicative (go from the facts to the principles).

   Know your dossier (including the details).

   Document what you say.

2. Negotiating with someone having an intuitive style

   Focus on the situation as a whole.

   Project yourself into the future (look for opportunities).

   Tap the imagination and creativity of your partner.

   Be quick in reacting (jump from one idea to another).

   Build upon the reaction of the other person.

3. Negotiating with someone having an analytical style

   Use logic when arguing.

   Look for causes and effects.

   Analyze the relationships between the various elements of the situation or problem at stake.

   Be patient.

   Analyze various options with their respective pros and cons.

4. Negotiating with someone having a normative style

   Establish a sound relationship right at the outset of the negotiation.

   Show your interest in what the other person is saying.

   Identify his or her values and adjust to them accordingly.

   Be ready to compromise.

   Appeal to your partner's feelings.

REFERENCES

Axtell, R. E. (1991). *The do's and taboos of international trade.* New York: John Wiley & Sons, Inc.

Casse, P., & Deol, S. (1991). *Managing intercultural negotiations.* Washington, DC: SIETAR.

Copeland, L., & Griggs, L. (1985). *Going international.* New York: Random House.

Foster, D. A. (1992). *Bargaining across borders.* New York: McGraw-Hill, Inc.

Herbig, P. A., & Kramer, H. E. (1991). Cross-cultural negotiations: Success through understanding. *Management Decision, 29*(8), 19–31.

Hofstede, G. (1991). *Cultures and organizations.* New York: McGraw-Hill, Inc.

Lewicki, R. J., & Litterer, J. A. (1985). *Negotiation*. Homewood, IL: Irwin.

Moran, R. T., & Stripp, W. G. (1991). *Dynamics of successful international business negotiations*. Houston: Gulf Publishing.

North American Free Trade Agreement Between the Government of the United States of America, The Government of Canada and The Government of the United Mexican States. (1992). Washington, DC: U.S. Government Printing Office.

Prosser, M. H. (1985). *The cultural dialogue*. Washington, DC: SIETAR.

12

Laws Affecting International Business and Travel

OBJECTIVES

Upon completion of this chapter you will:

- understand the difference between home country laws and host country laws.

- understand why a contract has a different meaning in different countries.

- understand how ethics and laws relate.

- know why international laws are being promulgated.

- understand the importance of the nonwritten laws.

- know how international travel is affected by the law.

Legal cultural research is the study of how societies develop their legal culture. The elements of legal culture include styles of legislation; court proceedings; adjudication (hearing and deciding a case); and the status, action, and acceptance of the members of the legal profession and of public officials (Blankenburg, 1988). Culture is relevant to the development of law. The current international trade agreements stress flexibility and a willingness to change, thereby showing an interest by participating countries in looking at the law from more than one country's point of view.

The world, with over 170 nations, has numerous laws that affect international business. Laws are used to regulate the flow of products entering and leaving a country. When a firm is engaged in international business, what the company representatives can legally do is controlled by both their nation and the foreign nation with which they wish to conduct business. Each nation can legally do as it wishes within its own boundaries without interference from other nations. This right is legally protected by the **Act of State Doctrine**.

HOME COUNTRY AND HOST COUNTRY LAWS

Business communication between persons of different national origins is governed by the laws of both countries. Because of the large number of countries and laws, a knowledge of not only your home country's laws but the host country's laws as well is important. **Home country laws** are the laws, treaties, or acts that govern business within your country of citizenship and those governing your business with other countries. **Host country laws** are the laws, treaties, or acts that govern business within the foreign country with which you wish to conduct business.

Imports and exports are regulated in some manner by most countries; therefore, having a lawyer who is knowledgeable of the laws of the foreign country with which you are doing your importing or exporting is important, as is having a lawyer who is knowledgeable of your home country's laws and agreements with the foreign country.

There are three important legal requirements that govern U.S. citizens' actions during negotiations: antidiversion, antiboycott, and antitrust requirements (Axtell, 1991).

The **antidiversion requirement** states that the bill of lading and the invoice must clearly display that the carrier cannot divert the shipment to a country the U.S. government considers restricted.

The **antiboycott regulations** prohibit U.S. companies from participating in boycotts between two foreign countries by refusing to do business with a friendly nation to comply with a foreign boycott. Furnishing information about their business relationships to either friendly countries or blacklisted companies is also prohibited.

Antitrust laws are primarily designed to ensure fair competition and low prices to U.S. consumers; they tend to affect exporters in such areas as mergers and acquisitions of foreign firms, raw material procurement agreements and concessions, knowledge licenses (i.e., intellectual information), distribution channels, joint ventures for research, manufacturing, and construction (Murray & Evans, 1992).

Written Information Laws

Written information is also controlled by most nations. The United States has several laws that govern the information that can be sent to specific countries.

The **Export Administration Act of 1985** requires federal licensing of technical information in business correspondence.

The **Arms Export Control Act of 1968** and the **Trading with the Enemy Act of 1917** prohibit the transfer of information on military material or defense-related materials.

The **International Emergency Economic Powers Act of 1977** governs information that is research oriented from being communicated to foreigners.

Technology Laws

The area of technology law is currently being dealt with in many countries. Mexico, Brazil, Venezuela, and the United States already have laws governing how technological knowledge may be transferred. The legal area of intellectual property licensing was helped considerably by the **Berne Convention Implementation Act of 1988,** which recognizes the copyrights of all the signatory nations to the act. Trademarks are protected by the countries that are signatories of the **Madrid Convention**; however, the United States is not a signatory (Presner, 1991).

Employment Laws

Employment regulations differ between nations. Most nations have legislation governing wages, hours, union–management relations, residence visas, and work permits. Restricting foreigners as to the number and types of jobs they may hold is common; however, a great deal of variation between nations exists. Some nations require a certain ratio of nationals to foreigners; other nations require proof that no one in the nation can do the job; other nations allow a limited time period. Questions that can be legally asked of a potential employee also vary greatly by country. In the United States, employers can ask if someone would be willing to work overtime; in other countries this is not the case.

Maquiladora Law

Mexico has a maquiladora program that is governed by the **Presidential Decree for the Development and Operation of the Maquiladora Industry Program, 1983**. The program is an international one that allows the duty-free import of equipment, machinery, and materials to assemble parts of products that are then returned to the home country. The U.S. Tariff Code allows the final product to be brought back into the United States with only the final value added to the goods being taxed. Pacific Rim and European countries are also taking advantage of the maquiladora program. An important consideration in this program is the difference in form of law. Although Mexico borders the United States, which practices common law (except in Louisiana), Mexico practices civil law. The difference is that the civil law rather than **precedent** (interpretations of the law in previous court decisions) is considered during litigation (Jarvis, 1990).

INTERNATIONAL LAW

The **International Court of Justice,** also known as the **World Court,** is a body of the United Nations that provides a way to settle international disagreements between countries rather than corporations. The **International Law Commission** is also a body of the United Nations that produces laws on international commerce, such as the Law of the Sea (rights of states in rules of navigation).

The European Economic Community (EEC), the North American Free Trade Agreement (NAFTA), and the General Agreement on Trade and Tariffs (GATT) are three cross-national agreements or laws that are trying to equalize the treatment of multinational organizations. A movement by institutions concerned with international business has encouraged the development of agreements and laws that are uniformly accepted in world trade. The institutions include the **International Chamber of Commerce, Incoterms (International Commercial Terms), ECE Standard Conditions**, the **Hague Convention**, and the **Vienna Agreement** (Presner, 1991).

Unified laws have not produced unified judicial practices. Judges currently lack training or experience in international trade. Even in the signatory countries of an agreement, the judicial practices are not equal concerning the interpretation of the agreement. Currently multinational corporations must be flexible and willing to learn concerning international contracts. Home country laws frequently have nothing in common with host country laws. Since different cultures may have divergent value conceptions, it is not surprising that they would also have divergent legal conceptions.

Quasi-international laws are rules for the relationship between legal entities and states that do not have national status, such as private corporations (Presner, 1991).

Negotiations in international business situations play an important part in determining which laws will be followed. These negotiated contracts will eventually help to define an international body of law. **Macaulay's thesis**, in fact, states that intercultural business cultures are developing that consider the long-term, mutually beneficial relationship more important than the contracts lawyers so laboriously draft. Macaulay explains that businesses' lack of consideration of the law is due to the long-term relationships and interdependencies that develop and their importance to the organizations involved. It is to the organizations' benefit to ignore, suppress, or compromise rather than litigate; few international contracts are litigated. Macaulay (1976) cites Luhmann's thematization process as applicable to his thesis. **Thematization** is the process by which a framework for mutual communication and satisfaction is reached; this process could be related to the law, economics, power, utilitarianism, or religion.

How the parties maintain their relationship over time is called the **governance structure** (Blegvad, 1990; Macaulay, 1976). There are four types of governance structures: (1) **market governance,** which is contract based; (2) **trilateral governance,** which adds an arbitrator; (3) **bilateral governance,** which may not spell everything out but has a strong recognition of a continuing economic relationship; and (4) **unified governance,** in which nothing is negotiated in advance, maximum flexibility is provided, and only one party sets terms for both parties involved. Depending on the frequency of transactions, market replaceability, the firms' tolerances for uncertainty, and the relationship of the firms, one of these governance structures would cover their transactions. Consumer transactions fit the market governance structure. Trilateral governance fits transactions that involve idiosyncratic goods or services or a situation in which the establishment of the relationship is expensive. Bilateral governance is good for long-term relationships that involve uncertainty due to the mixture of goods or services that are to be included. Unified governance is appropriate for subsidiaries of a single organization (Blegvad, 1990).

The desire organizations have for long-term economic relationships that are privately governed is emerging as the preference over international laws and public governance. However, the time period that statistics have been kept is short; so this is an area that is still evolving. Modern business wants future-oriented solutions and cooperation rather than legal constraints. Time will tell if economic norms can acquire the rank of laws or if laws will have to be written to guide private governance.

CONTRACTS

In the United States, a **contract** is defined as an agreement between parties to do something that is oral, written, or implied through conduct. If a supplier ships goods to a customer that the supplier believes the buyer needs and the buyer accepts the shipment, the buyer enters into a contract. Purchase orders that are commonly used for the written form of a contract must contain a statement such as: Confirmation of contract entered into between the buyer and seller (with date of the oral contract). The word *contract* is important to legal enforceability particularly in the United States (Murray, 1992).

In the United States, an oral contract is legally enforceable if the parties admit that the contract was made even if no written contract was made. Oral contracts are also enforceable if the contract is for custom-manufactured goods, and special materials have been purchased that are usable only for the custom order. An oral contract that has been partially fulfilled through shipment and acceptance of goods is also enforceable (Lewicki & Litterer, 1985).

In Japan a contract can also be made verbally, in writing, or by conduct, but it is always considered open for renegotiation. Because Japanese corporate personnel are accustomed to working within trading companies (which are very difficult to join and look out for each other forever), when problems occur they are discussed and resolved without legal intervention.

Formerly in the states of the Soviet Union, little need existed for contracts. Goods were allocated, which means the companies had to accept what was sent to them whether they needed the goods or not. With reforms, companies now have a right to refuse unneeded allocations and can modify or cancel contracts. When the Soviet states moved to the theory of property rights, they recognized the eventual costs to the buyer and the consumer. By allowing the companies to plan and order what they needed, central planning and binding annual production plans were eliminated. The companies now operate very much as Western companies do, in that they are responsible for their operational costs, income, expenses, and profit. Since the economic climate in the Soviet states is still changing, contract perception may also change and should be taken into consideration when negotiating contracts in the Soviet states (Kroll, 1989).

Because of numerous differences that exist in various countries, having legal counsel to advise you on the proper way to negotiate contracts in individual countries is recommended. Reading a book on contract law for the particular country with which you will be conducting business would also suggest questions to ask your legal counsel.

NONWRITTEN LAW

Often the interpretation of the law is different between countries; for example, countries that communicate as high context versus those that communicate as low context, such as the United States, would consider the situation as more important than the letter of the law. In a high-context culture, little emphasis would be given to the written word; the situation would determine whether to adhere to the law or not. The individual interpretation of the situation would be more important than external rules and regulations. Oral agreements would be considered binding, and written contracts would be considered flexible. Japan is an example of such a high-context culture. In a low-context culture, such as the United States, what is written is expected to be followed. Laws are binding; the situation is not considered. In the United States, laws determine how people respond to each other. In view of the difference in attitudes toward the law, it is not surprising that the United States and Japan have had their share of problems trying to understand each other in negotiations. While many agreements have been crystal clear to both sides, the enactment of the agreement generally gives rise to many problems.

Unwritten business laws are called **drawer regulations** in Brazil because they operate from unwritten operational codes rather than laws (Rachid, 1990).

In China they have written some joint venture law; however, the old ways still are controlling how the joint venture law is interpreted. Mexico's transfer of technology and foreign investment laws have been changeable; they were written in 1973 and changed in 1976, 1982, 1989, and 1991 and still have not been implemented (Rachid, 1990).

Sometimes the interpretation of the law can be a problem or a solution depending on your position. An example of such a problem occurred when the European Community punished the United States for months of battling over trade matters by determining that U.S. meat inspection practices were not adequate, thereby halting U.S. sales of meat to the European Community. Since Canada had said its meat inspection was equivalent to that of the United States, the European Community had to decide whether or not it should cut off Canadian imports also. The Canadian Inspector offered a way to distance Canada from the United States by saying *equivalent* meant *equal to or better than*, thus allowing Canadian meat imports to continue.

FIGURE 12.1   Drawer regulation.

ETHICS AND THE LAW

Since people throughout the world are culturally diverse, it is not surprising that what is considered ethical behavior in one culture may be seen as unethical in another culture. Missner (1980) cautions that when you are negotiating, it is important to understand the differences between ethics-based judgments and judgments based on concern and practicality.

Ethics judgments are based on some standard of moral behavior as to right and wrong. Practicality judgments are based on what is easiest, best, or most effective to achieve an objective. Lewicki and Litterer (1985) state that judgments are subjective, and the distinction between ethical or unethical is measured in degrees rather than absolutes; reasonable people disagree as to where the line is drawn between ethical and unethical acts.

In the business world, four motivations for unethical conduct exist: profit, competition, justice, and advertising (Missner, 1980). The three dimensions of negotiation ethics are means/ends, relativism/absolutism, and truth telling. The means/ends question is measured by utility. The moral value and worth of an act are judged by what is produced—the utility. The players in the negotiation game and the environment in which the negotiators are operating help to determine whether the negotiators can justify being exploitive, manipulative, or devious. The relative/absolute question considers two extremes: either everything is relative or everything is without deviation from the rule. Although most people are somewhere between the extremes of relative and absolute, they debate which point between the two extremes is correct. Of course, it is a matter of judgment as to what particular point on the continuum is correct.

Truth telling considers whether concealing information, conscious misstatements, exaggeration, or bluffing when you are in negotiations is dishonest. Judging how honest and candid one can be in negotiations and not be vulnerable is difficult.

Intercultural negotiations have the added problem of different business methods, different cultures, and different negotiation protocols. While the decision to be "unethical" may be made to increase power and control, whether the decision was made quickly, casually, after careful evaluation, or based on cultural values is important (Lewicki & Litterer, 1985).

The U.S. government has taken a strong stance concerning bribery and the accounting practices used in international business. The **Foreign Corrupt Practices Act of 1977** requires U.S. companies to account for and report international transactions accurately and prohibits bribes that are used to gain a business advantage. Bribes can include gifts and entertainment. A U.S. firm giving a Mexican utility official money under the table for the Mexican's personal use in order to speed up the installation of an electric line to a new construction site would be an example of bribery.

The U.S. Department of Commerce's 1985 booklet *Foreign Business Practices* lists foreign laws by country and offers the following guidance on distributor agreements:

- What is legal in the United States may not be legal in another country.
- Translations should be checked for concise meanings.
- If possible state the jurisdiction that will handle disagreements.
- Settle disagreements through an arbitrator; the arbitration body should be identified.
- Provisions of foreign laws that are to be waived should be stated.
- Benefits to both parties should be stated.
- The agreement should be in writing.

Another source of information to help distributors is *Export Administration Regulations*; a subscription is available by writing to the Superintendent of Documents, U.S. Government Printing Office, Washington, DC 20402.

The **Doctrine of Sovereign Compliance** is an international legal principle that can be used as a defense in your home country for work carried out in a host country when the two countries' legal positions are different. For example, a U.S. manager working in Canada may have to trade with Cuba; however, it is illegal to do so in the United States. If prosecuted, the manager could use the Doctrine of Sovereign Compliance as a defense. The defense is necessary because U.S. citizens or corporations are held accountable to U.S. law beyond the boundaries of the country, though the Trading with the Enemy Act, and the application of the act beyond the U.S. border is called **extraterritoriality**.

The **Export Trading Company Act of 1982** allows companies that normally would not be allowed to participate in joint ventures to develop trading companies similar to those in Britain, the Netherlands, and Japan (Axtell, 1991). As an example of this act, General Motors, Ford, and Chrysler make parts with European and Japanese car manufacturers in order to jointly produce and sell cars.

How legal and ethical practices are viewed by different countries is best explained by an example Axtell (1991) has used:

A Latin businessman, commenting on the U.S. attitude toward morality in international business, once confronted me with this rather different perspective. Take the word "contraband," he said. Here in the United States it is a very bad word. It suggests breaking the law by smuggling. However, in my country, the Spanish word is *contrabando*. It comes from the word *contrabandido*, which means literally, "against the bandits." When I was a child in the villages of my country, we were taught that the bandidos, the bandits, were the land and shop owners. I remember that even candy was illegally brought into our village and we were taught to favor that contraband candy because it was a way of fighting back against the bandidos. So, you see my culture was raised to view contraband as a good thing. That may help explain why there are differing values and differing perceptions of morality between our continents.

Intercultural business communication is affected by the laws of the countries in which companies do business and the growing body of international law. Because laws and rules develop from and are a part of cultural beliefs, values, and assumptions, interpretation and discussion of legal issues can cause communication problems between intercultural business negotiators unless they are completely prepared.

INTERNATIONAL TRAVEL AND LAW

Your passport is the most important document you can carry with you when traveling outside your native country. A **passport** is your proof of citizenship. To obtain a passport, you must have a copy of your birth certificate and current photos and apply in person the first time. As a precaution, make a copy of your passport so that if the original is lost or stolen you can give the copy to the embassy to facilitate getting a replacement (Skabelund, 1991).

Citizenship is the state of being vested with certain rights and duties as a native or naturalized member of a country. Proof of citizenship may be needed if you were born in another country, your parents are citizens of another country, or you are a naturalized citizen of the country that you consider your home country. If the country to which you are traveling considers you a citizen of that country, because it is the country of your birth or because your parents are citizens of the country, it may require you to do military service or pay income taxes (Skabelund, 1991).

A **visa** gives you the right to enter and stay in a country for a period of time for a specific purpose. If you are a tourist, most countries do not require a visa; however, for business purposes a visa may be required. The country you are visiting issues the visa, and the visa may be obtained from the embassy or consulate of the country you wish to visit. A **consulate** is made up of individuals sent by the government to other countries to promote the commercial interests of their home country (Skabelund, 1991).

All countries have **customs** agents who enforce export and import laws of the country; they have the right to search and confiscate anything you may have with you. Be sure to get a list from your embassy of items that are illegal to bring back into your home country. The host country's embassy can provide a list of restricted items. When returning home, you will be asked to declare the value of everything purchased that you are bringing home with you. Most countries have items for which they charge duties. **Duties** are an import tax. The host country's embassy can also give you immunization requirements and the verification needed for prescription drugs you may need to take. U.S. citizens should be aware that they cannot legally carry more than $10,000 out of the country without registering with U.S. customs officials before departing (Axtell, 1991).

To drive abroad, find out what type of license you may need and become familiar with the country's driving laws. If you obtain an international driver's license, it will help you learn about international driving.

To be sure you do not break the law in other countries, the following tips can be beneficial (Axtell, 1990):

1. Because of political unrest in the world, register with the U.S. embassy or consulate when you arrive in a foreign country.
2. If you have any kind of trouble, turn to the embassy or consulate for legal, medical, or financial problems.
3. The American consul can visit you in jail, give you a list of attorneys, notify family, and protest any mistreatment; however, the consul cannot get you released or provide for bonds or fines.
4. Remember that you are subject to the laws of the country while you are there.
5. If you stay for a prolonged time period, you will have to register with the local authorities. You may be requested to leave your passport overnight or to complete a data sheet.
6. Use authorized outlets for cashing checks and buying airline tickets; avoid the black market or street money changers that you will see in many countries.
7. Ask before you photograph anything to be sure it is permissible.
8. Notary publics in many countries have broader powers than in the United States.
9. Common infractions of the law include trying to take historic artifacts or antiquities out of the country, customs violations, immigration violations, drunk and disorderly conduct, and business fraud.
10. If you need to drive, obtain an international driver's license. Travel agents can assist with this. Many countries require proof of insurance while driving.
11. Dealing in drugs is a serious offense in all countries and penalties can be much more serious than in the United States, including death.
12. Keep a list of credit card numbers and traveler's check numbers in a safe place in case they are lost or stolen.
13. Obtain a copy of *Know Before You Go* and *Customs Hints for Returning U.S. Residents* from the U.S. Customs Office, P.O. Box 7118, Washington, DC

20044. For foreign country customs information, write the Office of Passport Services, Department of State, Washington, DC 20514, for *Country Information Notices*.

14. Telephone numbers/addresses that may be beneficial include:

The U.S. State Department, Washington, DC, 202-635-5225 or 202-632-1512

A copy of *Key Officers of Foreign Service Posts*, available from the Superintendent of Documents, U.S. Government Printing Office, Washington, DC 20402

Amnesty International, New York, 212-807-8400

International Legal Defense Counsel, 1420 Walnut Street, Suite 315, Philadelphia, PA 19102, 215-545- 2428

COUNTRY-SPECIFIC TRAVEL TIPS

Before you travel to a foreign country, find out what documents are needed, what hotel accommodations and modes of transportation are available, what laws affect behavior (such as the legal drinking age), and other information to assure personal safety and comfort so that your sojourn is a pleasant one. Books by Braganti and Devine (1992) and Devine and Braganti (1986, 1988) and Brigham Young University's *Culturgram* (1994) contain country-specific information that will make international travel easier. Because space does not permit an extensive examination of numerous countries, the travel tips that follow have been limited to the six countries with which the United States conducts a majority of its international trade.

Canada

U.S. citizens need no passport when traveling to Canada from the United States but do need one when coming to Canada from another country. Although visas are not required for visits of up to 180 days, U.S. citizens do need proof of citizenship, such as a birth certificate or voter's registration card, and identification containing a photograph.

Hotel accommodations in the large cities are comparable to those in the United States. Voltage connectors and plug adaptors are not needed for small appliances.

Public transportation systems in Montréal and Québec City are very good. Montréal's Metro system is one of the best subway systems in the world. The underground system includes miles of underground shopping malls; you can buy anything you want without going above ground. Since public transportation cannot accommodate the many isolated regions in the north, domestic air transportation is used to reach these areas. People who drive in Canada should remember to leave their radar detectors at home as they are illegal in that country and will be confiscated if detected.

Additional information about traveling in Canada can be obtained from:

Canadian Consulate General
1251 Avenue of the Americas
New York, NY 10020

Embassy of Canada
501 Pennsylvania Avenue, N.W.
Washington, DC 20001

England

A valid passport is required for travel in England. However, U.S. citizens do not need a visa for visits lasting no longer than six months. Vaccinations are not required.

If staying at a hotel, you may be asked if you would like early morning tea delivered to your room. Larger hotels may include a continental breakfast in the room price. Electrical converters and plug adaptors are needed to use small U.S. appliances in England.

Public transportation includes the Underground (subway) and taxis. To drive in England you do not need an international driver's license. Remember that people drive on the left side of the road. In rural areas gas stations may be scarce so fill your tank when you see a station.

The legal age for drinking in England is 18. The English police are known for being friendly and helpful; ask them for directions or assistance with travel-related problems (Braganti & Devine, 1992).

More information on traveling in England is available from:

British Tourist Authority
40 West 57th Street
New York, NY 10019

Embassy of the United Kingdom
3100 Massachusetts Avenue, N.W.
Washington, DC 20008

British Information Service
845 Third Avenue
New York, NY 10022

France

To travel in France, a valid passport is required; but U.S. citizens may travel in the country without a visa for up to three months. Vaccinations are not required.

Hotels in France do not always have a bath in the room nor are they always air conditioned. To use small appliances, such as a hair dryer, you will need to have a voltage converter and plug adaptor.

Public transportation in France includes the Métro (subway), buses, streetcars, taxis, and the TGV (*train à grande vitesse,* a high-speed train connecting 36 European cities). Exercise care in choosing only an "official" taxi; unauthorized taxi drivers have no meters and charge whatever they wish. Driving a car in France does not require an international driver's license. Avoid honking the horn in cities since this is illegal; turning right on red is not permitted.

The drinking age in France is 18. Women should exercise care when using the Métro at night since it is considered unsafe; ask about other unsafe areas in France before exploring the locality (Braganti & Devine, 1992).

Additional information about traveling in France is available from the French Government Tourist Office in New York and the French Embassy in Washington:

French Government Tourist Office
610 Fifth Avenue
New York, NY 10010-2452

Embassy of France
4101 Reservoir Road
Washington, DC 20007-2185

Germany

A valid passport is required for travel in Germany; however, U.S. citizens do not need a visa to travel in the country for up to three months. Vaccinations are not required.

If you stay at a hotel, the price of the room generally includes a continental breakfast; heat may be an extra charge. When making your reservation, inquire about bathroom facilities; some rooms do not have a bath so you will use a communal facility. Electrical converters and plug adaptors are needed to use small appliances in hotels.

Public transportation includes buses, streetcars, subways, trains, and taxis. Tickets for mass transit are purchased in advance. Since the conductor often checks your ticket during the ride, have your ticket available for inspection. An international driver's license is required for driving in Germany. Since service stations in Germany are quite competitive, except on the Autobahn (freeway), shop around for the best prices on gasoline.

Jaywalking is illegal in Germany. Biking, hiking, or hitchhiking along the Autobahn is illegal. Since the tapwater in towns along the Rhine contains dangerous chemicals, do not drink it. Always use bottled water (Braganti & Devine, 1992).

More information on traveling in Germany is available from:

German National Tourist Office
747 Third Avenue
New York, NY 10017

Embassy of the Federal Republic of Germany
4645 Reservoir Road, N.W.
Washington, DC 20007-1998

Japan

Although no visa is needed for visits of less than 90 days, U.S. citizens need a valid passport when traveling to Japan. Vaccinations are not required.

Numerous Western-style hotels are available in the large cities. They will probably have private baths, but expect some differences in accommodations. Faucets and door handles, for example, operate in the opposite direction from what is considered the norm in the United States. The same toilets are often used for both genders and are quite different from those people of the United States are accustomed to using. Small appliances usually work in Japanese electrical outlets.

Public transportation in Japan includes trains, subways, and buses. The "bullet train," which runs between major cities, offers regular and first-class service. Taxis are available at larger hotels and in commercial districts (Devine & Braganti, 1986).

Additional information about travel in Japan is available from the Japan National Tourist Office in New York and the Japanese Embassy in Washington:

Japan National Tourist Office
630 Fifth Avenue
New York, NY 10111

Embassy of Japan
2520 Massachusetts Avenue
Washington, DC 20008

Mexico

U.S. citizens may stay up to three months in Mexico with no visa but need proof of citizenship. Although no vaccinations are required, they may be advisable when traveling in certain parts of the country.

Numerous excellent hotel accommodations are available in the resort towns and in larger cities. Since many people from the United States visit Mexico over the Christmas and Easter holidays, hotel reservations should be made well in advance.

Public transportation in Mexico is quite varied, from the subway of Mexico City to the crowded buses. Trains are a good choice for longer distances, such as between Mexico City and Monterrey. Driving a car in many parts of Mexico is not advisable. Driving can be hazardous, especially at night, because of bicycle riders, robbers, and problems with getting help should your car break down. In addition, you need to be aware that at various checkpoints, men dressed in military or police garb may stop you, expecting money, cigarettes, or other bribes before permitting you to proceed. Failure to offer the bribe may result in lengthy delays while your car and luggage are searched (Devine & Braganti, 1988).

Additional information about traveling in Mexico is available from:

Mexican Government Tourist Office
405 Park Avenue, Suite 1002
New York, NY 10022

Embassy of Mexico
2827 Sixteenth Street, N.W.
Washington, DC 20009-4260

When traveling in other countries, the best advice is to obey the laws of the host country, be courteous and helpful to all you meet, and remember it is *their* country so if you cannot speak positively about the country, remain silent.

TERMS

Act of State Doctrine
Antiboycott regulations
Antidiversion requirement
Antitrust laws
Arms Export Control Act of 1968
Berne Convention Implementation
   Act of 1988
Bilateral governance
Citizenship
Consulate
Contract
Customs
Doctrine of Sovereign Compliance
Drawer regulations
Duties
Export Administration Act of 1985

Export Trading Act of 1982
Extraterritoriality
Foreign Corrupt Practices Act
   of 1977
Governance structure
Hague Convention
Home country laws
Host country laws
Incoterms (International
   Commercial Terms)
International Chamber of Commerce
International Court of Justice
   (World Court)
International Emergency
   Economic Powers of 1977
International Law Commission

Macaulay's thesis
Madrid Convention
Market governance
Passports
Precedent
Presidential Decree for the
    Development and Operation
    of the Maquiladora Industry
    Program, 1983

Quasi-international law
Thematization
Trading with the Enemy Act of 1917
Trilateral governance
Unified governance
Vienna Agreement
Visa

Exercise 12.1

Instructions: Match the following terms with their definition.

__ 1. Gives permission to stay in a country
     for a specified time and purpose

__ 2. Unwritten business laws

__ 3. Contract relationship

__ 4. Includes an arbitrator

__ 5. Nothing negotiated in advance; one
     party sets terms for both

__ 6. Persons sent to other countries to
     promote commercial interest

__ 7. Enforces export and import laws of
     the country

__ 8. Document that shows proof of
     citizenship

__ 9. Agreement between parties to do
     something that is enforceable by law

__10. Considers long-term cultural
     relationship more important than
     written legal contract

A. Bilateral governance
B. Consulate
C. Contract
D. Customs
E. Drawer regulations
F. Host country laws
G. Macaulay's thesis
H. Market governance
I. Passport
J. Trilateral governance
K. Unified governance
L. Visa

Exercise 12.2

Instructions: Match the laws with their major provisions.

___ 1. Prohibits bribes to gain a business advantage

___ 2. Prohibits transfer of information on military materials

___ 3. Legal right of each nation to do as it wishes within its own boundaries

___ 4. Protects trademarks of countries who are signatories

___ 5. Requires federal licensing of technical information in business correspondence

___ 6. Recognizes copyrights of signatory nations

___ 7. Prevents research-oriented information from being communicated to foreigners

___ 8. Affects exporters involved in mergers/acquisitions of foreign firms

___ 9. UN body involved in laws on international commerce

___ 10. Regulates differing legal positions of home and host countries

A. Act of State Doctrine
B. Berne Convention Implementation Act
C. Corrupt Practices Act
D. Doctrine of Sovereign Compliance
E. Export Administration
F. International Emergency Economic Powers Act
G. International Law Commission
H. Madrid Convention
I. Trading with the Enemy Act
J. U.S. Antitrust Law

QUESTIONS AND CASES FOR DISCUSSION

1. Explain the difference between home country and host country laws.
2. Describe how a low-context and a high-context culture view a contract.
3. Are ethics the same around the world? Explain why they may vary.
4. Explain differences among the four governance structures.
5. Why are nonwritten laws difficult to learn about before going to another country to do business?

6. Explain the importance of citizenship. Include in your answer how differences between countries in interpretation of citizenship could affect an individual.
7. What is the difference between a passport and a visa?
8. Who governs a multinational corporation's operations?
9. Why is legal counsel important when doing business in a foreign country?
10. Which act prohibits a corporation or individual from circumventing the Arms Export Control Act of 1968?

Case 1   A famous doctor's parents emigrated from Russia in the early 1900s before she was born but eventually became naturalized citizens after all their children were born. They also changed their last name to an English-sounding name. The doctor practiced medicine during the 1950s and 1960s. She spoke and wrote seven different languages and was very involved in research and education in her field of study. As the doctor became sought after for educational seminars around the world, she was invited to Russia to speak. The doctor refused to go. What are the legal, cultural, and political issues that could have caused her to reach this decision?

Case 2   Your corporation has sent you to another country to build a manufacturing facility. A representative of the government with whom you have been working informs you it will take six months to get the necessary permits to allow work to begin. You explain that you have a deadline to begin manufacturing in nine months and that three months is not sufficient time. He explains that certain people if compensated may be willing to help things progress at a faster pace. You must determine if it is illegal to do so. How would you respond? Explain why you have chosen your answer and whose laws you are considering.

Case 3   Aerobus, a French airplane manufacturer, and Boeing, a U.S. airplane manufacturer, have reached an agreement to jointly manufacture a new airplane to carry 600 people. Which country's laws will govern the manufacturing of the plane? Where will litigation of any disagreements take place? What form of thematization will be used? What should the governance structure be?

Case 4   A major corporation uses a great deal of a derivative from high-grade petroleum. Because of the cost of the high-grade petroleum and a decrease in the use of other derivatives that come from the cracking process, the cost of the derivative is going to increase. Substitute products are available if the cost increases sufficiently to make those products cost efficient. The purchasing agent for the corporation without the direction of his superiors has verbally agreed with his supplier to purchase a six-month supply of the derivative at the current cost. In the meantime, the research department has found a cheaper substitute that can be available for shipment in two months. The purchasing agent is told to purchase the substitute beginning in two months. What are the legal ramifications concerning the four extra months of the derivative that have been ordered and the supplier has begun to produce?

ACTIVITIES

1. Bring to class a critical incident related to international law.
2. Secure forms for obtaining passports and visas for a country of your choice. How will you find out about nonwritten laws of this country before you travel there?
3. Interview students from another culture; ask them to identify at least one law in their own country that differs from that in the United States.
4. Ask a professor of international law to address the class on variations in contracts in various cultures.
5. Prepare a list of books or journal articles related to international law.

REFERENCES

Axtell, R. (1990). *The do's and taboos of hosting international visitors*. New York: John Wiley & Sons, Inc.

Axtell, R. (1991). *The do's and taboos of international trade* (pp. 111–135). New York: John Wiley & Sons, Inc.

Blankenburg, E. (1988, October). *Zum Begriff "Rechtskultur."* Paper presentation, 24th meeting of the German Sociological Association in Zurich.

Blegvad, B. (1990). Commercial relations, contract, and litigation in Denmark: A discussion of Macaulay's theories. *Law and Society Review, 24*(2), 397–411.

Braganti, N. L., & Devine, E. (1992). *European customs and manners*. New York: Meadowbrook Press.

Devine, E., & Braganti, N. L. (1986). *The traveler's guide to Asian customs and manners*. New York: St. Martin's Press.

Devine, E., & Braganti, N. L. (1988). *The traveler's guide to Latin American customs and manners*. New York: St. Martin's Press.

Jarvis, S. S. (1990). Preparing employees to work south of the border. *Personnel*, pp. 59–63.

Kroll, H. (1989). Property rights and the Soviet enterprise: Evidence from the law of contract. *Journal of Comparative Economics, 13*, 115–133.

Lewicki, R. J., & Litterer, J. A. (1985). *Negotiation*. Homewood, IL: Irwin.

Macaulay, S. (1976). An empirical view of contract. *Wisconsin Law Review*, pp. 465–482.

Missner, M. (1980). *Ethics of the business system*. Sherman Oaks, CA: Alfred Publishing Company.

Murray, J. E. (1992, March 19). What exactly is a contract? *Purchasing*, pp. 25, 27, 29.

Murray, M. E., & Evans, D. (1992). United States laws affecting business communication at home and abroad. In R. V. Lesikar, J. O. Pettit, Jr., & M. E. Flatley (Eds.), *Basic business communication*. Homewood, IL: Irwin.

Presner, L. A. (1991). *The international business dictionary and reference*. New York: John Wiley & Sons, Inc.

Rachid, R. (1990, June 15). Unwritten laws govern business in some nations. *The Journal of Commerce, 384*(27250), 5A(1).

Skabelund, G. P. (Ed.). (1991). *InfoGram: Travel and international law*. Provo, UT: Brigham Young University.

Appendix A _____

Glossary

Acculturation   the process of becoming adapted to a new and different culture.

Acronyms   words formed from the initial letters or groups of letters and pronounced as one word.

Act of State Doctrine   each nation can do as it wishes within its borders.

Antiboycott regulations   prohibit firms or employees from refusing to do business with friendly nations.

Antidiversion requirement   bill of lading and invoice must clearly display that the carrier cannot direct the shipment to a U.S.-restricted country.

Antitrust laws   affect the merger or acquisition of foreign firms, raw material, licenses, distribution channels.

Argot   a vocabulary of a particular group; it is often regional.

Arms Export Control Act of 1968   prohibits transfer of military- or defense-related materials.

Attribution   something seen as belonging to or representing something or someone.

Attribution training   focuses on explanations of behavior from the point of view of a person in the host country.

Authority   the power to give commands and make decisions.

Backstage culture   cultural information that is concealed from outsiders.

Berne Convention Implementation Act of 1988   recognizes the copyrights of all the signatory nations.

Bernstein Hypothesis   explains how social structure affects language; speech emerges in restricted or elaborated codes.

Bilateral governance   strong recognition of a continuing economic relationship.

Bribery   to give or promise to give something, often money, to influence someone's actions.

239

Buffer   a paragraph used to begin a bad news letter; tells what the letter is about, is pleasant, but says neither yes nor no.

Caste system   rigid system of class in India. The society is divided into castes determined at birth. Each caste has its own status, rights, and duties.

Chromatics   use of color to communicate nonverbally.

Chronemics   use of time to communicate nonverbally.

Citizenship   the state of being vested with certain rights and duties as a native or naturalized member of a state or country.

Cognitive-behavior modification approach   applies principles of learning to specific adjustment problems in other cultures.

Cognitive dissonance   logic and reasoning differences, normally due to cultural differences; may generate frustration, regression, fixation, resignation, repression, projection, and aggression.

Collectivism   the political principle of centralized social and economic control.

Colloquialism   informal words or phrases often associated with regions of the country.

Communication barriers   obstacles to effective communication.

Consulate   made up of individuals sent to other countries to promote commercial interests.

Continental style of eating   a manner of eating; place the fork in the left hand and knife in the right; use the knife to push food onto the back of the fork then move the food into the mouth, with the tines of the fork down.

Contract   an agreement between parties to do something.

Conversation taboos   topics considered inappropriate for conversation with people in certain cultures or groups.

Cultural awareness approach   includes a comparison of values and behaviors of people in the home country and the host country.

Cultural heritage   values, ideals, and beliefs that one inherits from one's culture.

Cultural noise   anything that would distract or interfere with the message being communicated.

Cultural synergy   when people of different cultures absorb a significant number of each others' cultural differences and have a number of similarities that merge to form a stronger overriding culture.

Cultural shock   the trauma a person experiences when he or she moves into a culture different from his or her home culture; a communication problem that involves the frustrations that accompany a lack of understanding of the verbal and nonverbal communication of the host culture, its customs, and value systems.

Cultural universals   formed out of the common problems all cultures have.

Culture   the structure through which communication is formulated and interpreted; deals with the way people live.

Customs socially acceptable ways of behaving; also refers to enforcement of export and import laws of a country.

Deductive method problem solving that goes from broad categories or observations to specific examples to determine the facts and then the solution to the problem.

Demeanor conduct, behavior, deportment, and facial appearance.

Directional model negotiation process that is based on the prediction that tough or soft moves will be reciprocated by the other negotiating party.

Doctrine of sovereign compliance international legal principle used as a defense in your home country for work carried out in a host country.

Drawer regulations unwritten laws.

Duties import taxes.

EEC European Economic Community; an expansion of the free trade zone.

ECE Standard Conditions organization that works toward development of laws that are uniformly accepted in world trade.

Ebonics a distinctive language of African Americans.

Economic system the way in which the products that meet the physiological needs of the people are produced, distributed, and consumed.

Educational system the formal or informal means of passing on the cultural heritage.

Elaborated codes messages low in predictability; verbal transmission is important.

Enculturation adapting to the cultural patterns of one's society.

Ethical standards guidelines established to convey what is perceived to be correct or incorrect behavior by most people in a society.

Ethnocentric management occurs when a firm is located in one country and all its sales are also in the same country; does not account for cultural differences in the workforce.

Ethnocentrism the belief that your own cultural background, including ways of analyzing problems, language, and verbal and nonverbal communication, is correct.

Etiquette manners and behavior considered acceptable in social and business situations.

Euphemisms inoffensive expressions that are used in place of offensive words or words with negative connotations.

Expatriate denotes a person who works or lives outside of his or her country.

Experiential learning approach affords participants an opportunity to actively experience the culture through field trips or such simulations as Bafa, Bafa.

Export as a verb, means to actively send a good or service out of one sovereign domain to another for purposes of sale (or from areas not designated as sovereign to those so designated); as a noun, a good or service actively sent from one sovereign domain to another for purposes of sale (or from areas not designated as sovereign to those so designated).

Export Administration Act of 1985 requires federal licensing of technical information in business correspondence.

Export Trading Company Act of 1982 permitted trading between competitors normally prohibited from association by antitrust laws.

Extended family consists of grandparents, uncles, aunts, and cousins.

Extraterritoriality application of laws, such as the Trading with the Enemy Act, beyond the U.S. border.

Foreign Corrupt Practices Act of 1977 law that makes bribing someone else's government a crime; applies to both parties involved.

Formality degree of preciseness, regularity, or conformance expected within the society.

Free trade zones areas of international commerce where foreign or domestic merchandise may enter without formal customs entry or customs duties.

Frontstage culture cultural information that you are willing to share with outsiders.

GATT General Agreement of Tariffs and Trade; multinational trade agreement of which the United States is a member. Deals with intellectual property, services, national treatment for services, market access for services, foreign investment, antidumping, subsidies, textiles, agriculture, market access, dispute settlement, and telecommunications.

Geocentric management type of management that requires a common framework with enough freedom for individual locations to operate regionally in order to meet the cultural needs of the workers; a synergy of ideas from different countries of operation.

Globalization the ability of a corporation to take a product and market it anywhere in the world.

Governance structure how parties maintain their relationship over time.

Gross domestic product (GDP) value of a country's goods and services produced by residents within the country during a specified accounting period, usually one year.

Gross national product (GNP) value a country's income earned by residents both within and outside the country during a specified accounting period, usually one year.

Group Decision Support Systems a business conference software package.

Group membership has two extremes with people belonging to many groups or very few groups and a middle ground between the two.

Hague Convention works toward developing agreements that are uniformly accepted in world trade.

Haptics use of touch to communicate nonverbally.

High context   communication that transmits little in the explicit message; non-verbal aspects are important.

Home country laws   laws of the nation in which your corporation is headquartered.

Homonyms   words that sound alike and have different meanings.

Host country laws   laws of the nation in which you are conducting business.

Host language   native language of the country.

Import   as a verb, means to actively bring a good or service into one sovereign domain from another, or from areas not designated as sovereign to those so designated, in order to be sold; as a noun, refers to the good or service.

Incoterms   International Commercial **Terms;**   standard definitions of international terms of sale.

Individualism   the pursuit of individual rather than common or collective interests.

Inductive method   problem solving that starts with facts or observations and goes to generalizations.

Information or fact-oriented training   gives participants facts about the host country using such instructional methods as lectures and videotapes.

Interaction approach   interaction with people in the host country, either nationals or U.S. persons who have been in the host country for some time.

Interaction model   negotiation process that includes environment, atmosphere, parties, and process.

Intercultural business communication   communication within and between businesses that involves people from more than one culture.

Intercultural communication   communication between persons of different cultures.

Intercultural negotiation   discussion between persons of different cultural backgrounds who work toward mutual agreement.

Intercultural negotiation process   involves defining, observing, analyzing, and evaluating what happens between negotiators.

Intermediaries   people who act as go-betweens with other people.

International Chamber of Commerce   international organization headquartered in Paris, France, that establishes a consensus on matters such as trading practices and procedures for handling trade disputes.

International communication   communication between nations and governments rather than individuals; quite formal and ritualized.

International Court of Justice (World Court)   specialized body of the United Nations that provides a means of settling international disputes peacefully.

International English   a limited vocabulary for international businesses using the 3,000 to 4,000 most common English words.

International Emergency Economic Powers Act of 1977   governs information that is research oriented from being communicated to foreigners.

International Law Commission   body of the United Nations that works toward laws on international commerce.

Intimate zone   physical distance between people; in the United States, less than 18 inches; reserved for close friends.

Intracultural communication   communication between members of the same culture.

Jargon   technical terminology used within specialized groups.

Johari Window   named for its creators, Joseph and Harrington; a way of looking at a person's inner world. It includes panes that represent the self that is known and unknown to oneself and the self that is known and unknown to others.

Keiretsu system   Japanese negotiating practices; a company group formed by the principal company and the partner companies that supply parts, equipment, financial support, or distribution of the final products.

Kinesics   term used for various types of body language including facial expressions, gestures, posture and stance, and other mannerisms used to communicate or to accompany verbal messages.

Lexical errors   language content errors.

Linear   has a beginning and an end; logical and object oriented.

Linguistic determinism   the assumption that a person's view of reality stems mainly from his or her language.

Low context   communication explicitly coded and given in more than one way to be sure it is understood by the receiver.

Macaulay's thesis   proposes that intercultural business cultures are developing that consider long-term mutually beneficial relationships more important than written contracts.

Macroculture   the larger society or culture.

Madrid Convention   trademarks protected by signatory countries.

Market governance   contract-based relationship.

Marriage and family system   attitudes, beliefs, and practices related to marriage and the family held by people in various cultures; importance placed on marriage and the family in a society.

Matriarchal   family that is mother oriented.

Mediation   the use of a third party in the negotiation process.

Melting pot   a sociocultural assimilation of people of differing backgrounds and nationalities; being or becoming the same.

Metacommunication   the intentional or unintentional implied meaning of a message.

Microculture   a subculture; a group of people possessing characteristic traits that distinguish them from others within the macroculture or larger culture.

Mindsets   a way of being that allows you to see and perceive things through your own filters.

Misperception   to perceive incorrectly.

Monochronic   a system of time that allows for performing only one major activity at a time.

Monogamy   family system that includes one husband and one wife.

Multicultural   learning more than one culture and being able to move between two cultures comfortably.

Multinational   composed of many nations or nationalities.

Multinational firm   corporation with operations and subsidiaries in many foreign countries.

NAFTA   North American Free Trade Agreement; an expansion of the free trade zone concept. Deals with trade in goods, technical barriers to trade, government procurement, investment, services and related matters, intellectual property, and administrative and institutional provisions.

Nationalism   (1) a desire for national advancement or independence; (2) devotion to the interests of one's own nation.

Negotiation strategies   plans organized to achieve a desired working relationship.

Networks   formed with personal ties and involve an exchange of assistance.

Nonlinear   circular; subjective; traditional orientation.

Nonverbal communication   nonword messages, such as gestures, facial expressions, interpersonal distance, touch, eye contact, smell, and silence.

Norms   culturally ingrained principles of correct and incorrect behaviors, which, if broken, carry a form of overt or covert penalty.

Nuclear family   family consisting of the father, mother, and children.

Oculesics   use of eye contact as a way of communicating nonverbally.

Olfactics   use of smell to communicate nonverbally.

Package deal model   negotiation process that includes background factors, process, atmosphere, and outcome.

Parables   story to convey a truth or moral lesson.

Paralanguage   the linguistic elements of speech, such as pitch, loudness, quality, rate, or dialect that interrupt or temporarily take the place of speech and affect the meaning of a message.

Parochialism   same as ethnocentrism.

Passport   proof of citizenship.

Patriarchal father-oriented family.

Perception   awareness or comprehension through the senses.

Personal constructs   individual belief systems and attitudes that are different for different cultures.

Personal zone   physical distance between people; in the United States, from 18 inches to 4 feet; used for giving instructions to others or working closely with another person.

Perspective   one's mental view of facts, ideas, and so on, and their interrelationships.

Platinum Rule   do unto others as they would have done unto them.

Political system   the governing system that originates from dictatorship, inherited rights, election procedures, consensus, or conquest.

Polyandry   one woman with many husbands.

Polycentric   centered on self.

Polycentric management   type of management that considers the culture of the country in which the firm is located.

Polychronic   a system of time that allows for performing several activities simultaneously.

Polygamy   one man with many wives.

Power   the ability to influence others.

Precedent   interpretation of the law in previous court decisions.

Presidential Decree for the Development and Operation of the Maquiladora Industry Program, 1983   allows duty-free import of equipment, machinery, and materials to assemble parts of products.

Principles model   or comparative model, assumes that the negotiators are problem solvers and that they share a goal that they wish to reach efficiently and amicably; the people are separate from the problem; the focus is on interests; the options have mutual gains; and the criteria used to judge the gains are objective.

Property   something that is or may be possessed.

Protocol   refers to customs and regulations having to do with diplomatic etiquette and courtesies expected in official dealings with persons in various cultures.

Proverb   sayings that express a commonplace truth.

Proxemics   communicating through the use of space.

Public distance   in the United States, physical distance between people of about 12 to 25 feet.

Quasi-international law   rules between countries and specific corporations.

Reentry shock   sometimes called reverse cultural shock; problems with readjustment to the home culture.

Regiocentric management   type of management that considers the region rather than the country in which the firm is located, realizing that countries can and often do have many different cultural backgrounds.

Repartee conversation   a conversation in which the parties take turns speaking and talk only for short time periods.

Repatriation   returning to one's country of citizenship.

Restricted codes   include highly predictable messages; use oral, nonverbal, and paralinguistic transmission channels.

Ritual conversation   involves standard replies and comments for a given situation, with little meaning attached to what is said.

Roles   include the behavioral expectations of a position within a culture and are affected by norms and rules.

Rules   formed to clarify cloudy areas of norms.

Sapir-Whorf Hypothesis   belief that language functions as a way of shaping one's experiences; includes structural and semantic aspects of a language.

Self-disclosure   a form of interaction that involves telling other people about yourself so they may get to know you better.

Semantics   the study of the ways behavior is influenced by the words and other symbols used to communicate.

Serial monogamy   family system that includes a number of different monogamous marriages through divorce or death.

Slang   idioms and other informal language vocabulary.

Social hierarchies   structure of a culture.

Social interaction   what is acceptable and unacceptable communication between people in a culture.

Social reciprocity   refers to the way formal and informal obligations are handled, ranging from the belief that people are forever indebted to others to those who feel no obligation to others.

Social zone   in the United States, physical distance between people of 4 to 12 feet; used for business situations in which people interact in a more formal, impersonal way.

Sociolinguistics   the sociology of language.

Socio-psychological model   a negotiation process that involves the goals the parties want to reach, the communication and actions leading to the negotiations, the expected outcomes for each, the preexisting relationship and cultural factors of both parties, and the conditions under which the negotiations are conducted.

Stereotypes   perceptions about certain groups of people or nationalities.

Subculture   groups of people possessing characteristic traits that set apart and distinguish them from others within a larger society (or macroculture).

Subgroup   groups of people possessing characteristic traits that set apart and distinguish them from others within a larger society/culture (or macroculture); groups with which the macroculture does not agree and has problems communicating.

Subjective interpretation   interpretation placed on a message that is affected by thought processes; influenced by personal judgment or temperament of a person.

Subnationalism   exists when a political body attempts to unite diverse people under one government.

Supernationalism   extending authority over more than one nation.

Syntactic errors   errors in language meaning.

Tactics   any maneuvers used for gaining advantages or success.

Thematization   process by which a framework for mutual communication and satisfaction is reached.

Trade agreements   laws under which U.S. businesses must function when exporting.

Trading with the Enemy Act of 1917   prohibits the transfer of information on military material or defense-related materials.

Transcultural   across cultures.

Transnational   corporations that cross the borders of countries in conducting their business.

Trilateral governance   allows for later redetermination of terms by using an arbitrator.

Uncertainty-reduction theory   creation of proactive predictions and retroactive explanations about our own behavior, beliefs, and attitudes and those of others.

Unified governance   no advance negotiations; provides maximum flexibility; terms for both parties controlled by one party.

U.S. style of eating   zig-zag style of eating used by people in the United States: cutting the meat with the knife held in the right hand and the fork in the left, then placing the knife on the plate, shifting the fork to the right hand, and eating.

Values   beliefs and attitudes held by a culture.

Verbal dueling   a friendly type of argument or debate.

Vienna Agreement   a multilateral treaty signed by states to protect intellectual property.

Visa   written permission to enter and stay in a country for a specified time and purpose.

Vocabulary equivalence   reasons for translation problems between languages.

World culture   involves the breaking down of traditional barriers among people of differing cultures, emphasizing the commonality of human needs.

Work   mental or physical activities directed to socially productive accomplishments.

Work attitudes   how people of a culture view work.

Work ethic   the attitude that hard work is applauded and rewarded, while failure to work is viewed negatively.

Appendix B _____

Answers to Exercises

CHAPTER 1 _____

Matching

1. D
2. C
3. I
4. B
5. A
6. H
7. F
8. G
9. K
10. J

CHAPTER 2 _____

True/False

1. F
2. T
3. F
4. F
5. F
6. T
7. T

8. T
9. F
10. F

CHAPTER 3

True/False
1. T
2. F
3. T
4. T
5. F
6. F
7. F
8. F
9. T
10. T

CHAPTER 4

True/False		*Identification*		*Matching*	
1.	F	A.	determination	1.	K
2.	F	B.	happiness	2.	F
3.	F	C.	interest	3.	I
4.	T	D.	disgust	4.	H
5.	F	E.	anger	5.	G
6.	F	F.	contempt	6.	E
7.	F	G.	surprise	7.	B
8.	F	H.	sad	8.	A
9.	T			9.	J
10.	F			10.	D

CHAPTER 5

True/False
1. F
2. F

3.   F
4.   T
5.   F
6.   T
7.   F
8.   T
9.   T
10.   T

CHAPTER 6

True/False

1.   F
2.   T
3.   F
4.   T
5.   T
6.   T
7.   F
8.   T
9.   T
10.   T

CHAPTER 7

True/False

1.   T
2.   F
3.   F
4.   T
5.   F
6.   T
7.   T
8.   F
9.   F
10.   F

CHAPTER 8

Matching		*True/False*	
1.	A	1.	T
2.	H	2.	F
3.	C	3.	T
4.	A	4.	F
5.	K	5.	T
6.	G	6.	T
7.	D	7.	F
8.	I	8.	T
9.	L	9.	F
10.	F	10.	T

CHAPTER 9

True/False	
1.	T
2.	T
3.	F
4.	F
5.	T
6.	T
7.	T
8.	T
9.	F
10.	F

CHAPTER 10

True/False	
1.	T
2.	T
3.	F
4.	F
5.	T

6.   F
7.   T
8.   T
9.   T
10. T

CHAPTER 11

Multiple Choice	*True/False*	
1. C	1.	T
	2.	F
	3.	T
	4.	F
	5.	T
	6.	F
	7.	T
	8.	F
	9.	T
	10.	F

CHAPTER 12

Matching		*Matching*	
1.	L	1.	C
2.	E	2.	I
3.	H	3.	A
4.	J	4.	H
5.	K	5.	E
6.	B	6.	B
7.	D	7.	F
8.	I	8.	J
9.	C	9.	G
10.	G	10.	D

Appendix C _____

Maps of the United States and the World

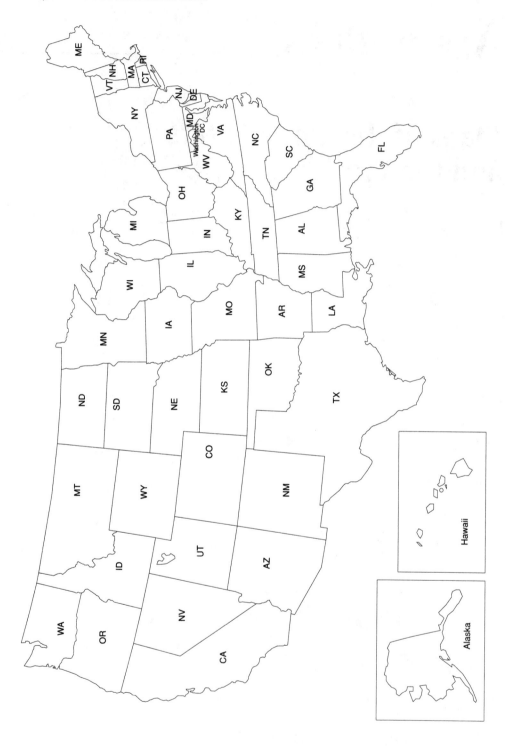

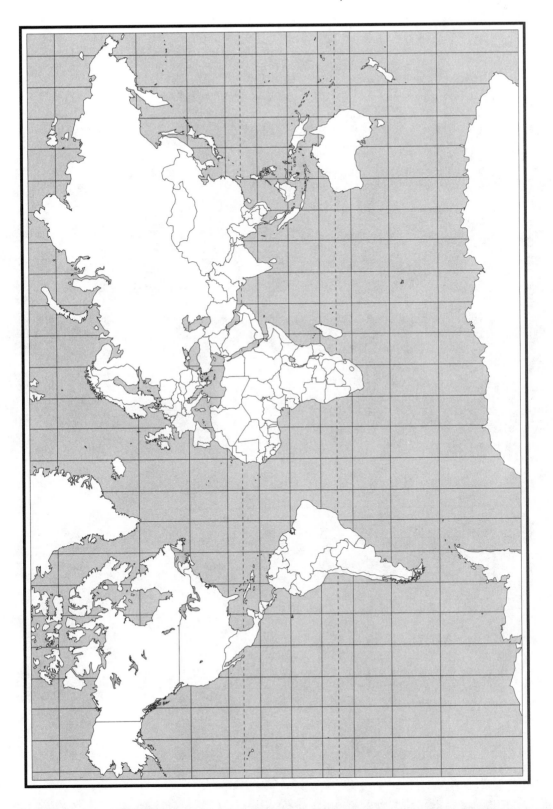

Index